New Priorities for Success of Armed Forces

Efficiency - A Key Requirement for the Military of the Future

Lars Naunheim

Imprint and Copyright

New Priorities for Success of Armed Forces
Efficiency - A Key Requirement for the Military of the Future

Author: Lars Naunheim

Cover: Lars Naunheim

1st Edition 2015

Self-Publishing

(Contact: lars.naunheim@yahoo.com)

ISBN-10: 0692416390
ISBN-13: 978-0692416396

Dedication:

To my wife Verena, for her love and support and to our wonderful children, Ben, Victoria and Jack.

Special Dedication:

To all of our military personnel and their families for the tremendous sacrifices they make so we can live a life in peace and freedom.

Acknowledgement:

I would like to thank Prof. Dr. Stefan Bayer for his incredible support and mentorship during this endeavor. This project would not have been possible without him.

List of Figures

List of Tables

Abbreviations

AVF – All-Volunteer Force
CentCom – United States Central Command
CINC – Composite Index of National Capabilities
DEA – Data Envelopment Analysis
DOD – US Department of Defense
DMU – Decision Making Unit
FCS – Future Combat System
FDH – Free Disposal Hull Analysis
FY – Fiscal Year
GAD – Generation-Adjusted Discounting
GDI – Gross Domestic Income
GNI – Gross National Income
IDF – Israeli Defense Force
IT – Information Technology
JDAM – Joint-Direct-Attack-Munition
KPI – Key Performance Indicator
MIT – Massachusetts Institute of Technologies
MRS – Marginal Rate of Substitution
MRT – Marginal Rate of Transformation
NATO – North Atlantic Treaty Organization
OECD – Organization for Economic Co-Operation and Development
O&M – Operations and Maintenance
O&S – Operations and Support
PLA – People's Liberation Army
PMF – Private Military Firm
PPBS – Program, Planning, Budgeting System
PR – Public Relations
PMC – Private Military Company
PMF – Private Military Firm
RMA – Revolution in Military Affairs
R&D – Research and Development

SIPRI - Stockholm International Peace Research Institute

TOC – Total Ownership Cost

TVI – Trade Value Indicator

USMC – United States Marine Corp

WVS – World Value Survey

1 Introduction

"The highest degree of military efficiency is our goal, and all of us should make every effort in our power to reach it."[1]

Major General John A Lejeune, USMC - 1920
Commandant of the US Marine Corps

1.1 Relevance of Topic

The nations around the globe spend an estimated total of $2.2 trillion on defense.[2] The US alone expects to spend more than $800 billion in 2014.[3] In the case of Germany with close to €30 billion, about 10 percent of the country's federal government spending is defense related.[4]

Despite these huge numbers, the efficiency of Armed Forces seems to be very rarely a focus of academic studies. This is surprising since a broad audience could benefit from understanding the efficiency stage of Armed Forces and factors that have an influence on it. Knowing the stage of efficiency can help politicians to make decisions around adequate funding of the military, and understanding its drivers can help them to positively influence the market and administrative environment in which they operate. The public of a nation should know whether its tax dollars are invested well and if not demand changes. Senior officers in the Armed Forces could learn how to get more capabilities with their given budget or cope with budget cuts in a manner that does not

[1] Lejeune, J.: Military Efficiency 1920
[2] see Global Security: World Defense Spending 2012
[3] see US Government:Federal Budget 2014
[4] see BMVg: Verteidigungsausgaben 2013

risk their operational readiness. Employees in the defense industry could understand their customers and better serve their needs. Military personnel in each hierarchy and position could better serve their nation and taxpayers if they better understood the financial impacts of their actions on and off the battlefield. The opportunities for beneficially applying the results of studies on efficiency of Armed Forces are almost infinite.

This discussion becomes even more important under consideration of current political developments as of early 2013. Facing a challenging economic environment and high public debt, the US government has announced steep budget cuts for the military. $46 billion alone is supposed to be cut in 2013 and a total of $500 billion over a 10-year timeframe.[5] Former Secretary of Defense Leon Panetta warned the US public that this will have serious impacts on military programs and military readiness.[6] There seems to be no doubt that the US needs to face the challenge of balancing the needs of the Armed Forces with the risks posed by a steadily increasing government deficit. Improving efficiency of Armed Forces would serve both purposes. And operating efficiently should not just be demanded from senior officers. This analysis will illustrate the complex environment and how political decisions and the private sector influence the Armed Forces as well. Indicators actually suggest notable areas for improvement in terms of administrating defense budgets in particular. According to Rumsfeld, the former secretary of defense of the US, $18 billion could be saved by better financial

[5] see Barrett, T./Cohen, T.: Spending Cuts 2013
[6] see Barrett, T./Cohen, T.: Spending Cuts 2013

management of the defense budget.[7] Other estimates even assume a saving potential of up to $30 billion and point out that due to the underlying confidentiality and critical necessity productivity improvements are rarely demanded in the area of defense spending.[8]

But why should economists have an interest in national security or any military matters? In economic terms, national security is a public good. This good has to be financed by the scarce resources available to the government of a nation. The efficient allocation of resources across all available options with the aim of improving the overall social welfare of a nation is the very basic question of public finances in the world of economists. Nations need to decide how much of other things to sacrifice in the interest of military strength.[9]

Even in times of peace, economic considerations have to be made with regard to defense budgets. It is still a question of how much budget needs to be allocated to defense and the military to help it fulfill its defined objectives during peacetimes. Armed Forces are not just used to fight wars but also to deter potential aggressors from starting them. Investments in the military can be compared with an insurance policy. Even in peacetime investments are required to maintain their capabilities in case required and to deter potential aggressors from starting a conflict. Government financials and the military are therefore very interdependent. According to Smith, the balancing of

[7] see Jones, J./McCaffery, J.: Financial Management 2007, p.97
[8] see Jones, L./McCaffery, J.: Financial Management 2007, p.97
[9] see Hitch, C./McKean, R.: Defense in the Nuclear Age 1960, p.3

resource allocation and commitments between both departments can even be a determining factor for military decisions.[10]

It seems that no matter from which angle governmental defense spending is being analyzed, efficiency apparently has to be seen as a key aspect that needs to be considered. In the end the question arises as to how efficiency can even be measured in the military environment. National Security is a public good provided by the government of nations. A commonly faced challenge in the area of public goods is that their benefit is often intangible and no market prices exist.

However for classical efficiency evaluations, costs and benefits have to be quantified and compared against. Scientists have developed multiple tools to do so for products and services that are traded on the open competitive market. Not so many have attempted a quantification of efficiency in the area of government services. And very few have even attempted studies around the efficiency of Armed Forces.

It shall be emphasized that this analysis is aspiring to provide a scientific and fact-based assessment of the efficiency stage of Armed Forces and is not written for a specific political agenda lobbying for more or less military in general. Armed Forces operate in a highly competitive environment for scarce resources and are at the same time facing increasing demands regarding their state of readiness for a myriad of missions. The reader shall not draw the conclusion that nations with inefficient Armed

[10] see Smith, R.: Military Economics 2009, p.8

Forces spend too much on defense. Efficiency is determined based on input factors as well as output factors and a nation can improve efficiency by either spending less or delivering more with what they have. Determining which way efficiency improvements should go, by either cutting costs, asking for improved capabilities or a combination of both needs to be a thoughtful decision of the government of a nation considering the specific national security goals.

1.2 Hypothesis and Research Question

The intention of this analysis is to approach the topic of military efficiency from multiple angles. The main goal is to develop and apply an economic model for measuring the efficiency stage of Armed Forces. This model will be based on a clear definition of efficiency in economic terms that will be achieved in a dedicated chapter of this paper. As a second step it will further be tested if certain factors exist that appear to have an impact on the efficiency of Armed Forces. For this a few selected factors will be defined to test the model with regard to this question.

This leads to two main hypotheses that are supposed to be tested as part of this analysis.

1.) Economic efficiency varies among the Armed Forces of nations

2.) Certain factors have a positive or respective negative impact on the efficiency of Armed Forces

1.3 Structure of Study

As a first step, this analysis will begin with a systematic review of the existing literature and theories in the field of public goods and how efficiency can be measured in this area. It will be outlined how challenging this endeavor is and how some of the obstacles could be overcome. A review of prior efficiency studies regarding public goods will complement this chapter with the benefit of providing best practices and lessons learned for the specific model that will be applied in this study.

Chapter 3 will focus specifically on the efficiency of Armed Forces and outline why efficiency is important and how it will be measured in terms of this study. It will further be described which input and output factors will be used in order to conduct this efficiency evaluation. Three approaches in particular have been identified following a single-factor, multi-factor and qualitative factor approach. The qualitative factor represents a new and innovative approach for measuring the output produced by Armed Forces.

Chapter 4 will then describe the actual efficiency model and the specific datasets will be applied. For six countries it will be attempted to provide a detailed interpretation of the results. In order to obtain a meaningful database to draw conclusions from, the three models will be created with 1995, 2000 and 2005 related figures, respectively.

Chapter 5 will cover a selection of potential drivers for efficiency, covering advances in technology, the governmental administration process and the model for sourcing service members. It will outline how these are linked to the Armed Forces and tested if they appear to have an influence on efficiency.

This analysis will be based on statistical models combined with qualitative assessments of scientific literature. Specifically the model for assessing the efficiency stage of the Armed Forces will be primarily based on empirical datasets in order to ensure validity and comparability of the results. The second part of the analysis concerning the drivers for efficiency will more heavily rely on qualitative assessments due to the fact that hardly any studies and databases are available, or suitable for a cross-country comparison. However, the qualitative arguments will still be supported in terms of numbers by proxy indicators to be identified in the upcoming chapters.

The potential impact of military specific factors will be covered in the outlook section of Chapter 6. This approach shall ensure a high quality of the empirical assessment in Chapter 5 while at the same time moving relevant topics into the focal point for future research. The private military industry is one example for such a factor. This topic is very relevant with a very likely impact on the efficiency of Armed Forces. Studies in this area are however scarce and if available limited to a subset of the industry. Force planning as a second topic requires substantial military expertise which is not the focal point of this economic analysis.

To ensure important and relevant topics like these are still addressed appropriately, the outlook section will lead into the discussion around the relevance of those topics and their potential impact on the efficiency of Armed Forces.

In order to evaluate the efficiency of Armed Forces it is important to understand the tasks and underlying requirements of the military and a nation's security policy. Therefore this analysis in general and Chapter 3 in particular will considerably leverage studies in the area of international politics, peace politics and to a certain extent military strategy to accompany the general economic research.

Some challenges are expected when it comes to the evaluation of the data for this analysis, given that not all countries may accurately publish their government financials and the definition of military expenses differ. The data sources that will be used for this analysis however are publicly accessible and provide transparent data and explanations on how they have been derived.

The aspired regional focus of this work will be around the countries US, UK, Israel, Russia, China and Germany. The main reason is that all these countries provide certain characteristics that will be helpful in the scope of this analysis. Germany used to be a conscript military until 2011, Israel still relies on conscripts today and is very active in preparing for local conflicts. Russia historically has been a mighty military power; the USA and UK were engaged in multiple military conflicts recently and still are at the time of this study. China finally provides a challenge since detailed data on government financials and the military are hard to come by and are actually only accessible through third party analysts. However, China is becoming a major power in the world and will therefore be considered as part of this analysis as well. The underlying data sources will clearly be highlighted and potential issues with regard to their accuracy will be identified.

With the structure and scope of this analysis defined, the following chapter will begin with a review and assessment of the theoretical basis for efficiency studies in the area of public goods.

2 Efficiency of Public Goods

2.1 Measuring Efficiency of Public Goods

From an economic perspective, national defense can be seen as a public good as it is provided by the government of a nation to all of its citizens. The measurement of efficiency in the public sector proves to provide some challenges compared to the rather straightforward approach in the private sector. Private enterprises typically produce goods with a given input and the output can in most cases be determined by market prices. Public organizations however utilize a huge variety of inputs and produce a good for which typically no market price exists. This results from the two basic criteria that are attributable to public goods as defined by Cornes and Sandler as follows:[11] Public goods are non-rival, meaning they can be consumed by one individual without detracting the slightest from the consumption opportunities of other individuals. As the second criteria they are non-excludable because preventing anyone from consuming the good is either very difficult or even impossible.

Several models have been developed in an attempt to answer the questions surrounding the efficient provision of public goods in order to maximize social utility. The Samuelson[12] condition shall be named as one of the most predominant models: The condition states that a public good should be provided for as long as the total benefit for all individuals exceeds the costs of providing the good. In other words it is the sum of all individual's willingness to pay and therefore the aggregated demand for a public good.

---

[11] see Cornes, R./Sandler, T.: Public Goods 1996, p.8
[12] see Samuelson, P.: Public Expenditure 1954

The condition is mathematically stated as: $MRS_1 + MRS_2 + \ldots + MRS_n = MRT$[13]

With n individuals indexed as 1,...,n, MRS_i stands for the individual *i*'s marginal rate of substitution and MRT stands for the economy's marginal rate of transformation. The MRS represents the marginal benefit that each consumer derives from a unit of a public good, measured in terms of units of private goods that he or she needs to give up. The MRT represents the opportunity costs associated with the production of the private good vs. the provision of the public good. With that, the provision of public goods is efficient when the marginal rate of transformation equals the sum of all individual's marginal rate of substitution as shown by the equation. This perspective analyzes if the public organization produces the right good and at the level required to maximize social welfare. In other words producing a lot of output in an efficient manner can still be inefficient for the society if excess output is produced and some of the input may be better invested in other areas of the economy.

While this model helps to explain the desirable level of provision for a public good for the society, it does not help answer the question whether the specific organization producing the good actually operates 'efficiently'. In other words, if the aspired output is achieved with the lowest amount of input or if with the used input a higher output could be produced. If either one is the case an organization has to be declared inefficient. Improvements in the input to output ratio of the producing organization could actually alter the marginal cost considerations and therefore increase social welfare by

[13] see Leach, J.: Public Economics 2004, p.160

producing even more units of the aspired good or by allowing the reallocation of input resources towards the production of other desired goods.

But can Armed Forces be seen as an organization as well following the classical view of organizational theory? An organization can be seen as a social system that structures available resources to achieve a common objective and fulfill a certain purpose.[14] Following that definition Armed Forces can in fact be seen as an organization as they produce the output of military capabilities utilizing inputs from the society and economy in order to fulfill their purpose of producing physical power to defend the nation's interests. An organization can further be considered a social subsystem embedded in the broader structure of a nation[15] interacting with the government, society and others. This highlights that Armed Forces can be seen as a separated unit that produces a specific output for a specific purpose but it is also highly interdependent with other systems and structures in a society and economy of a nation. In the end Armed Forces follow the directions from its society, formulated through the public governing process. While today's Armed Forces mainly focus on sustaining peace and conducting humanitarian missions, in the end in its core the purpose of the military organization is to threaten and, if required, use forceful actions at a moment's notice.[16] Accordingly, the output produced by Armed Forces is the provision of security to the homeland as well as the capability to project a nation's will through potential and/or actual physical and violent actions. Given that Armed Forces can be seen as an organization that is utilizing input factors to produce an output, they can be subject to efficiency analyses.

[14] see Hill, W./Fehlbaum, R./Ulrich, P.: Organizational Theory 1974, p.17
[15] see Hill, W./Fehlbaum, R./Ulrich, P.: Organizational Theory 1974, p.24
[16] see Gareis, S./Haltiner, K./Klein, P.: Organisationsmerkmale von Sreitkraeften 2006, p.14

Furthermore, the definitions also highlight the high influence from other parts of a society on the organization Armed Forces.

Leibenstein and Niskanen are two authors who claim for different reasons that government organizations and therefore the provision of public goods are prone to inefficiencies.

Leibenstein has identified a type of (in)-efficiency that may occur specifically under market conditions with limited or no competition. The government providing 'national defense' can be seen in analogy also as the single provider of a good to the nation's citizens. Leibenstein claims that under this market condition so called x-inefficiency can occur on the side of the production unit. This inefficiency refers to uneconomical use of resources due to the absence of competition and therefore lack of market forces that would otherwise foster efficiency.[17] An organization that is the sole provider for a product does not have to 'work' as hard, as it would have to under competitive market circumstances. Leibenstein further claims that this x-inefficiency can be seen as a very common phenomenon.

Also Niskanen[18] claimed in his 'Budget-maximizing' hypothesis that certain inefficiencies are very predominant in the public administration and are therefore impacting the provision of public goods. To him, social efficiency is reduced, because rational bureaucrats will always aspire to concrete their power by increasing their

[17] see Leibenstein, H.: X-Efficiency 1966, p.413
[18] see Niskanen, W.: Bureaucracy 1971

budgets and are therefore contributing to the growth of governments. Cansier and Bayer describe the model as follows:[19] Bureaucrats will be successful in maximizing their budget B(X)→max for as long as the costs for providing the public good C(X) do not exceed the citizen's willingness to pay WP(X). An efficient provision of the public good however is already achieved at a lower spending level X_0, resulting in a loss of social welfare for the society due to an overproduction of the public good. The result is illustrated in Figure 1.

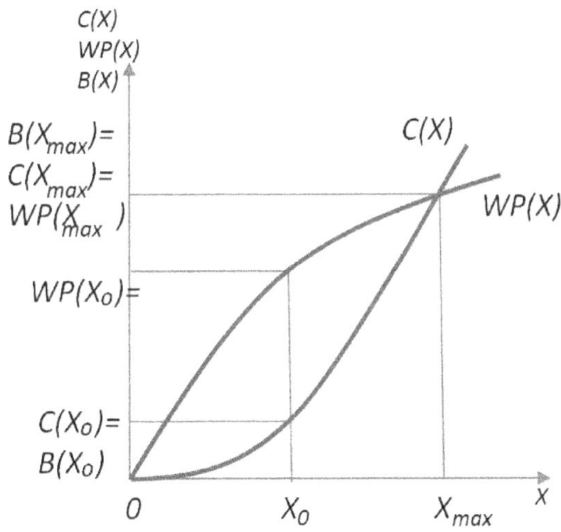

Figure 1: Niskanen – Budget-maximizing Hypothesis
(see Cansier D,/Bayer S.: Finanzwissenschaft 2003, p.207)

While these models highlight important conceptional aspects of public goods, they do no help to answer questions around efficiency on the level of individual organizations. In his context product possibility frontiers are a commonly used tool.

19 see Cansier D,/Bayer S.: Finanzwissenschaft 2003, p.207

In economic terms efficiency can be defined with further precision: In the scope of efficiency measurement tools the organization that is under review is called decision making unit or short DMU. The same naming shall therefore be used in the upcoming chapters. In the scope of this analysis DMU will refer to the Armed Forces of any given nation that is part of this research. Farrell in particular shall be named as a pioneer in the context of economic efficiency. His work provided a basis for many recent models around efficiency analysis. His groundwork regarding frontier efficiency will therefore be briefly described and is illustrated in Figure 2. Farrell characterizes DMUs as technically inefficient if less than the achievable output is achieved with a given input and as price inefficient if the best package of inputs is not used given its prices and marginal productivities.[20] Murillo-Zamorano more recently replaced the term price efficiency with allocative efficiency referring to the same content.[21]

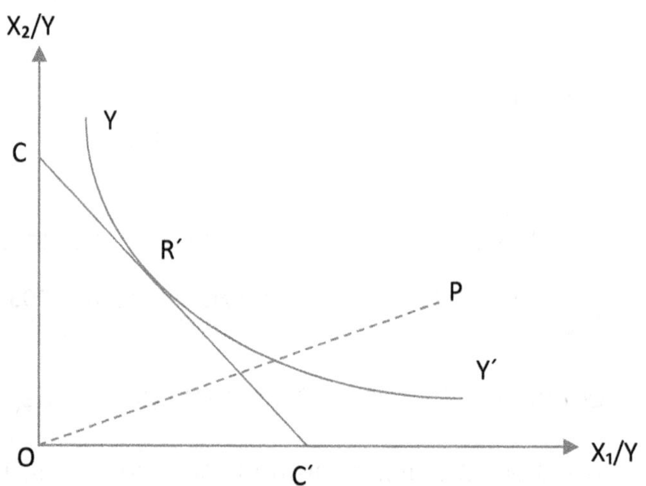

Figure 2: Technical and Price Efficiency

(see Farrell, M.J.: The Measurement of Productive Efficiency 1957, p.254)

[20] see Farrell, M.J.: The Measurement of Productive Efficiency 1957, p.255

[21] see Murillo-Zamorano, L.: Frontier Techniques 2004, p.33

The isoquant YY' captures the minimum combination of inputs per unit of output needed to produce a unit of output. Any element to the right of that curve is considered inefficient, since the same amount of output could just as well be produced with a lower input. Point P in the figure is therefore technically inefficient to the degree of OR/OP. If information on market prices is known and a particular behavioral objective such as cost minimization is assumed in such a way that the input price ratio is reflected by the slope of the isocost-line CC', allocative inefficiency can also be derived from the unit isoquant plotted in the chart.[22] The relevant distance to measure is S to R and the degree of allocative inefficiency accordingly OS/OR. Therefore the overall efficiency or more recently called economic efficiency (EE) can be stated as:

EE = TE x AE = OR/OP x OS/OR = OS/OP[23]

The results of EE range between 0 and 1 - mathematically stated as $0 \leq EE \leq 1$. 1 represents perfect efficiency, therefore as the scoring descends towards 0 the less efficient it becomes.

Specifically the distance SP can be further analyzed with regard to how cost reduction measures could improve the efficiency[24], since this distance purely reflects the costs for the input factors used in the production process. The difference SR represents changes to the used set-up of input factors which presumably require more substantial changes to the set-up of the production process.

---

[22] Murillo-Zamorano, L.: Frontier Techniques 2004, p.34
[23] Murillo-Zamorano, L.: Frontier Techniques 2004, p. 34
[24] see Murillo-Zamorano, L.: Frontier Techniques 2004, p. 34

One important limitation to the model above is that it requires a known best possible degree of efficiency with which to compare organizations. This however is a rarely available determinant. Therefore this basic concept of the efficiency frontier had been developed further in recent years. Most of the new approaches determine efficiency by comparing the performance of a given organization with the performance of others in form of benchmarking. If the other organizations produce either the same output with less input or a higher output with the same input, they can be seen as relatively more efficient.

The application of efficiency frontiers requires some further clarification of the framework for this study. The clear definition of input and output factors has to be addressed in particular, combined with the challenge of evaluating public goods in general. The specific model used in the context of this study will therefore be developed further and with more precision in the upcoming chapters.

2.2 Problem of Measuring Non-monetary and Future Benefits

One challenge in the public sector is that a lot of goods and services unarguably provide an essential benefit to citizens, but no market prices for these exist. Monetary quantification however is a basic requirement for the application of most economic models. And even though some benefits of public goods and services may come with an explicit price, this price is often not determined by the means of a free market given the absence of competition.[25] This challenge applies to issues like health care services and public education but especially to the benefits of investments in the Armed Forces. There is no market price for national security and citizens perceive security differently with some people favoring higher defense spending and others opposing it. This provides a challenge when it comes to measuring the actual output produced by Armed Forces.

Humanitarian missions for example can save the lives of foreign citizens in a short-term view. But they can also in the long term provide political stability in order to deter potential threats through terrorism which again leads to higher security at home as well. But which dollar amount should be assigned to each human life that is being saved? How could it even accurately be evaluated how many lives were at stake at the time the Armed Forces received their order to proceed with their mission?

On the input side we face the same issue in the context of military involvements. A dollar amount can be assigned to the military equipment used, logistics, fuel, oil and ammunition. But how do we factor in the potential loss of human life in combat or severe injuries? And how should potential economic damages caused by increasing oil prices be factored in or even be accurately predicted? If measuring the benefit of a single military mission already proves challenging, the measurement of national security and national power for a country in general has to be even more difficult.

[25] see Chote, R./Emmerson, C./Simpson, H.: Public Sector Efficiency 2003 p.106

A further aspect that needs to be considered is that lots of military objectives are cost-effective in one period but have the goal to provide a future benefit, e.g. political stabilization of a region or country. Today's developed and industrialized nations reside in fairly peaceful environments and conduct military operations on a rather voluntarily basis.

The US waged the war in Vietnam for the reason of deterring the diffusion of communists' ideas[26], the Alliance fought in Afghanistan to deter future terrorist attacks[27] and ongoing missions of various nations in Africa are supposed to provide improved security for humanitarian organizations as well as protection for commercial ship lines against pirates.[28] It is out of scope of this paper to evaluate the reasoning for nations to engage in the Iraq war, but economic reasons around the future oil supply[29] are often mentioned along the lines of these discussions as well. All of these missions have significant cost impacts on the military at the time of the missions and the perspective benefit in each case is expected in the future and difficult to quantify.

Studies around the economic impact of ecological damages provide parallels to the issues faced in this analysis and suggest a structure for deriving the total economic value of non-monetary goods considering all of the stated above. The following

[26] see Pentagon Papers: Kennedy Commitments 1971
[27] see NATO: ISAF's Mission in Afghanistan 2013
[28] see EUNAFOR Somalia: Mission 2013
[29] see BBC News: Poland seeks Iraqi oil stake 2003

explanations follow Bayer's outlines and structure around the quantification of ecological damages with parallel application on national security:[30]

I. **Use-values**

a. Direct use-values

b. Indirect use-values

c. Option values

d. Quasi-option values

II. **Non-use-values**

a. Existence values

b. Bequest values

Figure 3: Economic Value of Non-monetary Goods

(see Bayer, S.: Ecological Damages 2003, p.4)

The category of use-values refers to goods that individuals can use or are supposed to use at some point in the future. Direct use-value in this area occurs when individuals benefit from the action. An example could be the security provided by the German naval forces at the coastlines of Africa to deter threats by pirates. These activities provide a direct benefit to companies and ship lines, since routes can be used that otherwise would be too dangerous to pass for commercial ships. This leads to increasing profits accordingly. Indirect values occur when the activity, in this case a military mission, is incidental for the benefit but unrelated. Bayer illustrates this with the

[30] see Bayer, S.: Ecological Damages 2003, p.4

example of a higher employment rate and revenue for private enterprises since the military provides them with a peaceful and secure environment in which to conduct their business.[31] Option values consider the factor time and represent the fact that individuals are willing to spend money today in order to benefit from their investments at some point in the future.[32] Investments in Armed Forces are comparable to an insurance policy where future risks and costs are minimized by investments made today.

The quasi-option value represents the value of actions that are actually not taken and are providing a benefit because it helps individuals to make better decisions at a later time due to better knowledge of specific circumstances.[33] Evaluating the impact of not acting is certainly a difficult one, since it has to be predicted what would have happened differently if a nation actually had acted in a certain way at an earlier point in time. The Cuban missile crisis may be one example where both the US and the Soviet Union decided to not take immediate reactive military actions, but kept working on a political solution avoiding the further escalation of a nuclear conflict. Examples of situations in which quasi option values were not realized are easier to find. The US may have reconsidered the way they engaged in the Vietnam War had they known how fiercely the resistance of the adversary turned out to be, which they learned through painful lessons taught by the enemy deep in the jungles.

[31] see Bayer, S.: Nutzen und Kosten von Auslandseinsaetzen 2009, p.239
[32] see Bayer, S.: Nutzen und Kosten von Auslandseinsaetzen 2009, p.239
[33] see Bayer, S.: Nutzen und Kosten von Auslandseinsaetzen 2009, p.240

Bayer further states:[34] Non-use values as the second category describe goods that provide a value to individuals derived out of their bare existence. Within the category of non-use-values one can also see a link to the problem of measuring future benefits. Maintaining Armed Forces in peacetime can ensure a life in peace and liberty for today's generation, since they have deterrence effects on potential adversaries. This benefit of safe living conditions is not consumed by individuals, but it benefits them out of its pure existence (existence value). Some military measures however may take time to take effect and could have a cost impact today, but actually only benefit future generations (bequest values). As an example a peacekeeping mission in distant areas of the globe may not necessarily benefit the citizens today but rather future generations through a stabilized and more peaceful world.

The mission in Afghanistan addresses probably a combination of both values, since the immediate termination of terrorists and destruction of their training camps ensures security in the short-term, while the aspiration to establish a democratic government has a rather long-term impact, ensuring a stabilization of the region to avoid future development of support for terrorists.

In the economic theory the total of both use-values as well as non-use-values derive the economic value relevant for further evaluations. As outlined above this is difficult in the context of military actions, since hardly any of the benefits provided by Armed Forces have a direct benefit for individuals and/or come with a market price. These outlines however provide a great basis for further analyses. They help to

[34] see Bayer, S.: Ecological Damages 2003, p.4

structure the benefits of public goods and emphasize the relevance of intangibles and complex interdependencies between these values.

The complexity of the evaluation of costs and benefits around military actions is illustrated in a study conducted around the Iraq War by Stiglitz and Bilmes. While initial estimates quoted the conflict well under $100 billion, Stiglitz and Bilmes computed that the true costs of the conflict had already ended up somewhere between $2.7 and $5 trillion by the end of 2009.[35] The big tolerance in their estimate makes it clear that they faced similar issues as outlined in this chapter when it comes to the accurate monetary evaluation of relevant cost and benefit aspects. Their estimate is an attempt to include a lot of the rather indirect aspects also mentioned in this chapter. The death and injury of soldiers, the indirect impact on the economy as well as financial implications for the macro-economy caused by impacts such as higher oil prices, loss in tax income and overall weakened economic growth are just a few.[36] This study also highlights that apparently not just the forward-looking estimation of military missions is a challenge, but even in retrospect accurately taking account of costs and benefits provides to be a challenge.

Also on a more operational level investments in the military context come with a high level of uncertainty. Military acquisitions are expensive and have a long-term purpose that is often aligned with the nation's security goal or with a specific threat. Since circumstances change, a nation might spend a lot of money on a specific piece of

[35] see Stiglitz, J./Bilmes, L.: The Three Trillion Dollar War 2008, p.31
[36] see Stiglitz, J./Bilmes, L.: The Three Trillion Dollar War 2008, p.31

equipment or strategy that can never be used because of changes to the circumstances. Surface to air missiles can only be used if an enemy actually uses aircrafts. Same applies to counter submarine devices or surface naval forces in general. Heavy investments in these areas make sense if a threat from an industrialized nation is expected, but not so much in terms of the current counterterrorism missions in the Middle East. On the other side one could argue that simply owning overwhelming capabilities in the area of naval and air warfare deter aggressors from even trying to achieve potentially dangerous capabilities in these areas. This refers to the deterrence function of Armed Forces in peace time. An evaluation of this impact is even more hypothetical since, it would have to be speculated what the enemy's capabilities were and what damage they would have caused had they existed in order to determine the appropriate deterrence level required. The takeaway from this rationale is that simply adding up the financial value of military assets owned by a nation does not say much about their actual value or, in economic terms, about their produced output. This is an issue that will need further evaluation as the model for this study is developed.

The discounting of investments is a further factor that complicates the monetary evaluation of public goods. From an economic perspective it is always a consideration to either consume today or invest for tomorrow. The open financial market enables the lending and borrowing of money for a fee – that being the interest rate. A dollar today is worth the equivalent of two dollars at some time in the future if it is not spent, but invested in order to generate income over time. The investments cannot just be made in the general financial markets, but also in technology though R&D. Accordingly Armed Forces in general operate under the constraint of either spending in today's military readiness by acquiring resources and training them or spending on improvements of future capabilities through R&D. And most importantly outputs and outcomes of R&D investment, i.e. knowledge, skills and experience, are intangible, immeasurable and furthermore, the realization of their benefits is delayed in time and their impact may even occur in seemingly unrelated areas.[37] One example for this is the political theory that sees military-related investments as a tool to stimulate the economy through increased public consumption and improve the performance of private enterprises through technological spillovers. The same issue is faced in terms of cost and future benefits of peacekeeping missions. These represent commitments, investments and benefits that are related to the future and need to be discounted accordingly in terms of economic analyses that are based on monetary evaluations.

Discounting practices shall ensure a fair and accurate evaluation of the benefits for investments that cause cost and incur benefits over longer periods of time. In terms of investments in defense and certain military actions the benefits can in fact be substantially far in the future and therefore potentially even be impacting only a second generation of citizens. A common criticism is that classical discounting methods tend to favor today's generation and stand in the way of sustainable decisions that cross generations of citizens.[38] This is caused by the fact that any type of discounting lowers the future value of an investment. Hence, the higher the discount rate, the less future generations will be considered – relatively speaking.[39] This opposes the concept of Non-Declining Welfare which mandates in the interest of sustainability that future

[37] see Mandl, U./Dierx, A./ Ilzkovitz, F.: Efficency of the Public Sector 2008, p.26
[38] see Bayer, S.: Generation Adjusted Discounting 2004, p.142
[39] see Bayer, S.: Generation Adjusted Discounting 2004, p.145

generations may not have to sacrifice welfare over today's generation caused by the decisions made today.[40] The concept of generation-adjusted discounting (GAD) introduces a tool that specifically recognizes the finite lifetime of humans and existence of generations of citizens. Under this concept the GAD leads to lower discounting rates than traditional approaches with therefore increased focus on future generations leading to investment decisions in the context of sustainability.[41]

Since the output of Armed Forces in economic terms is non-monetary and in a lot of cases provides a future benefit, all of these challenges will be faced in the research section of this analysis. Due to the challenge of assigning monetary values to each of the aspects of output generated by Armed Forces, the model used for this study will have the requirement to handle non-monetary outputs. Respectively, indicators will need to be defined that measure the output of Armed Forces in the absence of explicit market prices.

2.3 Tools for Measuring Public Efficiency

Considering the above outlined circumstances, several tools have been developed that are supposed to help determine efficiency in the public sector. In particular these need to meet the high demands of empirical studies while solving the challenges faced with non-monetary measures. All of these methods commonly use a production frontier as the basis to calculate an efficiency frontier.

[40] see Bayer, S.: Generation Adjusted Discounting 2004, p.153
[41] see Bayer, S.: Generation Adjusted Discounting 2004, p.156

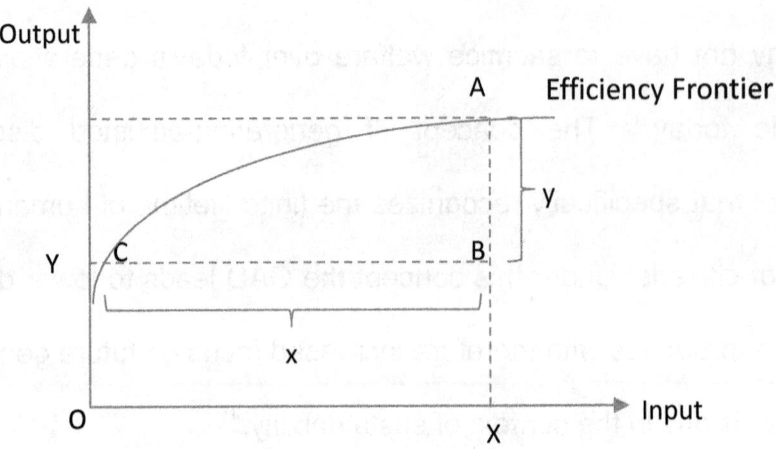

Figure 4: Efficiency Frontier

(see Mandl, U./Dierx, A./ Ilzkovitz, F.: Efficency of the Public Sector 2008, p.8)

The illustration above visualizes the concept of the efficiency frontier. The vertical axis reflects the output and the horizontal axis reflects the input. A, B and C are representing the input-output combinations that three given nations achieve in their current state. The big advantage of this model is that the respective data used do not need to be measured in monetary terms. In the absence of monetary measures, a Key Performance Indicator (KPI) can be applied to the model as well.

By comparing the position of the DMUs relative to the frontier, conclusions can be drawn with regard to their respective efficiency. Nations A and B have the same level of input, but Nation A reaches a much higher output. Consequently, Nation A operates more efficiently than nation B. Nation C reaches the same level of output as Nation B, but with significantly less input. Therefore nation C operates also more efficiently than Nation B. Nation B could improve its efficiency in two ways now. One option is to keep the input steady and improve the output to reach at least the level of Nation A. Or the second option would be to reduce the input at least to the level of Nation C, while maintaining the same level of output. If Nation B would in fact be able to produce an even higher output than Nation A or the same with even less than Nation C, Nation B would in fact be altering the shape of the frontier and be representing a new benchmark to others.

In other words, in an efficiency frontier model a DMU is called inefficient, if there is one or more DMU that dominates with fewer expenses and at least the same output or by achieving the same output with fewer expenses.[42] If a DMU is dominated by more than one, the dominating one with the fewest input is called most-dominating in the context of an output centric efficiency model.[43] Efficiency in these models refers to the absence of a better performing DMU with at least as much output.[44]

In order to determine the position of DMUs relative to the frontier, the frontier has to be defined in a first step. Depending on the problem at hand and/or available insight into the conditions of the market that is analyzed, researchers have different options for constructing the frontier. Besides the collection of appropriate data, the consideration of frontier shape is certainly one of the more complex tasks that are required.

Today's approaches can be either classified as a parametric or nonparametric method. The main difference between the parametric and the non-parametric approach is that parametric frontier functions require the ex-ante definition of the functional form of the efficiency frontier.[45] Through statistical estimates the form and shape of the

---

[42] see Eeckaut, P./Tulkens, H./Jamar M-A.: Belgian Municipalities 1993, p.304
[43] see Eeckaut, P./Tulkens, H./Jamar M-A.: Belgian Municipalities 1993, p.304
[44] see Eeckaut, P./Tulkens, H./Jamar M-A.: Belgian Municipalities 1993, p.306
[45] Mandl, U./Dierx, A./ Ilzkovitz, F.: Efficency of the Public Sector 2008, p.8

efficiency frontier is predefined by the researcher and the actual performance of the DMUs is compared against this frontier.

Non-parametric methods do not require a predefined efficiency frontier, because the actual sample data will provide the required input for this. However a DMU called efficient in this context may indeed be more efficient compared to other DMUs, while it is still not achieving an optimal input-output relation.[46] This is because a best possible efficiency position on the frontier is simply not known. This situation is called efficient by definition and a situation that a model cannot identify, if only existing organizations are compared with each other in absence of a known best possible constellation of input and output.

Within the parametric class of models it can be further subdivided into deterministic or full frontier models and stochastic models. The deterministic view considers all variances as being under control of the organization, while the stochastic model incorporates factors that account for external factors like regulatory-competitive environments, weather, luck, socio-economic and demographic factors or uncertainty.[47] Models can be further classified by their approach regarding the construction of the production frontier through econometric or mathematical programming. The econometric approach is stochastic and attempts to distinguish noise from inefficiency, while the programming method lumps all those factors into one.[48]

---

46 see Crawford, I./Klemm A./Simpson H.: Public Sector Efficiency 2003 p. 107
47 Murillo-Zamorano, L.: Frontier Techniques 2004, p. 36
48 see Lovell, C.: Production Frontiers 1993, p.19

Non-parametric methods have a further characteristic that has to be noted and carefully considered, when the data sample is analyzed. Depending on the choice of input and output they can produce outliners, extreme data points on the frontier, which do not fit into the pattern of the observed set of data. This may be caused by errors in the database that have to be fixed, but may also be the result of unlikely, but fully correct data that actually provide valuable insight for the study. This can e.g. be the case if one DMU has in fact found a way of operating much more efficient than others. Outliners on the efficiency frontier therefore need to be analyzed carefully. Since USA and China are in scope of this study this phenomena needs proper attention. Both nations spend a significantly higher amount on defense than most other nations in the study, which will put them in the area of the frontier that is more prone to outlier effects.

Deterministic frontier functions can be solved either by the usage of mathematical programming methods or by means of econometric techniques, while the stochastic models use econometric techniques only, as the following example of the Stochastic Frontier Analysis illustrates.[49]

A common parametric approach is the Stochastic Frontier Analysis (SFA) as a statistical method to fit the frontier based on econometric methods. Mandl (at al) define this model as follows:[50] This approach assumes a specific functional form for the relationship between input and output. The advantage of this method is that it is able to cover the effects of exogenous shocks, i.e. nondiscretionary factors, because it can

[49] See Murillo-Zamorano, L.: Frontier Techniques 2004, p. 36
[50] See Mandl, U./Dierx, A./ Ilzkovitz, F.: Efficency of the Public Sector 2008, p.9

specify the equations based on such assumptions. This approach is shown by the solid line in Figure 4. A through F shows the input/output relation of a given set of organizations. The solid line presents an optimum ratio predetermined based on assumptions before the actual data are applied to the model. The deviation is shown by the brackets. As outlined, the SFA method explicitly allows the consideration of exogenous factors, like measurement inaccuracies or other errors also called noise in the model. Therefore any deviation of an organization from the frontier is caused by either noise and/or inefficiency. The respective degree of noise versus inefficiency is one further factor that has to be predefined before the data are applied. Based on this the requirements for the SFA Analysis include the ability to actually create the ideal input/output ratio in form of the SFA Frontier and also give insight into noise deviations expected during the study.

The non-parametric approaches have been traditionally assimilated into Data Envelopment Analysis (DEA), a mathematical programming model applied to observe data which provides a way for the construction of production frontiers as well as for the calculus of efficiency scores relative to those constructed frontiers.[51] The Frontier is determined by the sample of data itself and any DMU below that frontier is considered inefficient. DEA do not accommodate for noise, and therefore can be considered as a non-statistical technique where the inefficiency scores and the envelopment surface are calculated rather than estimated.[52]

[51] Murillo-Zamorano, L.: Frontier Techniques 2004, p. 35
[52] see Murillo-Zamorano, L.: Frontier Techniques 2004, p. 37

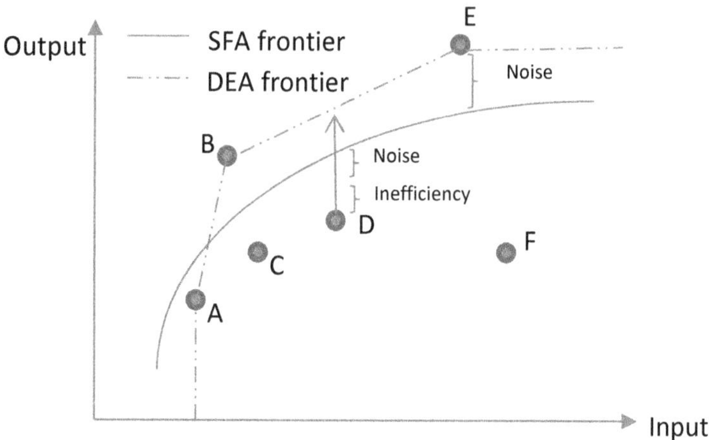

Figure 5: SFA and DEA Analysis

(see Crawford, I./Klemm A./Simpson H.: Public Sector Efficiency 2003 p. 108)

In a simple way the DEA is illustrated in Figure 5 by the dashed line. The DMUs on the line produce the highest level of output with the least input in the data sample. All DMUs below that line are therefore considered inefficient, since benchmarks achieve a better input/output ratio.

The initial DEA model was originally presented by Charnes, Cooper and Rhodes (CCR) (1978), and is based on the work of Farrell (1957)[53] which has already been described in Chapter 2.1 as the basis for research around efficiency frontiers. Since the initial study by Charnes, Cooper and Rhodes more than 400 articles have appeared in the literature and according to Seiford and Thrall such rapid growth and widespread acceptance of the methodology of DEA is testimony to its applicability for economic analyses.[54]Within the scope of DEA models the CCR model after Charnes, Cooper and Rhodes (1978) has a specific characteristic as it allows for the use of multiple input and

[53] see Charnes, A./ Cooper, W.W./Rhodes, E.: Efficiency of DMU's, p.429
[54] see Seiford, L./Thrall, M.: Developments in DEA 1990, p.10

output factors. The essential characteristic of the CCR construction is the reduction of the multiple-output/multiple-input situation (for each DMU) to that of a single virtual output and virtual input.[55] This model imposes three restrictions on the frontier technology: Constant returns to scale; convexity of the set of feasible input-output combinations; and strong disposability of inputs and outputs.[56] In this model (see Figure 6) all DMUs produce the output level Y through a combination of input X1 and X2. Line DG provides the efficiency frontier. The technical efficiency of A can be derived as OA*/OA. A* represents a deviation of A based on the performance of its peers B and C, which is computed as their proportional input X1 and X2. The efficiency of E is deviated by direct comparison to C, since both are on the same ray of the efficiency isoquant with OC/OE.

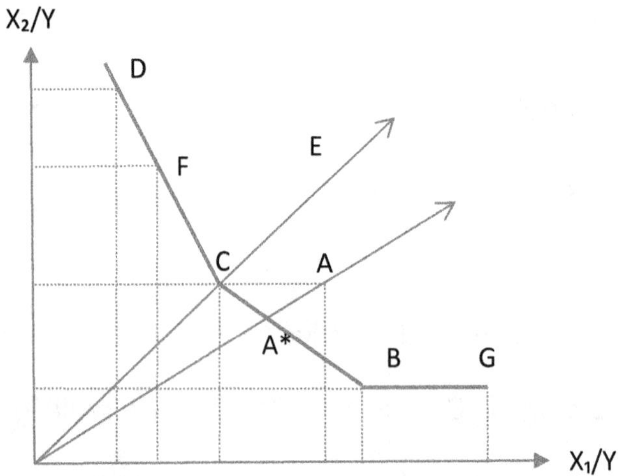

Figure 6: CCR Model as illustrated by Murillo-Zamorano

(see Murillo-Zamorano, L.: Frontier Techniques 2004, p. 38)

[55] see Seiford, L./Thrall, M.: Developments in DEA 1990, p.10

[56] Murillo-Zamorano, L.: Frontier Techniques 2004, p. 37

Even though G is located on the frontier it cannot be seen as technically efficient, since it uses the same input X2 as B but a higher input X1 to produce the same level of output. Overall, the model provides some room for criticism. For one it does not allow for external impacts which are considered as noise e.g. in the SFA model. Furthermore, since it operates under the restriction of constant scale it does not allow for economies of scale on the input side, a factor that actually has to be considered pretty common in most markets.

An advantage of this model is however that it can be used to evaluate input as well as output efficiencies. The illustrated examples use the input oriented perspective and evaluate how DMUs reach their output with current input volumes and how the input vector relates to that output from an efficiency perspective. The DEA model explicitly allows for output-oriented analysis as well, which relates to an analysis of how much output is achieved with the given input and if in an efficient situation more output would be feasible. However studies like the work of Coelli and Perelman (1996) have shown that both input as well as output models lead to similar results.[57] Under the assumption of constant return even parametric and non-parametric methods show the same results, but results do differ for parametric approaches if return of scales is considered.[58]

Deciding on one of the two approaches seems to be up for discretion based on the analyzed field of business. Highly regulated markets where the output is a fixed

---

[57] see Coelli, T/Perelman, S.: Parametric and Non-Parametric 1999, p 332
[58] see Coelli, T/Perelman, S.: Parametric and Non-Parametric 1999, p 332

exogenous factor like the power supply are probably more suitable to be analyzed through the input-oriented approach, since the input is the variable factor that drives efficiency in a business model with a fixed exogenous output factor.[59] In scope of Armed Forces this can actually be argued both directions depending on the way the budget is been derived. Some countries allocate a certain percentage of their GDP to defense; therefore it would be desirable to achieve the maximum output with that amount. In other cases a nation may specifically determine the security goals as a given output and then backward engineer to the respectively required defense budget.

Weighting the ramifications of the available approaches, the non-parametric area is the best fit for the purpose of this study. Since there is no ideal production function available in the context of national security that nations could be benchmarked against, having the data sample itself create the frontier is an ideal approach. The details provided by the parametric approach would certainly provide attractive additional information, however the demands on ex-ante knowledge required for the analysis limit its applicability for this study.

Within the non-parametric area of models the researcher needs to make one further specification in terms of the form and shape of the frontier that shall be constructed. Since in the non-parametric area of frontiers the data points determine the frontier, the frontier is shaped based on the way the data points are connected. The respective method has to be chosen based on the assumed returns to scale or as a free

---

[59] Murillo-Zamorano, L.: Frontier Techniques 2004, p. 42

disposal if the returns to scale are unknown. The following figure will illustrate these options.

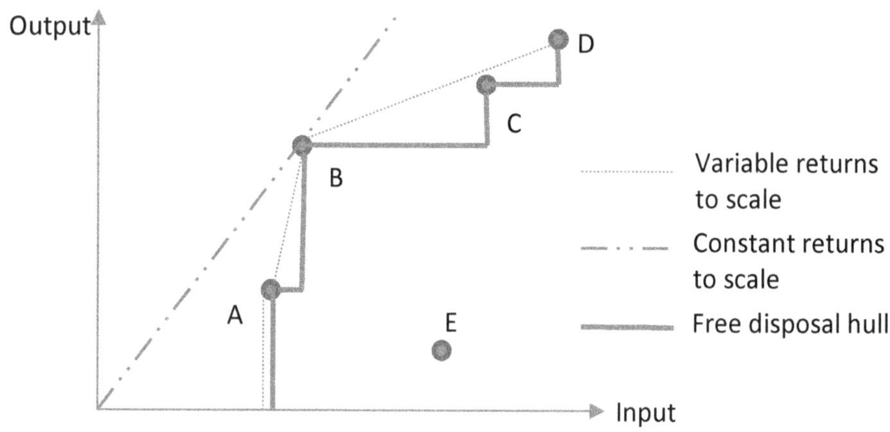

Figure 7: Efficiency Frontier and Returns to Scale

(see Murillo-Zamorano, L.: Frontier Techniques 2004, p. 38)

While there are several variants to the shape and form of the efficiency frontier, essentially they go back to any of these three basic models. Constant returns to scale are illustrated by the ray from the origin through the data point with highest efficiency, defining effectively only one efficient DMU in the example above. Variable returns to scale connect data points since they assume variances within the input to output relations across the frontier. The FDH approach simply connects the data points and avoids the requirement of having to specify any returns to scale assumptions. The FDH approach is therefore a special form of the DEA model in its concept and represents an alternative option for research areas with unknown returns to scale. Between all approaches it is a common definition, that data points along the line of the frontier are efficient. Any points between the data points along the frontier are further possible constellations that are considered efficient.

Understanding the returns to scale in the military environment is a challenge. Models that require constant returns to scale are likely not applicable for defense spending analyses. Military assets are expensive and one can presume that there are critical mass levels that are required to achieve progress at certain levels. On the one hand adding more infantry soldiers to the army may have a rather linear relationship, since the costs are mostly cost-per-head for salary, training, equipment and overhead. Aircraft carriers on the other hand are considered one of the most powerful weapon systems currently on the market. These investments come with an immense price tag in terms of initial investment and ongoing maintenance. They presumably allow for much more power projection capabilities than a standing, rather immobile infantry battalion. Unleashing the power of this highly mobile weapon right in the backyard (technically shoreline) of an enemy elevates the capabilities of the Armed Forces to a whole new level.[60] Similar is the case with a nuclear arsenal, which is tremendously expensive to acquire and maintain as well. This situation however can also be an opportunity for smaller nations to leverage the resource pooling within alliances as a measure for driving efficiency gains. A recent McKinsey study indicates that nations with resources in subcritical mass could drop capabilities all together and rely on their partners to provide those capabilities.[61]

[60] Aircraft carriers are just used as an example to illustrate the financial implications of investments in military assets. The example shall not diminish the capabilities that a well-trained infantry unit can bring to the battlefield. In the end both units fulfill very different functions.

[61] see McKinsey& Company: The Future of European Defense 2013, p.12

Given that the economies of scale for defense spending are not understood yet, also variable returns to scale are not an option for the model in this study as the choice could not be supported by scientific evidence.

This leaves free-disposability as the basis for return to scale assumption in this study and therefore the free-disposal hull analysis as the model of choice. In this research the main focus is to study if and how performance levels differ between nations in terms of operating their Armed Forces. Understanding the full shape of the frontier is no requirement to answer this question as the actual datasets themselves and their comparisons provide the evidence required.[62]

Based on the upcoming specifications the FDH model will be more clearly defined in Chapter 4 for the scope of this research subject.

2.4 Current State of Research

Tools that measure efficiency in the public sector have been applied on a variety of topics in recent years. Researchers have specifically identified the variants of the DEA method as suitable in the context of measuring efficiency in markets without market prices. Given that this paper aspires to apply a similar approach on Armed Forces, this chapter will provide information around the current state of research regarding non-parametric tools that have been applied on efficiency studies in the scope

[62] Chapter 2.4 will furthermore show that existing studies indicate that the outcomes of FDH and DEA with variable returns to scale are very similar in terms of comparing existing DMU's and their efficiency performance.

of public goods. From this, lessons learned and parallels will be identified in order to build the specific model that will be applied to the data set collected for this study.

The most notable examples of studies in the public sector cover the efficiency of the education system.[63] McCarty and Yaisawarng as a specific example conducted research on the efficiency of New Jersey school districts. Even though they based their research on existing models, they made some notable enhancements. Most notably they added a Tobit Analysis[64] to their approach in order to distinguish between factors that are under control of the school management and those that are not manageable. They summarize that both approaches lead to similar results as to their efficiency ranking and their positive correlation.[65] Removing the potentially unmanageable components of the data set however produced different results and some districts that were considered efficient in the full data set are now classified as inefficient. They point out that these differences need to be analyzed carefully due to the fact that they can either be intended and relevant or seemingly unrelated.[66] To summarize these findings and draw a lesson for this study, using Tobit analysis and adjusting for non-manageable factors does not change the results to the extent of identifying the ranking of DMUs. Only when specific actions to improve efficiency or organizational target settings are considered, removing non-controllable aspects would become important, since the individual actors should only be held accountable for things they can actually influence.

---

[63] For examples, see Bessent A. and Bessent W.: Efficiency of Schools 1980 and Faere, R./Grosskopf, S./Weber, W.: School Performance 1989

[64] The model itself is not relevant for this paper, just the relevant conclusion drawn from its application in this referenced study.

[65] McCarty T./Yaisawarng, S.: New Jersey School Districts, 1993 p. 285

[66] McCarty T./Yaisawarng, S.: New Jersey School Districts 1993 p. 286

In the context of this analysis this underlines that distinguishing between these two is not relevant for this particular study, since the goal is to determine where nations are today in terms of efficiency and what factors are potentially driving efficiency independent of who is responsible.

The DEA application on education provides also a fundamental general similarity to the context of Armed Forces, since in both cases the benefits provided are public and non-monetary and results occur in the future. The public education system, just as Armed Forces, operates under the fiscal budget restrictions of the government.

Further similarities can be found with regard to a study around Belgium municipals and their respective efficiency. Eeckhaut, Tulkens and Jamar applied the FDH and other DEA analyses on the dataset of Belgium municipals. The datasets contained their respective budgets on the input side and performance indicator as their output. These indicators were not quantifiable in monetary terms given the lack of available market prices for governmental services, which presents similar circumstances that are faced in this paper in the scope of Armed Forces. They further adjusted the input factors based on one-time effects, like investments which tend to be irregular, to make the data set of the different DMUs more comparable.[67] Respective one-time effects could be seen in the context of Armed Forces as well, e.g. with regard to incremental costs for foreign deployments. Based on this, in the scope of this analysis it has to be considered that some of the analyzed nations in fact do operate under certain one-time influences. This specific research work also underlines the

[67] Eeckaut, P./Tulkens, H./Jamar M-A.: Belgian Municipalities 1993, p.301

reasoning for applying the FDH method in the scope of the research conducted in this paper. As part of their research multiple tools were applied and the results compared. Besides FDH, the DEA method with various restrictions regarding returns to scale had been applied as well. In comparison the authors state that the DEA method, which assumes variable return of scale, is the closest to the FDH definition and both together provide similar results that can be seen as realistic under consideration of qualitative evaluations. In combination with the various already described advantages of the non-parametric approach in context of this analysis, this indicates that the FDH method is suitable to evaluate the efficiency of Armed Forces.

Also, military-related topics have been analyzed regarding the efficiency of Air Force Maintenance Units for the US by Charnes, Clark, Cooper and Golany (1985) and for Israel by Roll, Golany and Seroussy (1989). Furthermore studies were conducted around military recruiting units in the US by Charnes, Cooper, Divine, Klopp and Stutz (1985) as well as Lovell, Morey and Wood (1999). In 1960, Hitch and McKean started a discussion around military efficiency and appropriate funding levels. They proposed early forms of production functions to make military funding decisions and presented an illustrative example for efficiency analysis in terms of military airlift capacities. The frontier analysis was remarkable base work, but did not even get close to the scope aspired by this analysis.[68]

[68] Hitch and McKean created a very simplified frontier based on two factors to create a model for illustrating efficiency analysis and decisions around resource allocations in the military context. They did not use a realistic database nor did they attempt to perform a cross-country comparison.

No study is available that has aspired to determine the efficiency of Armed Forces on a cross-country comparison, which underlines the necessity of the particular study conducted with this analysis.

3 Efficiency of Armed Forces

3.1 Introduction

Carton claimed in 2001 that the US military potentially is far better than any other military in the world, but that the government owes to the public not just a better military but the best military for the money that is being spent.[69] This highlights that efficiency and determining the sources for efficiency is an important basis for policy decisions in public as well as private organizations.[70] Given the ongoing budget constraints of nations, politicians are always interested in finding a way to fight and win conflicts with the lowest level of resource investment.[71]

Talking about efficiency is often received with a negative touch – at least for those parties that receive the task to show improvements in efficiency. To them it means enforcing changes and giving up resources and getting the same done with less. One should not forget though that understanding efficiency in the military context can be of great benefit for military leaders. If a budget reduction is handed down from the government, the military can understand how to cope with this situation with limited negative impacts on their readiness.

Furthermore it can also help them to better understand their enemies as described by Gholz. He points out that over the long term, improved studies on military

[69] see Carter, A: Keeping the Edge 2001, p. 3
[70] see also Lovell, C.: Production Frontiers 1993, p.5
[71] see Gholz, E.: Military Efficiency 2003, p.5

efficiency can actually help to determine the level of threat posed by a hostile nation's economy and military state.[72] Given that simply comparing the stock of military capital is not sufficient to fully grasp a nation's capabilities, analyzing the efficiency stage can be a determining factor. If the enemy operates with high efficiency it poses a bigger threat, since the nation could get easily more out of its Armed Forces for any additional resource it allocates to them in times of conflicts. An inefficient enemy may not be able to achieve increases that quickly.

Along with productivity, efficiency is also an important measurement that can be used to evaluate the performance of an organization. This paper distinguishes between productivity and efficiency following Farrell's and Forsund's definition. Productivity is the index output divided by the index of input.[73] Efficiency actually goes beyond that scope and considers that an organization can be performing at a higher level through transforming the function for producing the output or even changing inputs. Therefore efficiency represents the success of a production unit in producing the largest possible output from an available set of inputs.[74] The following example will illustrate the distinction in a military context. A nation's Armed Forces may maintain a fleet of supply airplanes productively with high capabilities at low cost, but the alternative of transportation using ships may provide the same output capability at even lower cost. Hence the transport by ship in this example is more efficient than the transportation by air. This simplified example can be transferred to the Armed Forces as a whole to

[72] see Gholz, E.: Military Efficiency 2003, p.5
[73] see Forsund, F. R.: Productivity Growth in Norwegian Ferries 1993, p. 352
[74] see Farrell, M. J.: The Measurement of Productive Efficiency 1957, p.254

determine how much output they produce as an organization for what is allocated to them in terms of resources.

To summarize, efficiency has to be seen as an essential tool for Armed Forces to stay competitive in times of scarce resources. It can also help military leaders to understand the state, professionalism and threat posed by one's adversaries. However to date no one has attempted an economic analysis of the efficiency state of Armed Forces on a cross-national basis.

In the following chapter an economic model will be built in order to address this open question at hand.

3.2 Perceived Security

According to Fredland (at al.) the dominant paradigm considers national defense from a neoclassical perspective as a production process.[75] In this view military power is the output that is achieved with the input of resources in the form of aircrafts, vehicles, people and further elements. Different combinations of input can hereby lead to the same output, like a few high-tech weapon systems can be equally effective as a lot of less sophisticated ones. These input factors are then used to produce military capabilities that ensure the national security goals. The main goal is in most cases, at least in democracies, a high perceived level of security by its citizens by either fighting a war or deterring potential aggressors from starting one.

[75] see Fredland, E./Kendry, A.: Privatisation of Military Force 1999, p.150

The output respectively is defined as the product or service an organization produces, while the outcome is the goal that the organization achieves with this output. The question for this study is now where a measure for efficiency should come into play. Is it the output produced? Or the outcome achieved?

The following outlines will determine if the outcome could be considered a suitable measure in an efficiency analysis. This is the purpose for the existence of the organization 'Armed Forces', after all.

One factor that describes and explains the level of perceived security is the so-called national security function, which according to Poast can be described as follows:[76] The security function assumes that a nation can decide how to allocate the given production capabilities between military goods and civil goods. For every additional unit spent on military goods, the perceived level of security increases, but at diminishing marginal returns of having more weapons. As soon as enough military assets have been built up to diminish the fear of an adversary's threat, additional weapons will not further improve the level of perceived security. This function is now further influenced through the decisions taken by adversaries. If they increase their spending on the military, the own level of spending is not sufficient anymore and therefore the national security function shifts down.

[76] see Poast P.: The Economics of War, p.73

This interdependence of defense spending among adverse nations can ultimately result in an arms race. According to Smith, an arms race typically involves two nations. In rare occasions it can span across several nations or occur for a single nation in case of exaggerates fears of a potential opponent.[77] The increase is military spending is then considered integral part of an arms race if it is specifically motivated by an anticipation of/or in response to military moves of perceived or potential adversaries.[78] This specifies that the increases are explicitly caused by the nation's relationship and interdependence with a rival nation. One would assume that it is unlikely that two partners are truly equally strong and that one side quickly prevails over the other and therefore citizens of that nation do feel safe and secure. In reality however the presumably weaker partners actually often end up gaining on initially stronger or wealthier opponents.[79] This 'Paradox of Power' can be explained by the fact that the initially weaker party is typically motivated to fight harder.[80] The implications of arms races will be described in more detail in an upcoming chapter.

A specific theory within this area of studies is the orthodox view on military spending which according to Smith assumes that a state recognizes a well-defined national interest and tries to defend this interest against potential threats through appropriate military precautions.[81] In this theory the national interest is defined as a result in the process of democratic and pluralistic systems to resolve problems of social

[77] see Smith, T.: Arms Race, p.255
[78] see Smith, T.: Arms Race, p.256
[79] see Hirshleifer, J.: The Paradox of Power 1991, p.177
[80] see Hirshleifer, J.: The Paradox of Power 1991, p.178
[81] see Smith, R.: Military Expenditure 1977, p 63

choice and conflicts of interest by creating a consensus which a neutral state administration acts upon.[82] Furthermore from an economic perspective this level of capability is supposed to be achieved at minimum costs, which emphasizes the relevance of the efficiency of military organizations. Smith also criticizes the orthodox view on military expenditures by claiming that it diverts the attention from private interests and avoids oppositions by assuming a general consent regarding the decisions and further ignores the political and economic function that military expenditures characterize as well.[83] So even if it is assumed that a national objective exists and can be identified, according to Smith it puts unrealistic demands on rationale and knowledge to actually define an objective optimal strategy.

Furthermore during peacetime the effect of military expenditures is rather psychological. It cannot reliably be determined if a certain amount of military expenditures was really necessary.

As a result of this the liberal view on military expenditures opposes the existence of consent in national interest according to Smith: The level of defense spending is determined as a result of bargaining and compromises between specific groups in nations that have a high stake of interest in military expenditures. In this view military threats which influence the perceived level of security do not determine the level of defense spending, but are rather created to justify them.

[82] In this view the public governance process would determine the perceived level of security of the nation's citizens and determine appropriate actions to change it, if necessary.
[83] see Smith, R.: Military Expenditure 1977, p 64

The statements above refer to a situation in which an increase in military capability is used to increase the perceived security by matching or exceeding the capability of a potential adversary. Overall the perceived level of security is also influenced by multiple further factors. Olsen and Zeckhauser are notable researchers in the area of national alliances and provide interesting insight into this topic.[84] According to their studies a nation that is close to the border of an enemy country might value security higher than a more distant nation. They argue that a nation with a large boarder might value ground forces higher than a more compact country that is more concerned with potential air strikes by enemy air assets. In the same manner they see the culture influence the willingness of citizens of a nation to invest in military assets as well. Militaristic or pacifistic cultures can lead to very different standpoints for contributions to the military.

While the perceived level of security is to a certain extent the ultimate goal of military investments in a democratic nation, it is apparently inadequate as an output measure for this study. Perceived security is not the output produced by Armed Forces and defense investments, but is actually the goal that a nation pursues by making these investments. For one a practical challenge is faced in order to obtain consistent datasets that can be used in an empirical study with cross-national comparison. However also from a logical perspective it cannot be the first step of an efficiency analysis. Perceived security is highly influenced by political and geographic circumstances. Two nations with equal rankings in citizens feeling safe and secure may

[84] see Olsen jr. M./Zeckhauser, R.: Theory of Alliances 1966, p. 271

have totally different levels of military expenditures. A large country may need more expenditure to reach the same level of security as a small nation. A nation fearing a current or perceived threat may have to maintain a higher level of defense spending to make its citizens feel as safe as another nation residing in a peaceful environment. And another nation may in general or for historic reasons feel more insecure in the first place.

The following diagram illustrates this relationship and also points out where efficiency becomes relevant in this value chain of producing an outcome. Output is set one step before the outcome and efficiency can be a measure in this transformation process. The outcome as the last step is the effective application of the output that has been produced. All of this is under the influence of external factors.

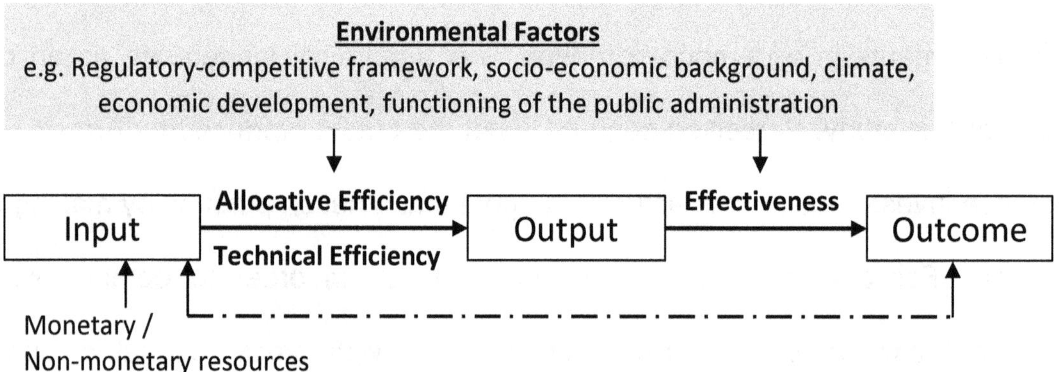

Figure 8: Framework for Effectiveness and Efficiency

(see Mandl, U./Dierx, A./ Ilzkovitz, F.: Efficency of the Public Sector 2008, p.3)

Even if not used as a measure for efficiency, understanding the citizen's satisfaction with their Armed Forces can provide valuable insight when the results of this study are being interpreted. It can for example provide insight into which way efficiency improvements of nations should go. Efficiency can be improved by either increasing output or reducing input. If the output proves to be sufficient, e.g. citizens are already feeling safe and secure, an increase of output would not make any sense from an economical perspective. The organization would be more efficient in terms of producing the output, but this increase is not necessary since the current output is already sufficient to produce the aspired outcome. Hence more output does not increase the benefit for the citizens and therefore the social welfare. It would be a wasteful use of resources for the economy.

In terms of this paper one source has been identified that will help to gain insight into the perspective of a nation's citizens with regard to their military. The WorldValueSurvey conducts questionnaires across different nations at different points in time and to some extent touches military matters and national security. These data points will be used as the efficiency scores of nations are analyzed. [85] An understanding of this definition and context will be relevant in this paper due to the fact that a public survey will be quoted and referenced as a supporting source to underline the interpretation of the empirical results of this study.

[85] The WorldValuesurvey is a global survey asking citizens of nations to comment on and or rank certain aspects of cultural or political interest. More details will be given in Chapter 4.2.1.

3.3 Defining Military Capabilities

Analyzing efficiency of organizations with production frontiers requires a clear definition of the input and output factors applied to the model. The output 'produced' by Armed Forces covers multiple facets and this chapter will aspire to create a common understanding as a basis for the upcoming research.

Several terms are used in this area by scientists, defense officials and the media. The term military effectiveness is probably the most commonly, but also the most inconsistently, used term particularly in politics and press. It sometimes refers to the readiness of troops, the success of a specific mission or presumed capabilities of a specific military asset. In other cases it is defined as victory in an armed conflict. However in the military context effectiveness is much more complicated than that. Victory is the outcome of a battle and therefore not a characteristic of an organization, but rather a result of an organization's activity.[86] Furthermore victory as the outcome of a war or military action cannot be the only measurement for military effectiveness, since Armed Forces fulfill a variety of tasks.

The term war itself already can actually be highly misleading since the definition of war is not very straightforward. A common approach to classify an armed conflict as war considers the amount of deaths and the involvement of at least one government organization in the armed conflict.[87] This distinguishes a war e.g. from peacekeeping missions or skirmishes between local tribes in a country. War can be further classified

[86] see Millet, A./Murray, W./Watman, K., Military Effectiveness 1986, p. 38
[87] see Smith, R.: Military Economics 2009, p.74

as a limited, local war when limited military actions are used to extend international politics.[88] This differs from a full-blown total war where a nation will put every effort to the battlefield e.g. in cases where their own liberty is at stake. If the economic aspect is considered, one can speak of economic warfare as defined by Smith as follows:[89] Economic actions can either be used to complement military actions, used as part of regular warfare or as a substitute for military action. Practical examples would be the destruction of crops and supplies during a campaign to avoid them being available for the enemy or blockades like the German submarine attacks on the supply routes in the Atlantic Ocean during both world wars. Sanctions are a typical example for a substitute usage of economic measures. Instead of a military attack on supplies, the supply to a certain nation is blocked.

North Korea is one very current example where ongoing tensions have shown that a nation better be ready in the military sense if it takes on economic actions. North Korea has made military threats several times opposing the economic sanctions to its country.[90] All these examples illustrate that today most western nations keep their Armed Forces busy in activities that are not necessarily a war in its precise political definition.

Considering non-violent military acts as part of warfare is becoming even more important in recent years since cyberattacks by foreign hackers into key government

---

[88] see Hitch, C./McKean, R.: Defense in the Nuclear Age 1960, p.13
[89] see Smith, R.: Military Economics 2009, p.168
[90] see Lorenz, A.: Pyongyang's Provocation 2003

facilities make it to the front of the newspapers more frequently.[91] The implication behind this is that not only do tanks and bombers have to be seen as military assets but so does computer proficiency. With this also comes a big challenge in terms of resources, since the skillset of software developers is also a scarce resource in the private sector. China underlines the importance of non-lethal force and states in its latest strategic discussions that non-kinetic actions with economic, financial, information, legal, and psychological instruments are part of modern warfare.[92]

In order to determine the output of Armed Forces, defining effectiveness in terms of war in the classical sense therefore does not go far enough. Some authors actually define military effectiveness more specifically as a sub-set of the actual output. In this view military effectiveness is the process by which Armed Forces convert resources into fighting power and a fully effective military is one that derives maximum combat power from the resources that are physically and politically available.[93] Judgment of effectiveness should thus retain some sense of proportional cost and organizational process.[94] This implies that effectiveness incorporates some notion of efficiency as well[95], underlying the importance of the research conducted within this paper.

Chang draws a similar conclusion while using slightly different terms. He distinguishes in this context between potential and actual power. Hereby is actual power derived from the potential power through intangible factors like will, capacity, mastery or

[91] see Greenwald, G./MacAskill, E: Target List for Cyber-Attacks 2013
[92] see Annual Report to Congress: China 2009, p.14
[93] see Millet, A./Murray, W./Watman, K., Military Effectiveness 1986, p. 37
[94] see Millet, A./Murray, W./Watman, K., Military Effectiveness 1986, p. 38
[95] see Millet, A./Murray, W./Watman, K., Military Effectiveness 1986, p. 37

skill.[96] Brooks provides a similar definition in context of the science of international relations. The capabilities of Armed Forces consist of the resources that are available, while military effectiveness describes the actual process of how a nation uses its resources and translates them into military power.[97]

Biddle actually tried to prove this point through the results of his research conducted on battles and wars of the last century. He emphasizes that according to his study material factors like the pure amount of troops are not solely determining the outcome of a conflict but that non-material factors specifically have to be considered as well.[98]

To summarize these statements, just simply summing up a nation's value of military equipment and adding the salaries of their soldiers is not a sufficient output to measure in context of this paper as these neglect the impact of intangibles. As a further conclusion the term military effectiveness has to be used with caution since it refers to the process of creating output and outcome and it is not an output of Armed Forces itself.

Broadening the perspective may help to derive a better definition of the military output for the scope of this study. Political scientists often use the wording national power which is defined as a country's capacity to pursue strategic goals through

[96] see Chang C., A Measure of National Power 2004, p. 3
[97] see Brooks, R./Stanley, E.: Creating Military Power 2007, p. 3
[98] see Biddle, S.: Military Power 2006, p. 191

purposeful action.[99] Biddle uses the term military capability as a subset of the broader national power which would also include other soft factors in addition to military ones.[100] One can think of economic strength or political weight in international relations. Military capabilities in this sense seem to be a suitable definition and measure for the scope of this paper since it in fact does refer to the actual output of the Armed Forces. Military capabilities therefore express the strength that a nation can activate to pursue its interests.[101] The following figure illustrates how in this context military capabilities can be seen as a subset of national power. In this definition intangibles are at least considered from a conceptual perspective.

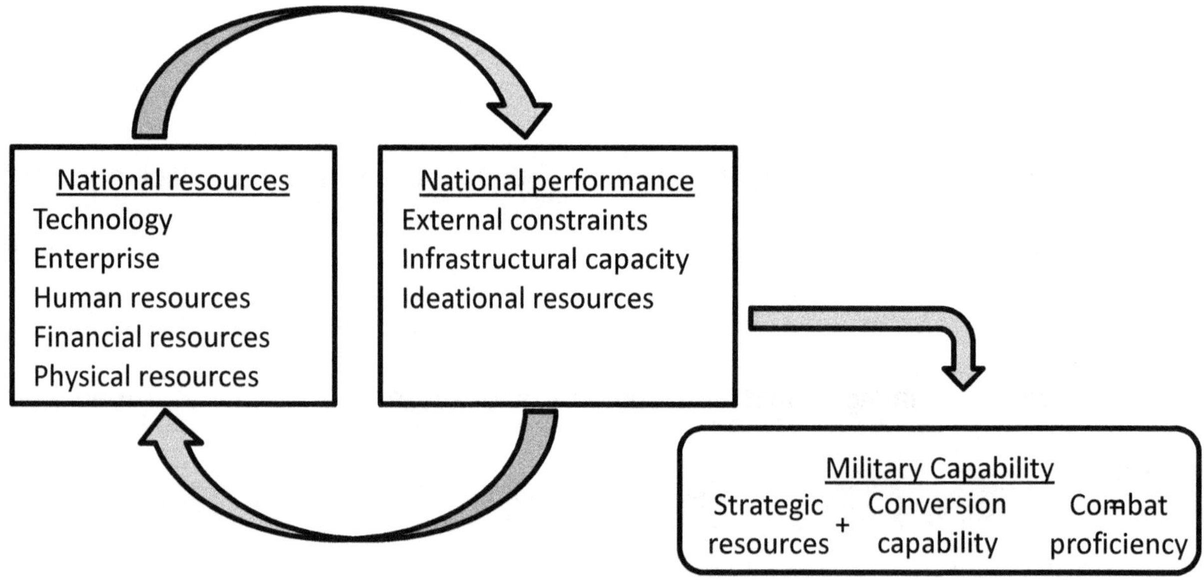

Figure 9: National Power

(see Tellis, A./Bially, J./Layne, C./McPherson, M.: Measuring National Power 2000)

[99] see Tellis, A./Bially, J./Layne, C./McPherson, M.: Measuring National Power 2000, p.44
[100] see Biddle, S.: Military Power 2006, p. 5
[101] see Tellis, A./Bially, J./Layne, C./McPherson, M., Measuring National Power 2000, p.47

Gholz supports these interdependencies and the importance of intangibles:[102] Military effectiveness captures the ability of a fighting force to execute its doctrine. This effectiveness is influenced by the amount and quality of the given set of resources as well as psychological factors such as morale and unit cohesion. It is further determined by a military's skill at employing combined arms, operational planning, logistical support, and other factors that increase the probability of successful outcomes to military operations.

The relevant conclusion for this chapter is that an output factor used for the model cannot be limited to an evaluation of military assets; it has to be able to capture in some way the intangible factors as well. Some of the most relevant intangible factors will therefore be described in more detail in the upcoming chapter. Furthermore the term military capability will be used to describe the output of Armed Forces considering resources as well as intangible factors for measurement of how much forceful power a nation retains.

[102] Gholz, E.: Military Efficiency 2003, p.10

3.4 Intangible Factors

3.4.1 Culture

Culture is a broadly used term and it is certainly out of scope for this paper to analyze every aspect of it. However this chapter will at least touch some aspects in order to highlight how culture can influence Armed Forces and how they may influence their capabilities and efficiency as well. The following outlines will touch selected examples of relevant cultural aspects from the national level over the organizational level down to the level of individuals in this order.

On the national level culture e.g. addresses the way citizens of a nation relate to their Armed Forces. Militarism describes to which extent military values are being absorbed by the broader public and therefore to which extent society supports the military and its interest.[103] The effects of strong militarism could be the topic of a separate detailed paper, but there are certain negative impacts on the economy and general society associated with high militarism.[104]

Culture can also be a factor in the context of international relations. The US is an example of a nation that is used to operating on its own. In the future the US expects to face an increasing number of missions with involvement of non-US military forces and even non-military organizations. However the culture of the US military system focuses on secrecy and its own internal procedures as a key factor to obtain a military

[103] see Smith, R.: Military Economics 2009, p.28
[104] see Smith, R.: Military Economics 2009, p.28

advantage over potential adversaries.[105] The US however has recognized the need for cultural sensitivity of their officers and the Department of Defense has stated that understanding the culture of adversaries as well as allies will be critical in the 21st century and the future of national security.[106] The example of the Operation Enduring Freedom proves this point. The allied forces initially successfully utilized local forces to diminish the Taliban regime. But after this initial success the local tribes were not willing to support ongoing missions to fight Al-Qaida in the Afghan backcountry. This points out that the model only works when the objectives of all parties are aligned, which apparently in this case was not sufficient enough to motivate the tribes to oppose a well hidden and furiously fighting enemy in the rough terrain of Tora-Bora in Afghanistan during the later campaigns of the war.[107]

Given the variety of missions that Armed Forces face today it in fact does make a difference whether to prepare troops for a conventional war or unconventional military actions. Tucker from the US Army War College describes that one soldier cannot be prepared for both given that conventional and unconventional warfare are characterized by completely different cultures that a soldier needs to fit into.[108] However other strategists point out that at least adding crowd control and civil-military operations to the skill-set of infantrymen could extend their skillset in that direction.[109] This last statement seems to neglect the fact that unconventional warfare certainly is much more sophisticated than adding police work to a soldiers skill-set. The role of specials forces

[105] see Sherwood-Randall, E.: International Relations, p.239
[106] see Gansler, J.: Democracy's Arsenal 2011, p.50
[107] see Shimko, K.: The Iraq Wars and America's Military Revolution 2010, p.138
[108] see Tucker, D. : Confronting the Unconventional 2006 p. 68
[109] see Horowitz, M. / Shalmon, D.: The Future of War 2009, p.316

as cultural diplomats and trainers makes it obvious that these tasks require a much different set of skills and capabilities than those a regular infantryman is being trained on.

Culture on the organizational level reflects e.g. the Armed Forces openness toward change. The following practical examples cited from Smith illustrate this:[110] During a once hold competitive bidding for a new tank model, a vehicle scored the highest among the defined criteria but wasn't selected by the US Army, simply because it didn't look like a tank. As a second example, during the Vietnam War it became clear that helicopters and jets are not a good option to provide close air support for the troops on the ground. With focus on endurance and survivability the A10 Thunderbolt was introduced as a well-armored slow-flying aircraft. While embraced by the troops on the ground, the US Air Force pushed back because they didn't like the look and feel of this plane which is also reflected in its nickname, 'warthog'.

Another more recent example was the focus of the US Air Force on high-performance fighter planes instead of unmanned reconnaissance vehicles. This decision was overruled by the office of the Secretary of Defense[111] and as can be seen today these unmanned military assets found broad usage and benefits in the recent conflicts.

A further cultural factor with impact on efficiency and effectiveness is the habit in the military to rotate service members between jobs frequently. This influences the

[110] see Smith, R.: Military Economics 2009, p.137
[111] see Gansler, J.: Democracy's Arsenal 2011, p.40

experience of military officers that are assigned to a task. In the US one reason for inefficiencies in the defense budget is appointed to the fact that the average duration of officer assignments to a staff job in the Pentagon with between 2-3 years is too short to have them fully understand and then improve any of the processes.[112]

A further cultural factor is the rivalry between branches in the Armed Forces which is typically organizationally structured in separate land, naval and air forces. As an illustrative example Smith uses the Italian Air Force:[113] Within the Italian military they used to be the only organization that was allowed to maintain winged aircraft military vehicles which created a monopoly with similar inefficiencies that are also attributed to monopolies in the public economy. This policy led to the fact that the Italian Navy was not allowed and able to operate aircraft carriers in their arsenal which might have been an increasing factor for their respective capabilities.

Inter-branch rivalry still persisted within the US Armed Forces in the 1990s. It was criticized that the military was focused on technological changes but did not work on organizational and doctrinal changes.[114] According to Weitz still during the First Gulf War the branches of the Armed Forces conducted their own planning for campaigns and did compete for attention and resources based on their own internally preferred tactics.[115] Cebrowski points out that this changed remarkably during the later missions in Afghanistan where not the actions of independent branches stood out, but rather a joint approach was directed by a Joint Chief of Staff of Central Command, orchestrating

[112] see Jones, L.; McCaffery, J.: Financial Management 2007, p.96
[113] see Smith, R.: Military Economics 2009, p.27
[114] see Shimko, K.: The Iraq Wars and America's Military Revolution 2010, p.140
[115] see Weitz, R.: Jointness and Desert Storm 2004, p.135

the forces at a level of teamwork not seen before.[116] This is also confirmed by Biddle, who describes the method as quite new and unprecedented; US commandos were the only ground forces and they fought at the side not of their countrymen but local Afghan people with support of their sister branch the US Air Force.[117] Boot points out similar examples for the Second Gulf War, where ground forces were supported by the Air Force with Close Air Support and Army Supply Troops were used to support the advancing Marine Corps Forces.[118] Cohen actually underlines this further and claims that specifically the senior military leaders of the post-Vietnam era are more confident and aggressive when it comes to the application of Information Technology and collaboration across branches.[119]

Culture can also have an impact on the operations of Armed Forces down to the individual soldiers. Dunnigan and Nofi call military tradition one of the key ingredients for military power since it contains a collection of habits that make Armed Forces effective in combat.[120] Traditions are an intangible factor very hard to measure and very difficult to maintain in peacetime.[121] Biddle specifically points out that this factor was an important one during the first Gulf War:[122] US junior officers had been trained and encouraged to make their own decisions, pursue opportunities and react based on their own hands-on judgment on the battlefield. This led to the fact that units were working towards the strategic goals without standing around and waiting for orders from the

[116] see Cebrowski A.: Battle Plan under Fire 2004 - Interview
[117] see Biddle, S.: Afghanistan and the Future of Warfare 2002, p.6
[118] see Boot, M.: War Made New 2006, p.400
[119] see Cohen, E.: transformation in Military Affairs 2004, p.400
[120] see Dunnigan, J./Nofi, A.: Shooting Blanks 1991, p.60
[121] see Dunnigan, J./Nofi, A.: Shooting Blanks 1991, p.61
[122] see Biddle, S.: Military Power 2006, p. 141

higher command. It was expected from them to understand their superior's intentions and operations and to find the best way to achieve them within their area of responsibility.

This is further underlined by the fact that changes are mostly driven from the bottom of the organization. According to Cohen a revolutionary change[123] cannot be applied top-down by senior leaders but has to develop bottom-up by giving junior leaders the ability to spontaneously apply people and technology in real military tactical circumstances to make them work and learn from them.[124] Along these lines it can also be argued that trust and honesty are critical attributes of a professional force given that this ensures the accurate and quick flow of information across the levels of command.[125]

Another intangible factor which is part of military culture is morale as Smith outlines:[126] Morale can be considered crucial in combat since confident, motivated troops that continue fighting despite dangers can make the difference between defeat and victory. Motivation can be defined as the belief in what the troops do and try to achieve. Adaptability describes the flexibility to react to changing circumstances on the battlefield and granting the troops responsibility for their actions. The element of confidence has several dimensions and refers to the trust of troops in their training, equipment and leadership. Specifically studies have found that the predominant factor

[123] The Theory around RMA – Revolution of Military Affairs will be outlined in more detail at a later point in this study.
[124] see Cohen, E.: Transformation in Military Affairs 2004, p.400
[125] see Millet, A/Murray, W/Watman, K., Military Effectiveness 1986, p. 51
[126] see Smith, R.: Military Economics 2009, p.153

for the willingness of troops to fight and die in war is the bond among the soldiers; they fight for one another and not for their country.[127]

This chapter touched a myriad of aspects and most of them are worth specific studies of their own. Specifically analyzing the culture on the organizational level of Armed Forces and its troops requires a lot of detailed insight and expertise. This chapter provided a base to ensure a common understanding of cultural aspects that are part of the qualitative measure applied in the efficiency analyses.

3.4.2 Education and Training

While training refers to the specific development and ongoing conservation of military skillsets of a soldier, education refers to the basic knowledge that the soldiers received in a nation before they joined the service. The rationale is that a better-educated population leads to more trainable military recruits that are better able to handle sophisticated weaponry and are more confident in battle.[128]

The general guidance on how to employ military assets is usually defined by the military's operational doctrines and fostered as part of military exercises. Specifically a gap in training and doctrine can be seen as a common problem in the military.[129] This describes a situation in which troops are insufficiently trained to use and apply the equipment and tactics of the operational units on deployment or actually in the theater

[127] see Brooks, R./Stanley, E.: Creating Military Power 2007, p. 5
[128] see Brooks, R.: Making Military Might 2003, p. 183
[129] see Millet, A/Murray, W/Watman, K., Military Effectiveness 1986, p. 67

of war. As an example, the importance of training became particularly evident after the Vietnam War was over and lessons learned were analyzed. Shimko states:[130] The Air Force discovered that their pilots had been lacking in air-to-air combat as well as surface-to-air missile avoidance situations. An Air force pilot was in very high danger of being shot down during his first 10 missions, but after that his survivability rate increased significantly. As a reaction to this finding, the so-called Red-Flag training exercise was implemented, which is a six-week training in Air combat under most realistic conditions including allied forces flying Soviet aircrafts posing as aggressor squadrons. This type of training is expensive for the nation since a modern fighter jet is estimated to cost $5,000-$20,000 per hour flight – not counting potential ordnance fired.[131] On the other side a shot down plane presents significant financial loss as well, not to speak of the potential loss of human lives.

Similar efforts were put in place by the Army in form of the National Training Center in Fort Irwin, Calif., which was supposed to help the Army to increase realistic training and help adjust to the newly established All Volunteer Force military.[132] Shimko draws the conclusion that these cases emphasize that training just as new technology can be a force multiplier in combat.[133]

As another facet, training or lack of training can also actually determine the selection of military equipment as one historic example illustrates best. In the 1500s the

[130] see Shimko, K.: The Iraq Wars and America's Military Revolution 2010, p.38
[131] see Dunnigan, J./Nofi, A.: Shooting Blanks 1991, p.61
[132] see Shimko, K.: The Iraq Wars and America's Military Revolution 2010, p.38
[133] see Shimko, K.: The Iraq Wars and America's Military Revolution 2010, p.38

bow and arrow was widely replaced by guns despite the fact that the bow up into the 19th century was still more effective and deadlier than guns.[134] The reason was mainly that a gun could more easily be used by the troops while handling a bow and arrow properly took a long time for a soldier to master.[135]

While military strategists independently point out the importance of military training, there are some reasons why training often comes short of attention. Wilson for example points out that training is an expensive, short-term investment and senior officers therefore prefer to spend money on new weapons systems instead in order to leave a legacy.[136] This tendency is particularly strong in countries that do not expect an armed conflict in the near-term future.[137] Dunnigan and Nofi link this to cultural aspects. The lack of immediate threats may make the service member avoid hard and sometimes dangerous peacetime training which is a bad habit that could be overcome with a strong devotion to military tradition.[138] This behavior has the risk to leave the military in an unprepared state during war times, given that conflicts often arise unplanned.[139]

The Revolution in Military Affairs or short RMA describes a current theory claiming that technological innovations have significantly improved the capabilities of modern Armed Forces like never before. Biddle claims that the success of the RMA is not just explainable though technology alone. To him the RMA is a combination of

---

134 see Smith, R.: Military Economics 2009, p.121
135 see Smith, R.: Military Economics 2009, p.121
136 see Wilson, G.: This War Really Matters 2000, p.50
137 see Biddle, S.: Military Power 2006, p. 50
138 see Dunnigan, J./Nofi, A.: Shooting Blanks 1991, p.61
139 see Biddle, S.: Military Power 2006, p. 50

technology and an improved skill-set of military personnel.[140] According to Biddle it would be a mistake to modernize a military at the cost of accepting less skilled personnel.[141] Biddle simulated and analyzed the 1991 Gulf War and based on his data he found that neither technology nor the skill-set alone can explain the military success and remarkably low casualty rates of that conflict.[142] The US Marine Corps equipped with their 1960 era tanks for example suffered lower casualty rates than the US Army with weapons of higher sophistication.[143] Biddle's conclusion is that specifically the combination of technology and skill with a high emphasis on the skill- set explains the remarkable success of the US troops.[144] Press draws the conclusion that Biddle's findings imply that technologically weaker but better trained adversaries could actually match the US forces if they are trained better.[145] However he also further outlines that in case of the Gulf War, the advantages of the US were high enough in both aspects, that skill-set alone as well as technological advantage alone would have led to the same outcome in the battles.[146] Press illustrates this with the example of a battle fought during the Gulf campaign in which the technological advantage of a USMC division was completely diminished. In a specific close quarter battle situation neither air support nor artillery support was available while still the USMC beat the Iraqi troops without suffering any casualties.[147] To Press this was mainly thanks to supreme training

[140] see Biddle, S.: Victory Misunderstood 1996, p.140
[141] see Biddle, S.: Victory Misunderstood 1996, p.141
[142] see Biddle, S.: Victory Misunderstood 1996, p.178
[143] see Biddle, S.: Victory Misunderstood 1996, p.153
[144] see Biddle, S.: Victory Misunderstood 1996, p.178
[145] see Press, D.: Lessons from Ground Combat 1997, p.137
[146] see Press, D.: Lessons from Ground Combat 1997, p.138
[147] see Press, D.: Lessons from Ground Combat 1997, p.141

specifically with regard to maneuvering troops on the battlefield.[148] Even though he criticizes Biddle's finding to a certain extend he comes to the same conclusion. In order to be competitive on future battlefields the United States has to find the right balance between R&D and training in order to be proficient in both and to win current as well as future battles.[149] This ramification has a significant impact on the force planning and defense budgets of nations.[150]

While the examples above outline the importance of training for combat readiness, there is also an implication for the efficiency of Armed Forces. In interdependence with the governmental purchasing process and privatization, military personnel may be involved in certain investment decisions and the monitoring of military services that are provided by third parties. This implies that the involved military personnel should have obtained the necessary education to negotiate with private suppliers and should have obtained the skills to monitor their respective performance and to take corrective actions if required. Singer points out that in a specific example during the Balkan conflict logistical support provided by third parties did overrun their initial budget by hundreds of millions due to a lack of training on the side of the supervising military officer.[151] In 2001 the DOD started to address this issue through initiatives that emphasize continuous learning and a focus on acquisition specialists as a career within the DOD to keep and expand the acquisition skill-sets of its

[148] see Press, D.: Lessons from Ground Combat 1997, p.141
[149] see Press, D.: Lessons from Ground Combat 1997, p.146
[150] see Biddle, S.: Victory Misunderstood 1996, p.140
[151] see Singer, P.W.: Corporate Warrior 2007, p. 154

employees.[152] These guidelines have even been formalized in policies which are aiming at sustained and successful career paths in the DOD.[153]

Also aside from the soldiering skills and training, successful coordinating, supplying and transporting forces in theaters of combat require skills in the context of management and analysis in order to determine and execute the most effective distribution of manpower and expenditures.[154]

As part of this analysis there is a significant challenge faced when it comes to evaluating the impact of education and training of troops. However since it is a key aspect of military capabilities, the output factors used to measure a nation's strength ideally incorporate to some extent intangible factors and therefore the impact of education and training.

3.4.3 Strategy and Tactics

Strategy in the military context defines how nations utilize their forces in peacetime and how they are being used to engage an enemy in conflict situations. These strategic decisions, specifically on the highest level called grand-strategy, are often crossing the border of military responsibility so that senior military leaders and military operations are only a piece of the bigger puzzle. This is important to consider when it comes to justifying certain political or military actions and decisions. The reason

152 see Lippitz, M./O'Keefe, S./ White, J.: Revolution in Business Affairs 2001, p. 175
153 see Snider, K.: Defense Acquisition 2008, p.33
154 see Beckley, M.: Economic Development and Military Effectiveness 2010, p.57

why strategy is important is its strong interdependence with economic decisions around the military budget. Hitch and McKean state:[155] Strategies outline ways of using budget and resources to achieve military objectives and that technology provides options for possible strategies. They also highlight the strong interdependence of military and economic decision even down to the operational level as they state that the process of economizing the Armed Forces goes hand-in-hand with military decisions. Strategy and costs are as interdependent as the front and rear sights of a rifle.[156] This seems to be a reasonable assumption since e.g. military planners cannot base their strategies on aircraft carriers if the government does not give them funding to acquire any. And military planners need to think within the borders of their available budget and budget decisions are ideally made in accordance with the military requirements.

Across all of this it is an economic problem to decide on the most efficient and economic approach.[157] For these reasons relevant aspects of strategy and tactics will be considered from the perspective of military capabilities and efficiency.

Some authors argue that strategies should be specifically aiming at the weaknesses of a potential opponent.[158] However given that the weaknesses might not always be known a strategy should be followed that at least lets the nation exploit its own strengths.[159] As a matter of fact there seems to be evidence that this approach would be more suitable anyhow, especially since today's conflicts are hard to predict

[155] see Hitch, C./McKean, R.: Defense in the Nuclear Age 1960, p.3
[156] Hitch, C./McKean, R.: Defense in the Nuclear Age 1960, p.3
[157] see Hitch, C./McKean, R.: Defense in the Nuclear Age 1960, p.3
[158] see Millet, A/Murray, W/Watman, K., Military Effectiveness 1986, p. 49
[159] see Millet, A/Murray, W/Watman, K., Military Effectiveness 1986, p. 49

and modern Armed Forces need to be mobile and flexible. Therefore having Armed Forces that are specialized on fighting one specific enemy only is not fulfilling today's needs. The US-Army e.g. faced a crisis after the Cold War ended since all the equipment and doctrines were specifically aiming at defending Europe against a potential Soviet invasion and were not suitable to oppose any of the threats they faced afterward.

Technological advancements are a further factor that influence strategic decisions. World War I was the first event in the 21st century that made evident how significantly technology can change military strategy and tactics. The industrialization enabled the creation of new weapon systems that made every movement in the open on a battlefield a devastating encounter for the troops with flying shrapnel.[160]

In more recent history during the Iraq War in 1991 the US Air Force was widely used to prepare the battlefield for the ground forces and was able to achieve that goal to an extent that was never before seen in military history.[161] According to military historian Keegan, 1991 has seen a revolution in accuracy that helped to achieve the goals sought by the Air Force since the beginning of the use of strategic bombing.[162] These improvements lead to the fact that strategists and military historians see the Air Force in a different role today. Lambeth sees in this development an increase of the relative combat potential of the Air Force in comparison to other forces.[163] Hallion attributes the Air Force not anymore just as decisive in war but actually as a determining factor for

[160] see Shimko, K.: The Iraq Wars and America's Military Revolution 2010, p.16
[161] see Budiansky,S.: Air Power 2004, p. 423
[162] see Keegan, P.: The Iraq War 2004, p.142
[163] see Lambeth, B.: The Transformation of American Air Power 2000

victory.[164] With less open movement of troops on the battlefield the maneuverability, concealment and suppressing fire are new elements that become important.[165] Cohen concurs stating that modern wars are fought without clear frontline and the use of air force, long range missiles and Special Forces aims at bypassing heavy resistance and to strike key vulnerable points of the enemy.[166] Since strategy and tactics are describing the way military assets are used, it implies that a good planner can get more out of the assets at hand if he or she deploys them wisely. Hence this is an intangible skill-set of Armed Forces that can strongly influence the power it can project and consequently increases the possible output produced.

Drawing the right conclusion and making the right decision shall be left to the military leaders since it certainly also depends on the specific mission at hand and a lot of other aspects. It shall be emphasized though that this topic cannot be neglected by civilians if it comes to efficiency evaluations. In western democracies, a civilian like the president or defense secretary has the last call on the directions of a military deployment. And furthermore civilians orchestrate the budgeting process and have a say in the purchasing process for military equipment.[167] Even though the expertise around strategy and tactics is certainly more with senior military leaders, there is an important take-away for this analysis. Most conflicts involve on the strategic level decisions that cross the border of military responsibility and the success or failure of missions should not blindly be appointed to the military leadership alone. Furthermore

[164] see Hallion, R.: Storm over Iraq 1997, p. 264
[165] see Hallion, R.: Storm over Iraq 1997, p. 264
[166] see Cohen, E.: Transformation in Military Affairs 2004, p.404
[167] This topic will be covered in a later chapter in more detail.

the topic does also become relevant in economic terms for military investment proposals. Investments in military equipment at the scale and price tag of new fighter plans, submarines or aircraft carriers are in most nations approved by civilian servants and they certainly need to understand the underlying rationale for their need in order to ensure the available defense budget is spent wisely and efficiently between all alternatives at hand.

3.5 Output: Measuring Military Capabilites

In order to analyze the efficiency of a nation's Armed Forces with a non-parametric model, appropriate output factors have to be defined. The factors have to measure the military capabilities and consider the important intangible factors beside the material ones. Measuring military capabilities is not necessarily an area of expertise for economists, but in political science and international politics multiple approaches are found that can be considered suitable for the scope of this study. Although a lot of theories try to measure these capabilities in monetary terms, some of them work under the assumption that military capabilities are a non-monetary public good and also account for intangible factors.

One early notable study approached the quantification of military output based on estimating the military capital of nations. A challenge around 1980 during the Cold War was to compare the military capabilities of the US with those of the Soviet Union. Hildebrandt used the theory of military capital to identify the military potential of both adversaries. He approached the topic as follows:[168] In order to get results he analyzed how military assets can be transferred and evaluated in monetary terms. Military capital stock is the aggregated monetary value of all physical assets, including military equipment, military facilities, spare parts and ordnance. He suggests to distinguish the military capital stock in K1, measuring the value of the assets at a given point in time and KL, measuring the long-term productivity over the remainder of their lifetime. K1 can be seen in analogy with the already mentioned term military readiness, since it describes the amount of military capability that can be called upon immediately. This capacity can be calculated through the military efficiency function. This function aggregates the capacity of all available military assets considering their respective individual capabilities. A modern piece of equipment in the stock may have a higher capability than an older one and the capabilities of existing assets are depreciated over time considering a decrease in capabilities through aging.[169] The long-term benefit in monetary terms is essentially calculated as the net value of benefit. The net present value of benefit is the asset's value minus respective repair and maintenance costs that occur.[170] While this approach certainly helps putting military capabilities in numbers, it does not go far enough in the scope of this paper. Specifically soft factors are not considered, like training and capacity of the troops and further a lot of the required data are hard, if not impossible, to obtain. Specifically the lifetime of assets, the expected maintenance and repair costs to just name a few.

---

168 see Hildebrandt, G.: Military capital 1980, p.1
169 see Hildebrandt, G.: Military Capital 1980, p.3
170 see Hildebrandt, G.: Military Capital 1980, p.4

Some scientists in the field of economics and political science tried to address the problem of intangibles and get to actual databases by utilizing discrete variables like population, GNP, size of Armed Forces, extent of land area and access to resources such as grain and steel.[171] These methods are a good fit to the approach used in this paper since the production frontier model allows for the usage of Key Performance Indicators in order to measure efficiency. In addition the databases are transparent, consistent and not simply a potentially subjective ranking.

The indicators defined by political scientists are commonly divided into two categories and classified based on the underlying variables as either single-variable or multi-variable approaches.

Most single-variable approaches use military expenditures or economic indicators in order to assess the military capabilities of nations. In the mid-1970s during the time of the Cold War, the CIA analyzed the capability of the Soviet military by estimating the share of budget the government devoted to defense.[172] This was estimated to be around 15 percent but ended up to be around 20 percent as research after the end of the Cold War showed.[173] However according to Smith these asset-related capabilities do not automatically translate into effectiveness, but rather intangibles like the grand strategy and leadership, training, tactics, logistics, morale and maintenance of equipment have to be considered as major factors as well.[174] This underlines the relevance of the outlines around intangibles as covered in the prior chapters. Since

[171] see Tellis, A./Bially, J./Layne, C./McPherson, M., Measuring National Power 2000, p.5
[172] see Smith, R.: Military Economics 2009, p.25
[173] see Smith, R.: Military Economics 2009, p.25
[174] see Smith, R.: Military Economics 2009, p.25

these intangibles are difficult to measure, a proxy will need to be identified that can still help to consider these. Beckley e.g. suggests covering intangible aspects through the general economic development status of a nation as an additional proxy for measuring capabilities.[175] The logic behind this is that a nation that dominates the cycles of economic innovation can utilize the fruits of these efforts to also produce effective military capabilities.[176] This is independent of how many weapons the nation in fact produces, because in this view in terms of war all economic capabilities could be converted to support wartime production. Respectively, a highly developed country is expected to have higher skilled workers and better factories to produce sophisticated equipment more efficiently.[177] Even though the military tends to be seen as a separate sector it is really embedded in the economy of a nation. Therefore countries that excel in producing commercial goods also tend to excel accordingly in the production of military equipment and skillful military personnel.[178]

Davis[179] and Organski[180] favor national income as the best indicator while Hitch and McKean advocate the use of a country's total output or GDP.[181] Alternatively Russett[182] proposes the use of fuel and energy consumption as an economic measure.

[175] see Beckley, M.: Economic Development and Military Effectiveness 2010, p.74
[176] see Tellis, A./Bially, J./Layne, C./McPherson, M., Measuring National Power 2000, p.36
[177] see Beckley, M.: Economic Development and Military Effectiveness 2010, p.12
[178] see Beckley, M.: Economic Development and Military Effectiveness 2010, p.12
[179] see Davis, K.: National Power 1954
[180] see Organski, A.: Word Politics 1958, p. 436
[181] see Hitch, C./McKean, R.: Defense in the Nuclear Age 1960
[182] see Russett, B.: Concentration in the International System 1968

Single-variable approaches have the advantage of ease-of-use and data are accessible through public databases. However some authors argue that these factors do not accommodate for the complexity of military capabilities in international politics.[183] Furthermore it has been outlined above that the nature of warfare has changed and today's military faces a myriad of different tasks. Economic factors therefore might be an indicator for a nation's capability to fight a full-blown war, but this does not necessarily match the actual requirements that Armed Forces face today. Furthermore these models presume that a nation's combat power can be increased by focusing its economic strength on military production. This however neglects the fact that combat proficiency is to a high degree dependent on intangible factors like experience and training, which an organization has to accumulate over time.

Beckley's research underlines at least the fact that economic development and defense spending is to some extent relevant and worth being analyzed: Economic development impacts military capabilities independent from their actual level of military spending.[184] This means that if two countries have the same level of military spending, the country with the stronger economic development will prevail in a conflict. This however does not imply that the economic level of development automatically allows for conclusions about military capabilities. If the spending level is not the same he does not answer the question as to how much more economically powerful a nation has to be to overcome the shortage in the defense spending.

[183] see Tellis, A./Bially, J./Layne, C./McPherson, M., Measuring National Power 2000, p.5
[184] see Beckley, M.: Economic Development and Military Effectiveness 2010, p.72

The second grouping of indicators works with a basket of factors and is classified as multivariable approaches. In 1956 Knorr proposed to measure national power by determining a country's ability to produce military manpower and supplies for a war.[185] However he did only provide a basis and did not specifically determine the level of power of nations or specifically list influencing factors. Clifford German in 1960 more specifically identified the factors of nuclear capabilities, land, population, industrial base and military size as relevant for determining the military power of nations.[186] In 1965 Fucks followed a similar approach and identified the three summation variables population size, energy production and steel production as relevant for the power of nations.[187]

In order to approach this topic in a consistent way that allows for cross-national comparison, the research project CINC has been identified as a useful proxy for measuring military capabilities. CINC stands for Composite Index of National Capacity and uses the three dimensions demographic, industrial and military indicators as the most comprehensive predictor of success in diplomacy, crisis or war.[188] The CINC index has been calculated for a multi-year time horizon starting with 1816 with the last update for the year 2007. The key variables are based on indicators that have been identified by many of the previously mentioned scientists in international politics as key components. These are namely a nation's iron and steel production, military

185 see Knorr, K.: The War Potential 1956, p.41
186 see German, C.: Evaluation of World Power, 1960, pp. 138-144
187 see Fucks, W.: Formeln zur Macht 1965
188 see COW: NMC Documentation V.4.0 2010, p.6

expenditures, military personnel, primary energy consumption, total population and urban population.[189]

It shall be encouraged though to see these factors also in the context of history and state of technology. Steel and grain production might have been key factors of military capabilities in the beginning of the last century but the advancements in information technology and innovations in this sector may be more prominent in determining the sophistication of products in recent years.

It is hard to determine which of the indicators described above is the best basis for an analysis in the context of efficiency of Armed Forces. If efficiency should be analyzed in the context of a current conflict, a qualitative method would probably be the most accurate one since it is not relevant how much military power a nation could create based on its economic power, but actually how much is currently deployable to a battlefield and, in economic terms, if these troops are maintained in a financially efficient way. These qualitative analyses are not easily accessible and come with some challenges as well. However this paper will propose a model and will analyze efficiency based on one specific qualitative assessment that is in fact available. This will be described in Chapter 4.3.4.

Furthermore any chosen factor should be seen in the context of the global political environment during the timeframe set for the scope of research. During the two world wars and to a certain extent during the Cold War nations did in fact try to convert

[189] see COW: NMC Documentation V.4.0 2010, p.1

as much economic power as possible into military capabilities because of an imminent threat to their homeland. In recent years however industrialized nations use their Armed Forces more as a political instrument and for peacekeeping as well as counterterrorism missions. Since the timeframe of this paper focuses on 1995 through 2005, this is important to be considered. Using the GNI as a potential indicator for a western industrialized nation e.g. would assume that these nations in the timeframe of research are willing to put their full economic power into play to fight a war. But most nations are currently not facing an immediate threat to their homeland and even though western alliances were at war in Afghanistan and Iraq, they still maintained their civilian industry with focus on production for the commercial sector. War is expensive, a strong economy is certainly the key ingredient to afford one, but it would go too far to use an indicator like the GNI to measure the absolute military capabilities of the nations under review in the context of today's political environment. However it again depends on the context of the research and what the data are being used for. Therefore this paper will propose one option of measurement for this area of indices as well.

In terms of this paper the CINC index will be used as the primary research model since it is a consistent set of data over centuries, frequently updated and commonly used in the literature. For comparisons the GNI data will be used as well, but not analyzed to the same degree as the CINC index as the primary indicator. To add to the current state of research this paper will show in addition an analysis of efficiency based on a qualitative evaluation of the capability of Armed Forces which will be described in Chapter 4.2.3.

3.6 Input: Defense Spending

In economic terms expenditures differ from costs, with costs referring to the flow of value caused by a good or action, and expenditures describing the underlying financial transaction in particular. Defense spending or military expenditures are therefore the money that is used to buy troops, weapons and the organization that manages them.[190] Costs caused by maintaining Armed Forces or military missions cover a broader area of relevant topics. Marginal cost calculations e.g. are a basic economic tool and can be used to evaluate specific military actions. In terms of military deployments marginal cost calculation can be used to determine the incremental cost of the deployment since some basic costs would have been incurred anyway purely by maintaining forces.[191] Notable cost areas in the military environment that go beyond financial expenditures are further for example the loss of life of soldiers or their injuries. Another example is the loss of productivity in the economy given that citizens serve their nation in uniform instead of producing goods for trade. Furthermore costs of an operation may or may not include the replacement of military equipment, extra interest on national debt, a risk premium added to the oil price and the future costs for care of wounded and killed soldiers.[192] Measuring these costs is in addition being made more difficult due to the high uncertainty of the outcome or further development of a military deployment. Case in point, besides the expectation of a casualty rate within the thousands[193] during the Iraq War in 1991, not more than 147 Americans and 99 other

[190] see Smith, R.: Military Economics 2009, p.24
[191] see Smith, R.: Military Economics 2009, p.30
[192] see Smith, R.: Military Economics 2009, p.31
[193] see Mann, E.: Thunder and Lightning 1995, p. 19

coalition soldiers were killed in action.[194] During the first three weeks which is considered the invasion part of the Second Gulf War, 137 American soldiers died.[195] Some sources show different numbers, but none of them change the message that even though every death is a tragedy, the actual casualties were significantly lower than expected by the military leadership of the United States. Instead of financials the casualty rate is actually a commonly used measure by political scientists to determine the cost of a war. See e.g. Shimko who specifically uses the casualty rate to determine the cost of the Gulf Conflicts.[196]

Military expenditures are a part of the total budget of a government and actually represent the money spent on military assets. Which government activities are actually accounted for as military expenditures can quite vary between different sources and nations. Some specific examples for items that are known to be treated differently between countries are the national intelligence service, paramilitary forces, nuclear and space-related research programs and pension for retired members of the Armed Forces.[197] This specifically makes it difficult to analyze and compare government financials if no consistent definition of military expenditures is followed. Not to speak of situations where countries follow different definitions or even intentionally report false data with the goal to overstate their potential military power or to hide certain activities. Examples for data sources that aspire to normalize datasets across countries are the SIPRI database or alliance reports such as those of NATO. These approaches also

[194] see Finlan, A.: The Gulf War 1991, p. 85
[195] see Van Creveld, M.: The Changing Face of War 2006, p.247-8
[196] see Shimko, K.: The Iraq Wars and America's Military Revolution 2010, p.158
[197] see Smith, R.: Military Economics 2009, p.90

adjust data for further factors that influence the way military expenditures have to be interpreted. These are notably financial factors like exchange rate effects and purchase price adjustments over time. Exchange rates have a major impact if military expenditures are reported in a single common currency like US-Dollars. Commonly used are therefore expenditures in absolute terms at constant currency and as a purchase price-adjusted number. Purchase price adjustments consider the factor of inflation and cost of living. These express that one has to spend more on an item today than one would have in prior years. Other commonly used approaches ensure comparability by setting the military expenditures in relation to a common basis. E.g. military expenses divided by population to get a per capita spend or divided by the absolute economic output as a percent of the GDP or GNI.[198]

There are further commonly used terms of measurement more specifically on the operational side. The capital intensity of the Armed Forces can be calculated by measuring the amounts of defense spending divided by the number of members in the Armed Forces to get a per capita spent.[199] Military expenditures are also often shown in form of subtotals. Smith provides an overview: wages for military and civilian personnel, operation and maintenance of weapons systems, housing and military base, R&D and investments in new weapon systems. He also states that specifically the labor-related piece can easily make up over half the spending and even up to two thirds in international comparisons.

[198] see Smith, R.: Military Economics 2009, p.92
[199] see Smith, R.: Military Economics 2009, p.93

Even the costs per soldier can significantly differ between the functions that they fulfill. A US Special Forces soldier like the Green Beret e.g. is estimated to cost about $260,000 over his 18 months of training alone.[200] One determining factor for the level of capital intensity of a nation's military is whether a conscript or volunteer army is maintained. This correlation will be described in more detail in a specific chapter of this paper. An alternative structural view that is commonly used refers to the metaphor of the tip of the spear. This metaphor classifies the closeness of military organizations to actual combat actions and helps to analyze requirements from an operational perspective. Infantry units as the tip of spear e.g. have different needs and requirements than support units in command and logistics.[201] Making sound decisions about an adequate split should be left to the military leaders. However civilians involved in defense decisions need to understand these basics as well since simple indicators can be a good snapshot of the health of the Armed Forces. If O&M costs increase and investments decrease, this is an indication for aging equipment and a threat for the military readiness. Old equipment tends to break and may not be able to be deployed at a moment's notice.

Above examples illustrated costs and expenditures specifically in the context of wars or actual deployments. However defense spending also occurs in times of peace and nations maintain a stock of military resources. The reason is that the defense budget can not only be used to attack and defend but also to deter and therefore

[200] see Poast P.: The Economics of War, p.101
[201] see Singer, P.W.: Corporate Warrior 2007, p.91

contribute to the perceived level of security of a nation.[202] In terms of deterrence the military expenditures can be seen as an insurance premium. Nations aspire to avoid an expensive conflict through maintaining a certain force level that discourages aggressors to take military actions. Smith outlines that a state must acquire the capability to deter potential aggressors as well as the ability to defend its interests in case deterrence fails.[203] This adds the precautious character to the definition of defense spending and points out that the stock of available defense resources are not only used to conduct armed conflicts, but also to avoid them. This is important in peacetime discussions around evaluations of potential budget cuts. The US still invests in fighter planes despite already dominating any other air force in the world. Appropriate investment levels are certainly open for discussion but dominance in this area has a deterrence effect only if other nations realize that they do not even stand a chance in air combat in the first place. And this deterrence level can only be maintained with state-of-the-art equipment which comes at a high price tag.

Defense spending is furthermore relevant in economic terms since certain views suggest a stimulating impact of the economy through public consumption. This covers the idea to smoothen and steer economic downturns, stimulate the economy overall or spill-over benefits through R&D efforts. Historically speaking a lot of technological inventions were in fact often implemented within the military environment first. Economists however still dispute whether the military investments induce and support economic growth and innovation or if innovation and economic growth would progress

[202] see Smith, R.: Military Economics 2009, p.24
[203] see Smith, R.: Military Expenditure 1977, p 63

in the same or even better fashion without the military.[204] The theory that war in particular considerably supports economic growth is known as the Iron Law of War[205], but this discussion is beyond the scope of this analysis. It just highlights that certain political parties and lobbyists may have more in mind than military capabilities when they discuss 'appropriate' funding levels for Armed Forces.

In the end the defense budget seems to be a reasonable indicator to use for an efficiency analysis. The data are commonly available and defense budget is in fact representative for the amount of monetary resources devoted toward military capabilities.

3.7 An Economic Perspective

Governments have to balance the money flows caused by revenues and expenditures that a nation has to manage. Hence if a government wants to increase military spending it has to select either one or a combination of the following options: reduce other government spending, increase taxes, print more money, borrow money by issuing more debt or sell assets.[206]

The history of economics as a discipline that considers military spending can be dated back as far as the year 1776 with Smith's work 'Wealth of the Nations' which already addressed military-related economical questions. One of his theories was that

[204] see Smith, R.: Military Economics 2009, p.167
[205] see Nordhaus, W.: War with Iraq 2002, p.74
[206] see Smith, R.: Military Economics 2009, p.160

not more than one hundredth of a nation's population can be employed as soldiers without ruining the economic basis which generates the funding for the military.[207] During World War II the US did have about 15 percent of its population in arms and was spending about 40 percent of its GDP on the war.[208] Also Syria and Israel are examples of countries that substantially spend more on their military than the 1 percent that Smith suggests as a critical level.[209] Even though these examples show that Smith's rule seems not to prove valid in general terms or at least not in the 21st century, it is notable that already in the 18th century defense spending has been part of his economic considerations.

Since then multiple studies have been conducted in order to analyze how war can be financed and how an economy should be managed during wartimes. Keynes tried to explain how World War II could be paid for.[210] Baran and Sweezy developed a theory in 1966[211] which stated that the expected recession after World War II did not follow because of relatively high military spending that remained among the major economies even after the end of the war.[212] Mosley is applying the term Military Keynesianism for this specific form of government driven economy stimulation.[213] In this view high defense related spending are justified by economic means rather than military or strategical means, a view which is not without controversy. In the year 1990 Dunn and Smith tried, but were not able to prove, this theory based on their studies on a

---

207 see Smith, A.: The Wealth of Nations 1776, p.885
208 see Smith, R.: Military Economics 2009, p.94
209 see Smith, R.: Military Economics 2009, p.94
210 see Keynes, J. M.: How to Pay for the War 1940
211 see Baran, P./Sweezy, P.: Monopoly Capital 1966
212 see Smith, R.: Military Economics 2009, p.100
213 see Mosley, H.: The Arms Race: Economic and Social Consequences 1985, p.7

correlation of military expenditures and unemployment rates within OECD countries.[214] Even though answering this question is not in scope of this paper, it is important to note that some decision makers involved in the defense budgeting process might try to achieve further goals besides just providing the military with sufficient funding for its military objectives.

From an economic perspective four ideal types of goods exist as well summarized by Brauer:[215] Defense can fit into each category under certain conditions. The four general categories are private goods, public goods, common-resource pool goods and club goods. The two criteria degree of rivalry and degree of exclusion are the differentiators for those classifications. A low degree of rivalry means that a good is available for everyone, while with a high degree of rivalry only one person can receive the benefits of the good. A low degree of exclusion means that a person cannot be excluded from receiving the benefits of a good, while with a high degree of exclusion a person can be omitted from the benefits.

Figure 10 illustrates how the four types of goods fit into these categories. Private goods are characterized by high exclusion and high rivalry. Public goods are characterized by low exclusion and low rivalry as they are available to everyone. Common-resource pool goods are goods which usage and allocation is administered within an economy. A club good is characterized by low rivalry and high exclusion. It describes a good that provides only benefit to people that belong to a certain group

[214] see Dunne, P./Smith, R.: Employment in the OECD 1990
[215] see Brauer, J.: Economic Perspective on Mercenaries 1999, p. 135

based on criteria such as entry fees, ethnic origin, loyalty oath or other means.[216] All non-members are excluded.

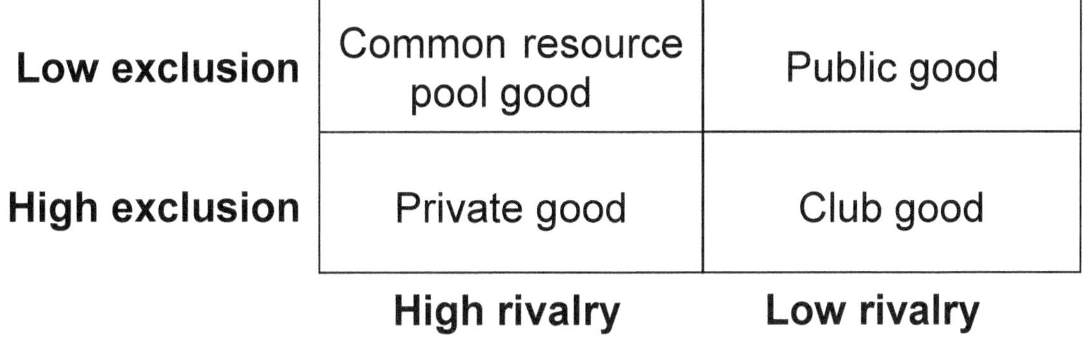

Figure 10: Characterization of Goods

(see Brauer, J.: Economic Perspective on Mercenaries 1999, p. 136)

As mentioned above, defense spending can fit in each of the categories under certain conditions and can actually even evolve over time from one to the other. Brauer illustrates this as follows: Starting with defining Armed Forces as a public good, the military offers protection to every citizen of a nation. However if the number of Armed Forces decreases to a level that not all areas of a country receive the same protection, the Armed Forces become a common-resource pool good which only provides benefits to those who reside within the regional area that is under protection.[217] From here, they can also move down to the lower half of the diagram if the regime of a nation substantially influences the Armed Forces. In certain extremes it might become a club good when it offers protection to a certain political or ethnical group only, and it may even become a private good when Armed Forces are specifically used to protect the

[216] see Brauer, J.: Economic Perspective on Mercenaries 1999, p. 137
[217] see Brauer, J.: Economic Perspective on Mercenaries 1999, p. 136

leader of a nation and his close cronies.[218] It is important to understand this differentiation, given that different countries around the world have Armed Forces that fit into the different categories of this diagram and that political changes can cause shifts in this classification from one area to another over time. Furthermore this classification becomes relevant in a later chapter of this paper when strategic defense alliances between nations are discussed.

From a macroeconomic perspective one important factor of defense spending is that it is characterized by a significant quick and strong increase and decrease before and after a nation is faced with an armed conflict.[219] This emphasizes that analyses should cover multi-year timeframes to avoid picking a specific period with significant one-time impacts.

Economists still dispute to which extent economic growth and defense spending are linked and how they influence one another. This dispute mainly focuses on the question of whether defense spending accelerates economic growth or is actually a burden on the economy. This paper is not aiming to take a stand on this topic in either direction. However outlining the scope of the discussion on this is helpful for understanding the efficiency of the military as well. Defense budget might be used as an economic stimulation instead of a military tool. More budget might become available than is actually required to fulfill certain tasks and any potential excess funds are spent anyway, which may negatively impact the evaluation of military efficiency. The view that

[218] see Brauer, J.: Economic Perspective on Mercenaries 1999, p. 137
[219] see Smith, R.: Military Economics 2009, p.160

military expenditures are necessary to stabilize the economy and offset stagnation is described as the Keynesian or underconsumptionist framework.[220] The same view however also sees some depressing impacts from defense spending on the economic growth rate.[221] According to Pivetti this provides a contradiction given that the defense expenditures are actually undermining something that they were originally meant to support.[222] He also points out that the USA experienced growth of defense spending and the economy simultaneously, but other advanced capitalist countries like Germany and Japan were performing better economically at lower rates of defense spending. However he also states that these examples do not necessarily indicate that defense spending has to be seen as a burden to economic growth in general. He lists the USA in the 1980s as an example where military purchases reached a peak at the same time as the economy showed signs of a strong performance.[223] But the statistical analyses also do not support the assumption that military expenses actively supported the economy e.g. by achieving a low unemployment rate.[224] To summarize these views: Military expenses are not a contradiction to economic growth but there is also no statistical evidence proving that they support growth either. According to Pivetti the specific situation of the US economy was the main driver for sustaining both economic growth and high defense spending. He attributes this to the closed and self-sustained US

---

[220] see Smith, R.: Military Expenditure 1977, p 61
[221] see Smith, R.: Military Expenditure 1977, p 61
[222] see Pivetti, M.: Underconsumptionist 1992, p.373
[223] see Pivetti, M.: Underconsumptionist 1992, p.375
[224] see Smith, R.: Military Expenditure 1977, p 68

economy powered by high internal demand for goods in general and not specifically the military expenditures.[225]

The view of seeing military expenditures as a burden argues along the lines of opportunity costs. Money spent on defense is not available to be invested or consumed in the private sector and the skills devoted to technological advancements in the military are not available in the civilian sector.[226] Sen points out that under a Keynesian view even though military expenditures as government spending stabilize the economy, the money would still be better invested in more fruitful sectors of government spends.[227] However Pivetti argues that other public spends may reach a limit with regard to capacities and a government could not reach the same high level of spending it could achieve by investing in the military.[228] To him limits have actually never been reached with military spending given that it seems to be fairly easy to scale. He also argues that technological advancements in the military context can transfer to benefits in the private sector in the long-term. Some researchers propose the usage of the economic performance of a nation as a measure of its military might. It is important to keep in mind that the impact of military spending on economic growth is not fully understood. If economic output is assumed to correlate positively with military capabilities such as with the GDI approach, it seems to contradict with the idea that high economic growth can only by achieved with low defense spending. How should a nation be called powerful if

[225] see Pivetti, M.: Underconsumptionist 1992, p.378
[226] see Blackaby, F.: Military sector and economy 1983, p. 19
[227] see Sen, A.: Defense Spending as a priority 1987, p 45
[228] see Pivetti, M.: Underconsumptionist 1992, p.380

a high measure for power can actually only be achieved by lowering the defense-related assets that are being acquired and maintained?

The concept of labor and capital is a further economic aspect with parallels to the area of defense. As outlined above, defense spending is an investment in resources that produces the good security to increase the social and economic welfare of a nation. With regard to this, military strategists face similar questions than do public entrepreneurs. Public entrepreneurs decide which and how much labor and capital they need and which product they produce in order to sustain themselves against competitors in the marketplace. The military strategist also has to decide which amount of troops and equipment he needs and how they have to be combined with technology in order to achieve the aspired level of military capabilities to provide the security level required for the nation.[229] Gholz describes this situation, considering the economic concept of the comparative advantage: [230] According to this concept a nation would use a combination that is most suitable to the individually available input factors. To him this means that a labor-abundant country, where labor costs are low, would focus on a high number of service members. Capital-abundant countries would use a more capital-intensive structure for their Armed Forces. Countries with a small but highly educated labor force might prefer a small, elite professional military like the example of the United Kingdom. A scientific, technology-focused country might prefer a technology-intensive military structure like the United States.

---

[229] see Smith, R.: Military Economics 2009, p.118
[230] see Gholz, E.: Military Efficiency 2003, p.9

3.8 Shortcomings

Policy makers and military officers are limited in their freedom to take actions that drive efficiency. Some of these limitations are not necessarily visible, nor are they explicitly recognized by those parties since they touch intangible areas in the social, cultural, economic and political environment of a nation. This chapter is called shortcomings because these limitations have the effect that no nation can be seen as fully free in its decisions and any particular evaluation of efficiency stages is influenced in particular by aspects in these areas.

An economist should ideally analyze each object of research unbiased and isolated to get objective answers to the problem at hand. However the following examples will show that some restrictions are embedded in the analysis. Since the study is based on benchmarks and presumably there will not be any country in the sample set that is free from all these limitations, determining a true degree of efficiency that is achievable from an economic perspective is not feasible.

3.8.1 National Values

The first grouping of shortcomings inherited in the data analysis will touch topics in the social and cultural areas as they extend to values and habits of nations. While their relevance for efficiency has already been defined in Chapter 3, this chapter will focus on those aspects of these areas that in particular provide shortcomings for the data analysis.

As a first example nations may have a different understanding of the value of a human life which can have significant influences on important decisions. If it is financially less expensive to sacrifice a soldier on a dangerous recon mission than using an expensive high tech drone, the intangible value of the human life becomes a critical part of the cost evaluation for performing this task. As another example it may be financially less expensive to use more soldiers for an attack than fewer, but better-trained, mechanized troops.

These are questions that military leaders face and for good reasons they may not always choose the financially 'cheapest'[231] one but rather one that they consider more human or right from a social perspective. And what 'right' and 'human' means may certainly differ between nations. Case in point the USA followed an asymmetric approach during the Cold War by matching the strength of the Warsaw Pact forces not with numbers but with superior technology.[232] This is known as the off-set strategy and was specifically reached through improvements in Information Technology.[233] Part of the reason certainly is the lower willingness of western nations in general to accept casualties.[234]

231 With financially 'cheapest' refers to the comparison of expenses for acquiring a piece of equipment compared with paying the salary and for training of soldiers from an armed forces point of view. This is opposed to a 'cost' view that would in fact also assign a value to the human life lost.

232 see Carter, A./White, J.: Keeping the Edge 2001, p. 9

233 see Carter, A./White, J.: Keeping the Edge 2001, p. 9

234 Even western countries today have different views in terms of the acceptance of casualties in war or peace keeping missions. This can stir some controversies within alliances as multiple instances showed in which NATO members felt the burden of missions is being shared unequally between the member states.

How does a nation consider the military overall? Citizens of some nations may scrutinize the actions of their Armed Forces more and more critically than others; this indirectly also influences the willingness of skilled members of the society to consider serving in the Armed Forces either temporarily or as a career. Questions of human rights and the use of specific weapon systems that could be considered inhumane are also a topic. Another example is a nation's willingness to accept collateral damage and to sacrifice lives of civilians (one's own and the enemy's) in order to reach the nation's goals through forceful actions.

Private military companies - sometimes used under the term mercenaries to give it a negative touch in political discussions - are another relevant aspect. It is not empirically proven if privatization of military force is 'efficient'. However, one way or the other national values influence if a country would even consider placing military tasks in the hands of a private company. Other examples are the use of child soldiers, foreign nationals or fanatic suicide bombers, which is still a price some nations or terrorists are willing to pay.

This listing of examples is not final and a detailed analysis of all of them is out of scope of this study. However the examples shall illustrate some of the shortcomings which will be expected in the empirical section of this paper. The use of the worldvaluesurvey for the interpretation of results will be a helpful tool to mitigate some of these expected shortcomings.

3.8.2 Global Political Environment

3.8.2.1 Potential Threats

According to Gholz, nations determine their public investment decisions in terms of military spending based on the global political environment of potential threats.[235] To him a government makes decisions on how much to invest and in which military assets based on the specific threats and opportunities that are potentially faced in the future. For this analysis, the term global political environment will be used to describe the concept that a nation operates in strong independence with other nations. These nations can either have concurring or contradicting goals which consequently determine their relationship and therefore the potential for cooperation or conflicts between them. The state of relationship can change quite a bit over the time and prior adversaries can become close partners as the formation of the European Union clearly illustrates. In terms of this analysis the impact of the political environment on nations represents a shortcoming. Its specific influence cannot be evaluated and the data for each nation are uniquely impacted by their individual political interdependencies. It is not possible to analyze and compare the state of nations without it. In this analysis the political environment will therefore be qualitatively evaluated as part of the interpretation of specific country results as a supplement to the statistical analysis.

The political environment can also determine the potential regional focal points of military conflicts.

[235] see Gholz, E.: Military Efficiency 2003, p.9

From the Vietnam era until today a regional and geographical change of focus impacted the US, given that instead of fighting in a tropical jungle, battles in the deserts of Middle Eastern countries became more probable. While for Germany during the Cold War a potential threat was to fight tank battles in middle and northern Germany, the new requirements focus on potential participations in missions conducted by global partnerships to which Germany belongs.

The reason for listing this topic as a shortcoming is that in reality all nations in the data set are influenced by potential threats. Either these threats are strong or they are weak, but no nation is without external influences. And two nations facing the same threat may even evaluate them differently. As a practical example, US troops stationed in the Middle East appear to receive stronger support from their citizens than the support German soldiers receive from their home.[236] And the threat of terrorist attacks may be more focused, but certainly not limited to the US homeland.

A military that evaluates the necessary budget requirements has not just to consider current threats but also potential changes in the global environment which could lead to new threats. General Sullivan, former chief of staff of the US Army, emphasizes that the requirements after the Cold War changed drastically and are characterized by increased frequency as well as higher diversity regarding objectives and regional location of the conflicts.[237] The pace of missions increased by 300 percent compared to the era of the Cold War and the Armed Forces had to deal with scenarios

[236] This hypothesis shall not be further tested in this paper as the statement is mainly meant as an example to illustrate the argument in general.

[237] see Sullivan, G.: "A Vision for the Future" 1995, p. 6

from the war in Iraq, to airlifting supplies in Somalia and hunting war criminals in Mogadishu, all with much fewer resources.[238]

The global environment can have a significant impact on the effectiveness as well as efficiency of Armed Forces. In order to have the right resources in the right place at the right time at the lowest cost it is relevant to anticipate future threats and to have the necessary resources available as quickly as possible. During the Cold War, the US was faced with a potential battle against Soviet troops in Europe. This allowed the US Army to establish forward-operating bases in western European countries to expedite the deployment of battle-ready troops in case they became necessary.[239] The above-mentioned uncertainty around potential future missions therefore makes it difficult to prepare similar precautions accordingly today.[240] Furthermore, the general political environment and relationships with nations may or may not even provide the option for countries to establish forward-operating bases.

Also the type of expected conflict can have an influence and is a further example for an external ramification that is not under the control of nations. Ron Smith considers the increase of economies to scale in military technology as a major reason for the fact that adversaries of the USA like terrorists consider asymmetrical warfare as an answer to the US' virtual monopoly in military technology.[241] In general asymmetrical threats can be divided into three categories, according to Carter and Perry:[242] The first category

---

[238] see Shimko, K.: The Iraq Wars and America's Military Revolution 2010, p.104
[239] see Shimko, K.: The Iraq Wars and America's Military Revolution 2010, p.105
[240] see Shimko, K.: The Iraq Wars and America's Military Revolution 2010, p.105
[241] see Smith, R.: Military Economics 2009, p.86
[242] see Carter, A./Perry, W.: Countering Asymmetrical Threats 2001, p. 120

belongs to the field of IT and refers to threats posted by adversaries to disrupt or destroy the reconnaissance capabilities through jamming communication systems, GPS or satellites. The second threat is caused by Weapons of Mass Destruction that are not just used on the battlefield, but as instruments of terrorist attacks on the American soil or any allied country. The third category describes terrorist-type attacks in general that can, but are not limited to, attacks with Weapons of Mass Destruction or biological weapons as part of a war-like act within the homeland of an allied nation. At this point it shall be noted that this classification follows Carter's and Perry's definition which were published in the year 2001 before the attack of Al-Qaida on the World Trade Center, which actually underlines the relevance of the asymmetric approach in today's global environment. Political analysts further state that it is difficult to precisely calculate the aggregate effects of these disparate elements and at the same time underscore the importance to reach judgment with regard to their relative effectiveness and efficiency. This is important since different options are available to military organizations of different nations due to different characteristics, problems and enemies. Each nation analyzed in this study is in a unique political and geographical environment; an exact comparison is limited to a certain extent.

Given that the study is based on a benchmark of nations, the shortcoming lies in the fact that to some extent nations are compared, that are in very different situations. The US may be mainly facing asymmetrical terrorist threats, but Israel in the same dataset actually prepares for a traditional ground war to defend its home country against hostile neighbors. The point here is that the dataset cannot be adjusted for these circumstances – it cannot be modeled as to how Israel's spending would have looked like if external threats would have been comparable to the ones the US faces. The interpretation of results will therefore need to address and account for these circumstances, which will be done with help of results from the worldvaluesurvey. The shortcoming can further be overcome by users of the results of this study by making educated decisions with regard to which countries are compared in order to determine potential actions to improve efficiency.

3.8.2.2 Global Alliances

The world of business has globalized at an immense rate in recent years and companies are acting on a global marketplace against global competition. A similar phenomenon can be seen with regard to Armed Forces, which have to interact in an environment of allies, partners, international organizations and non-governmental groups. Even the US, as a nation with an immensely advanced and powerful military, works under the premise that most, if not all, missions in the upcoming future will involve non-US forces or non-military organizations.[243]

Formal coalitions are called global alliances refering to international organizations with contributions of their members toward a common goal.[244] The idea of coalition warfare as part of alliances carries with it the problems of deriving full benefit from the partnership through the integration and coordination of member's individual

[243] see Sherwood-Randall, E.: International Relations, p.235
[244] see Olsen jr. M./Zeckhauser, R.: Theory of Alliances 1966, p. 267

contributions.[245] These coalitions can cause very relevant implications with regard to the efficiency and effectiveness of their resources.

In analogy to the already outlined characteristics of defense and security as a public good for citizens of a nation, Olsen and Zeckhauser argue that the security provided by a defense alliance generally presents a public good too, only that the benefiting members are rather defined in terms of nations than individuals.[246]

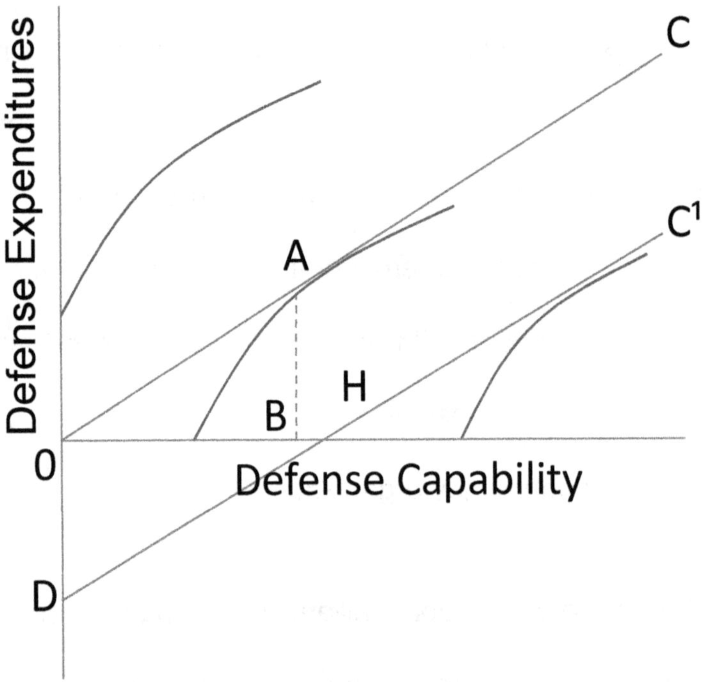

Figure 11: Indifference Map

(see Olsen jr. M./Zeckhauser, R.: Theory of Alliances 1966, p. 268)

[245] see Millet, A/Murray, W/Watman, K., Military Effectiveness 1986, p.48
[246] see Olsen jr. M./Zeckhauser, R.: Theory of Alliances 1966, p. 267

Figure 11 illustrates the model Olsen and Zeckhauser use to describe the correlation of defense spending between members of an alliance. This model shows the indifference curve of the nation considering the marginal value it places on the good security. The horizontal axis presents the defense capabilities and the vertical axis the defense expenditures contributed. The cost curve is represented as a linear function C and C^1 in this model. Without alliance, the nation would depict defense spending of the amount at the intersection, where the indifference curve is tangental to the cost curve at 0B. Olsen and Zeckhauser explain the hypothesis as follows:[247] The amount a nation spends on defense in an alliance is affected by the amount its allies provide. The spending of an ally is represented by moving the cost curve down on the vertical axis. So if an allied nation spends 0D on defense, it will receive defense of 0H at no cost, which is a direct equivalent to an increase of that nation's income. Accordingly, the more the allies contribute to defense, the more the cost constraint moves to the lower right section of the chart and the less the nation spends on defense. By recording all the points of tangency between the cost curve and indifference curves a nation's reaction function can be obtained. This reaction function indicates how much defense the nation will produce for all possible levels of defense expenditure by its allies. By overlapping the reaction functions of both allies, the model's equilibrium can be determined. However the curves do not have to overlap and if they do not, this shows that one ally values security that high that its contribution in the alliance is identical to what he would contribute alone. If the curves do intersect, the equilibrium presents a situation in which

[247] see Olsen jr. M./Zeckhauser, R.: Theory of Alliances 1966, p. 268

both nations contribute, but the larger nation which places a higher value on security will pay a share of the cost that is larger than its share of the benefit.

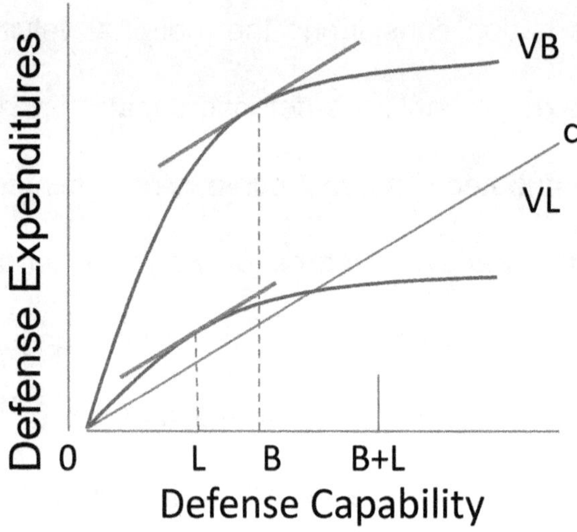

Figure 12: Evaluation Curves

(see Olsen jr. M./Zeckhauser, R.: Theory of Alliances 1966, p. 269)

The model above visualizes this situation, with B representing a bigger ally who values the common good defense higher than its little ally L. If both allies produce a defense output according to their individual preference, both nations would enjoy a defense output of B+L. However in this situation each nation values a marginal unit as less than its marginal costs. Nation B stops contributing as soon as the sum of the contribution of L and B reaches the point B in the model. At the same time country L has no incentive to produce defense at this level whatsoever since the individual preference level is already reached through the sole contribution of the bigger nation. Therefore this model would only reach equilibrium if nation B provides the whole defense capabilities on its own, which reflects exactly its preference based on the indifference curve.

Therefore from an economic perspective global alliances can create incentives for some countries to free-ride at the expenses of other nations. When an alliance grows, the individual benefits that the members receive shrink and they can therefore consider decreasing their own contribution given that other countries continue to support the alliance.[248] Sandler specifies this statement by predicting that if the public benefit of an alliance grows, the incentives for small economies to free-ride, increases given that they can rely on the contribution of their allies.[249] Free-riding in general describes a situation in which a party is taking benefits from the actions of others without contributing its respective share. To clarify, it shall be noted that free riding does not necessarily refer to a situation in which a benefit is entirely free, but it means that the free rider contributes less to the common goal than his individual benefit would warrant.[250]

Belonging to an organization of allies can increase the cumulatively available military power against a potential threat. It was already outlined that the perceived level of security of a nation increases with the amount of available defense resources against that potential threat. If several nations collaborate to oppose a potential threat together, the critical amount of defense resources necessary could be reached with a lower level of individual contribution by each nation.

However this certainly works only if each member can trust that their partners live up to their promises and actually take actions if the situation requires them. Missions

[248] see Brauer, J.: Economic Perspective on Mercenaries 1999, p. 142
[249] see Sandler, T.: Sharing Burdens 1988, p. 31
[250] see Sandler, T.: Sharing Burdens 1988, p. 31

like the ones in Afghanistan or very recently in Libya are often coordinated by and initiated through global organizations like NATO. Within the context of these organizations there are a lot of interesting factors that can influence the Armed Forces and their budget and efficiency situation. E.g. some organizations request a certain military spending contribution by their members and nations have to decide whether to obey and maintain defense budgets on a certain level or consider ignoring them. Within this context Germany for example is historically way below the level requested by NATO with regard to percentage of GDP defense spending; Switzerland did not even join NATO at all given that it already resides regionally within the borders of friendly NATO countries. Furthermore certain nations may belong to an organization but do not support a possible joint decision to act. This would be reflected by the recent missions in Libya which had been declared by NATO, but e.g. Germany as a NATO member decided to not get involved in.[251]

There is another downside to the collaborative waging of a war. If it is already difficult to get a nation's military branches to work together, it is presumably even harder to align these across the organizations of multiple nations with language and cultural barriers. The literature also specifically points out that a gap in the stage of military technology can make it highly inefficient for a technologically advanced nation to collaborate with a military of lower sophistication.[252] While the Kosovo conflict was fought by NATO as an alliance of nations, the actual Air Operations, which were the main strategy for the war, had to be carried out in 80 percent of the cases by US Forces

[251] see Burns, N.: Berlin's Stance on Lybia 2011
[252] see Sherwood-Randall, E.: International Relations, p.238

alone, because most other nations were lacking the competence in laser-guided bombing.[253] Further issues became evident as part of the after action report subsequent to the 1999 Kosovo conflict as Sherwood-Randell identified:[254] Secure communication, exchange of information and incompatible equipment were identified as the key weaknesses of NATO besides multiple years of joint preparation for a war. In fact, sensitive air tasking orders actually had to be printed out and exchanged daily in paper form between the involved nations, which then entered them manually for further communication within their respective organizations. During the actual air missions on which NATO heavily relied, the pilots between nations had to use open frequencies for their communication, which the Serbian forces could easily intercept.[255] In order to avoid the leak of critical information around the missions of B2 bombers, F117's and cruise missiles, information was not even shared by the US with allies which caused quite some confusion at times.[256]

From an economic perspective alliances seem to support the efficient use of military resources in peacetime through joint contribution to the perceived level of security. From an operational perspective this seems to be a different story in terms of the impact on military capabilities.

According to Sherwood-Randall, maintaining a powerful military can prove to be quite a contradiction for the US with regard to its international relations. She presumes that the US is involved in multiple peacekeeping missions around the world because

---

[253] see Lambeth, B.: The Transformation of American Air Power 2000, p.213-214
[254] see Sherwood-Randall, E.: International Relations, p.240
[255] see Sherwood-Randall, E.: International Relations, p.241
[256] see Tirpak, J.: Air Campaign 1999

nations turn to it for its high military capacity and capability.[257] Furthermore she argues that US politics rather limit the capabilities of the UN, which ironically brings the US into the position of having to further increase military capacities to compensate for the limitations of the UN.[258] It has even been argued that the US should promote the capabilities of its oversee partners to close this gap; the European nations were supposedly in 1999 not even at a capability level that the US had already reached during Desert Storm in 1991.[259] This can significantly limit the military capabilities of the US and put forces at risk.[260] This specific example shall not just describe an issue in a historic context, but actually point out that these kinds of issues can arise at any point in time when potential allies grow their military capabilities in a different direction or at a different pace. The potential efficiency gains through joint operations can easily be offset by incremental risks and the fact that allied forces cannot fight safely to execute missions alongside their partners.

For this study the implications are that some nations belong to one or more global alliances and to that extent it is difficult to assess their efficiency on a standalone basis. If they benefit from contributions of other nations, their own spending can be hold at a lower level while still achieving the required output. This would certainly in itself already be an interesting finding as it implies that belonging to an alliance drives efficiency. However the challenges explained above make it difficult to assess if and to what extent these benefits actually truly turn out to be effective. If the full combat

[257] see Sherwood-Randall, E.: International Relations, p.238
[258] see Sherwood-Randall, E.: International Relations, p.239
[259] see Gombert, D/Kluger, R./Libicki, M.: Mind the Gap 1999, p.4
[260] see Gombert, D/Kluger, R./Libicki, M.: Mind the Gap 1999, p.50

potential of the alliance cannot be carried out due to operational difficulties, generating savings through alliance would not help the cause. As a further implication, the alliance can provide benefits on a different level and that is to the extent that military assets can be sourced from close allies instead of having the home defense industry produce all the required goods. This can help countries leverage the competitive advantages of nations and potentially generate efficiencies due to lower prices for military assets achieved by economies of scale and scope in the production process. More details on this will be given in Chapter 5 of this study.

3.8.2.3 Arms Race

Military spending differs from regular government activities, since it can't be seen independently from the spending of other nations. It is an integral part of foreign politics and therefore strongly linked to the actions and spending of other nations.[261] This situation can go so far that nations stimulate each other to increase defense spending until they end up in a situation called an arms race.

Arms races can be explained with models of the game theories. Given that arms races can considerably impact the national security and can constrain the defense budget of a nation, arms races will be described as an influencing factor in this chapter.

International disputes can cause countries to spend a continuously increasing proportion of their GDP on military expenditures as a reaction to the behavior of other

[261] see Jones, L.; McCaffery, J.: Financial Management 2007, p.76

nations. Within the game theory this situation is called the security dilemma.[262] Especially between strong rivals an arms race can easily develop if one adversary increases the defense spending with the specific goal to exceed the spending of one's adversary. If the other party acts the same way, no one will ever achieve the goal of defense superiority and both parties keep putting effort and resources on defense without reaching the goal of defense domination.[263] In context of economic opportunity costs, nations in an arms race put a premium on defense and value it higher than any other public good – otherwise an arms race would stop as soon as one nation reaches a level of defense spending at which the marginal rate of return has deteriorated so much that no further spending makes sense. The nation would not be willing to sacrifice more of other goods in favor of national defense.

Figure 13 illustrates the options that two countries have in a situation of defense rivalry with the example of the US and Soviet Union. The two available options are to arm or to disarm, which consequently leads to four different scenario outcomes. In this described situation both parties try to achieve defense domination in order to increase their own security level. The numbers will help to illustrate the model and represent spending on national defense for each nation accordingly. Arming consequently increases a nation's defense spending and security level, disarming will decrease it. Looking at the options of each nation independently, the dominant strategy for each party is to arm, given that this strategy will lead to an increase in the perceived level of security. And even if the nations would reveal their intended actions to each other, they

[262] see Poast P.: The Economics of War, p.70
[263] see Smith, R.: Military Economics 2009, p.85

would still choose to arm. This is because if their adversary disarms, the best strategy is still to arm in order to achieve the aspired goal of superior power. If the adversary chooses to arm, arming becomes also the dominant strategy in order not to be dominated by ones adversary. Therefore arming is the dominant strategy for each nation individually as well as under consideration of other party's actions. This situation in the model is called the Nash-Equilibrium[264] and both nations continue arming.[265]

		USSR	
		Arm	**Disarm**
US	**Arm**	1/1	1/0
	Disarm	0/1	0/0

Figure 13: Game Theory: Arms Race

(see Poast P.: The Economics of War, p.71)

An arms race can be classified in various ways. A quantitative symmetrical arms race considers the pure amount of specific weapons that are being acquired in large numbers by both adversaries, like the amount of nuclear missiles, number of ships and

[264] For more details on Nash's Theory: Nash, John (1950) "Equilibrium points in n-person games"
[265] see Poast P.: The Economics of War, p.71

others.[266] The party with the higher number of a certain weapon type dominates the other. A qualitative asymmetrical arms race on the other side considers technological aspects and can be illustrated with the middle age example of a build-up of fortifications as a reaction to progress in siege equipment.[267] In this view the specific capabilities to deter each other's military threats is the determining factor and not the pure number of a specific type of weapon. O'Hanlon further claims that arms races are also fueled by the uncertainty and inaccuracy of the measurement of military capabilities.[268] Since it is already hard to accurately measure one's own military effectiveness, one can easily overestimate the capabilities of one's adversaries if too much precaution is being taken. And this again increases one's own feel of inferiority, thus fueling further spending on defense.

Later in this analysis the phenomenon of private military firms will be outlined in more detail. The topic shall at least be mentioned in the context of this chapter as well, since it is not necessarily obvious to think about them in the context of arms races. However in most recent arms races the private military firms became a dominant factor. In Africa the two adversaries Eritrea and Ethiopia extended their arms races to the open market for military resources and competed by contracting the best private military resources they could get and afford.[269] Given that these resources are often easily and

[266] see Smith, R.: Military Economics 2009, p.85
[267] see Smith, R.: Military Economics 2009, p.86
[268] see O'Hanlon, M.: The Science of War 2009, p. 64
[269] see Singer, P. W.: Corporate Warrior 2007, p. 175

quickly available, Singer claims that private military firms can even accelerate the development of arms races compared to the historically conventional arms races.[270]

However some authors also see positive impacts in arms races as they presumably foster technological progress in an economy. The following outlines explain this logic according to Pivetti:[271] Technological change is a reaction to a technological problem and these problems tend to arise much more frequently in an arms race situation, given that in a high pace on a continuous basis one's own capabilities have to be improved in order to dominate those of the opponent. Without an arms race the demand for new technological solutions would drop and the technological progress itself would slow down. Also military projects in arms races are often seen as essential and a new technological capability is being implemented in weaponry by contracting private production facilities basically at all cost. Consequently the private firm gains knowledge quickly in the new technology and can implement this knowledge in products for the private sector as well.

The examples above outline situations in which both adversaries are aiming for power dominance and trying to actively and aggressively be stronger than the adversary. However there are also situations in which nations realize the risk of an arms race and actually actively work together to keep the armament in a balance, so that neither side has to increase its spending on defense and both feel safe. The nuclear reduction program can be seen as one situation in which particularly the US and former

[270] see Singer, P. W.: Corporate Warrior 2007, p. 175
[271] see Pivetti, M.: Underconsumptionist 1992, p.380

Soviet Union realized, that an increase of nuclear war heads was inevitable, but at the same time should not be an aspired goal. This reduction program is seen by many as a great success.[272] The perceived level of security increases for all parties given the fact that the potential threat decreases. It can be noted that given the rather unsecure border of the Soviet Union[273], by reducing the overall amount of warheads also the potential threat caused by third-party nations is reduced, given that less nuclear warheads become available on the black-market. Along the same lines also missions to prevent the smuggling of weapons and enforcing export controls against potential rouge states[274] can increase the perceived level of security by simply decreasing the amount of weapons that are made available to adversaries. From an efficiency perspective this can be seen as preemptive measures to avoid an armed conflict in the future. This is a very relevant subject in this context, given that investments to avoid future threats are constraining the current defense budget of a nation to avoid a future event.

While arms races are not necessarily a phenomenon of the analyzed nations in the analyzed timeframe, it is important for the reader to understand the ramification since the database includes multiple countries, with some of which are potentially in an arms race situation. Accordingly the results for those countries may be shaded, given the special impact of intense defense spending.

[272] see Sherwood-Randall, E.: International Relations, p.262
[273] see Sherwood-Randall, E.: International Relations, p.235
[274] see Sherwood-Randall, E.: International Relations, p.267

4 FDH Analysis applied on Armed Forces

4.1 Definition of FDH

The prior chapters have provided the basis for the data analysis by highlighting challenges and limitations that will be faced in the area of research around defense spending. Building on this, this chapter will now define the specific model to which the datasets will be applied.

This analysis will use a non-parametric model in order to conduct efficiency studies in the context of a market with unknown production functions and non-monetary output factors. The free disposal hull as a non-parametric approach is in particular a good fit in terms of this analysis since it is primarily data-driven and constructs an efficiency frontier using input/output data for the whole sample following a mathematical programming method.[275] In the absence of further assumptions regarding the cost-output relation other than free-disposability, the frontier created with this method is called 'Free Disposal Hull'.[276]

By assumption, the frontier determines best practices and all nations can calculate their level of efficiency by measuring their distance to the next best DMU on the frontier. These are exactly the results that are required to test the first hypothesis of this paper and will help determine to which extent the efficiency of Armed Forces differ among nations.

---

275 see Mandl, U./Dierx, A./ Ilzkovitz, F.: Efficency of the Public Sector 2008, p.9
276 see Eeckaut, P./Tulkens, H./Jamar M-A.: Belgian Municipalities 1993, p.304

While chapter two already illustrated the non-parametric models in general, a more specific description of advantages and disadvantages of the FDH approach is required in order to outline the implications for this study in particular.

The main advantage of this approach is its transparency and its ability to handle multiple outputs without requiring a specific functional form of the production function as it relies on the input and output data only.[277] The main disadvantage of this approach is its deterministic nature. Results tend to depend heavily on the composition and size of the sample as well as the selection of input and output variables used.[278] Moreover, non-parametric methods in general tend to be sensitive to measurement errors, statistical noise and outliers.[279]

Another characteristic of the FDH model is its lack of insight with regard to specific data points on the created efficiency frontier. One example is called efficiency by default and occurs in a situation in which a DMU is called efficient solely because of a lack of a comparable data sets.[280] This is the case for the DMUs with the lowest of the observed inputs and largest observed output as well as for those that are neither dominated by others nor are dominating another DMU themselves. This can potentially be seen in the context of this paper as well, since in particular the US defense spending is high in absolute terms, followed by China and then other nations at a far distance. Given that the context of this paper, besides evaluating absolute efficiency, is the aspiration to identify influencing factors, the data for those nations can still provide

[277] see Mandl, U./Dierx, A./ Ilzkovitz, F.: Efficency of the Public Sector 2008, p.9
[278] Mandl, U./Dierx, A./ Ilzkovitz, F.: Efficency of the Public Sector 2008, p.9
[279] Mandl, U./Dierx, A./ Ilzkovitz, F.: Efficency of the Public Sector 2008, p.9
[280] see Eeckaut, P./Tulkens, H./Jamar M-A.: Belgian Municipalities 1993, p.308

useful insight even though they are prone to 'outlier' characteristics. This additional evaluation is a further advantage of the FDH method. Due to the fact that results are based on the actual sample, the data can be further analyzed to determine the actual drivers of efficiency from a qualitative perspective.[281]

For the operational analysis of the datasets the EMS software is used. EMS stands for Efficiency Measurement System and is a Microsoft Windows run software that is able to compute several different efficiency scenarios. Besides conducting scenarios of the DEA analysis with return on scale assumptions it is also capable of calculating the efficiency of DMUs in a Free-Disposal-Hull scenario.[282] The data are being fed into the tool via Microsoft Excel spreadsheets and the results show the efficiency score in percent as well as a breakdown of the DMUs that are referenced as benchmarks. Processing the data is certainly not the biggest challenge of this research. The actual challenge for researchers in this area is to identify the right input and output factors in order to build the model. This will be done in the upcoming chapters.

[281] see Eeckaut, P./Tulkens, H./Jamar M-A.: Belgian Municipalities 1993, p.315
[282] see Scheel, H.: EMS Analysis 2000, p.2

4.2 Database

4.2.1 Introduction to Research and Chapter Overview

This analysis will analyze the efficiency of Armed Forces within a multi-year timeframe. The study will therefore be based on a comparison of datasets for the three periods 1995, 2000 and 2005. Newer datasets are not available for all the required figures as of today. Analyzing timeframes ensures that the results are up-to-date but also helps to identify efficiency factors that may only be visible over time. The introduction of this paper outlined how rapidly the environment of Armed Forces changes and the potential impact of the phenomenon of 'Revolution of Military Affairs' on their operation. The datasets for each year therefore need to be analyzed separately and cannot be aggregated into one sample set e.g. to create more data points for the production frontier.[283]

While six specifically identified nations will be the focus of this paper, analyzing only six countries in scope of a FDH analysis would provide a very narrow view of the world's situation in terms of defense spending. So in order to obtain a more suitable database for comparisons, six countries will remain to be the focus of the analysis in terms of results, but the actually used sample size will be defined in a broader scope. The dataset will consist of all nations for which consistent sets of data are available. For some nations the availability of data is limited to just a few of the analyzed years, but all six focus nations are consistently considered for each year. The data accuracy for

[283] If the factor time would not matter, all data points could be added into one sample to get more data reflecting the 'possible' input output combinations for armed forces.

China is questionable, but a pragmatic approach has been found to address this situation by working with a low and high level defense spending scenario as alternatives to the numbers officially reported in commonly used databases. The distances between nations shall illustrate to which extent it is plausible to use production frontier techniques to determine efficiency performance differences between Armed Forces of nations. Results shall not be taken too literally by the numbers given the shortcomings described in Chapter 3. In more manufacturing oriented processes e.g. one can draw the conclusion that a DMU operating at 80 percent efficiency could feasibly reduce its input by 20 percent to catch up with the dominating DMU. Military capabilities are a very complex phenomena and variations in efficiency in this study shall mainly illustrate that there is a difference in efficiency and not suggest specific dollar amounts for appropriate spending levels. Furthermore this study attempts to create a production frontier for military capabilities across the whole global sample set. This implies that developed industrialized nations are benchmarked as well as developing and Third World Nations. If a nation were to analyze its individual performance more specifically it shall certainly be suggested to analyze the respective position on the frontier compared to nations in similar political circumstances or economic development stage. Nations have intentionally not been pre-selected for this study to show the global picture. Accordingly some nations will score fairly low in terms of efficiency on the frontier. The conclusions drawn shall mainly be that there is a difference in efficiency for producing military capabilities; the distances to other DMUs are shaded by the shortcomings identified in Chapter 3. The six focus nations will in fact prove to be appropriate benchmark nations for the most part; the above outlines shall simply caution users of the data as they extend the interpretation into other areas of the production frontier.

On the output side there are some limitations to the availability of datasets. GNI as an output factor will be included, but as outlined above will not be the focus, since it is too narrow of an assumption and correlates military capabilities just to one single economic factor. However GNI is a broadly reported factor and the World Bank provides GNI information for all nations for which also defense spending information is available. Therefore this dataset is the broadest. The CINC is a separate research project, which however still covers most of the countries that are included in the World Bank database as well. It varies slightly for each year but still around 150 nations are available with consistent data to run a FDH analysis with defense spending as percentage of GDP as input and the CINC results as output. The third data category represents a qualitative review of the capabilities of Armed Forces by defense specialists. This data will also be run in correlation to defense in percentage of GDP in the FDH analysis to provide an alternative view of the efficiency stage of Armed Forces.

With these FDH analyses the following two hypotheses of this paper are being tested:

1.) The efficiencies of Armed Forces differ between nations around the globe.

2.) Certain factors have a positive or respective negative impact on the efficiency of Armed Forces.

Along the lines of this analysis, the World Values Survey (WVS) will help interpret the results of this study. The World Values Survey grew out of a study launched by the European Values Survey group (EVS) under the leadership of Kerkhofs and de Moor in 1981.[284] The WVS is a global research project that gathers empirical datasets around multiple cultural aspects in countries around the world. The survey includes two questions that can be related to the topic of this paper. One question asks people about their confidence in the Armed Forces of their nation. The second question asks for their opinion regarding the priorities for their country with one of the options being 'strong defense forces'. The survey is conducted in waves and not for each country are datasets available for each given year. The US as an example has been surveyed in 1995, 1999 and 2006. The data sets for 1999 and 2006 will therefore accompany the results of the FDH analysis for 2000 and 2005. The political, social and global environment could certainly have an influence and vary even between two years, but the WVS results are used for supplementary information and not as a primary factor. This area leaves room for further analysis as more datasets become available in the future.

4.2.2 Input Key Performance Indicator

There are different options that can be considered on the input side of the FDH analysis. One option is the use of defense spending in absolute dollar terms either at actual rates or constant currency over time. Constant currency pretty much converts

[284] World Values Survey: Introduction 2012

non US-Dollar figures to US-Dollars based on a single denominating exchange rate to eliminate differences in numbers over time strictly driven by varying currency values. The issue with these absolute numbers is that they do not carry additional implied information that would help to further interpret them. The two following alternatives will illustrate how other factors actually help to find a figure that can also carry a 'signal'. Defense spending as a percentage of total government spending can be a consideration. The advantage of this view is that this KPI can also be seen as an indicator for the importance that the Armed Forces have within the nation. If a government spends a high share of its budget on defense, the Armed Forces can be seen as having a high importance and vice versa. However this data is hard to come by and very inconsistent. In addition to dealing with different definitions of military expenditures also the definition as well as general structure of government spending is different from nation to nation and needs to be normalized. Also a lot of nations differentiate between central government spending and regional government spending and nations do not consistently classify items as one or the other. So, while defense as a percentage of government spending would be a good view to consider, inconsistencies in the datasets make it a risky figure to use for cross-country comparisons. Defense as a percentage of government spending can however be used as an accompanying indicator. It is a very useful indicator if used in the correct context. Even though numbers cannot be compared among nations, the development of this percentage over time within a specific nation is a great indicator for the importance of national security.

Military spending as a percentage of GDP proves to be the most suitable input KPI to use for this study. The factor is commonly used as a proxy for the importance that national security and therefore the military has in a nation. Given that it correlates the spending with economic factors and not public spending itself, it may not be an indicator as strong as percent of government spending, but still a good sign for its importance. Just for the GNI model of the FDH study actual military spend in US-dollars at constant currency will be used. Military expenses as percentage of GDP or GNI would not make sense from a statistical point of view, as input and output would be determined by the same driver: economic performance.

Military- and defense-related information is characterized by its confidentiality. Therefore the quality of data varies and certain limiting factors have to be kept in mind when data are analyzed. The UK established an accrual type accounting system for defense budgets which treats them more like a public company. Costs are considered when they are being incurred rather than when cash is paid and also the equipment is amortized over time with impairment adjustments, etc..[285] While this is a helpful instrument for public companies to accurately reflect their value, there are restrictions to its application on defense assets. Companies can reliably evaluate the value of their assets with common measurements like historic value, market value and going concern value. For military equipment this is often hard to predict. If equipment has no civil usage, a market value is difficult to determine. Also the duration of usage for military

[285] see Smith, R.: Military Economics 2009, p.114

equipment tends to be longer and often more unpredictable than it is for public goods.[286] More generally speaking, not all countries are necessarily following the same budget structure, which is a challenge when numbers across nations are compared as described by O'Hanlon:[287] The USA e.g. reports the numbers of the Marine Corps within the numbers of the Department of Navy and a lot of military intelligence-related expenses are embedded in the Air Force budget. Also the review of the defense budget by activity can be challenging, since in some cases the distinction might not be that clear. Some forces can be used for conventional war and nuclear war, or some Battalions of the US Army and Marine Corps are suitable for conventional duties, but are also qualified for special operations tasks. However O'Hanlon suggests that these data at least provide a directional indicator and this seems to be a reasonable approach to follow.

Furthermore, countries like China are not very transparent when it comes to the communication around its defense budget. The officially reported numbers exclude R&D expenses, foreign weapon purchases, nuclear weapon programs and paramilitary forces, all of which typically are included by western standards.[288] Another important factor is that given the lower cost of living in countries like China, a direct comparison of soldier-related cost requires a purchasing power adjustment.[289]

---

[286] see Smith, R.: Military Economics 2009, p.114
[287] see O'Hanlon, M.: The Science of War 2009, p. 13
[288] see O'Hanlon, M.: The Science of War 2009, p. 46
[289] see O'Hanlon, M.: The Science of War 2009, p. 47

Multiple sources are available to obtain military expenditures in absolute terms as well as percentage of a nation's GDP. However the data for the same time period may vary from source to source due to the fact that military expenditures can be defined differently by the reporting countries and may also have been compiled differently by the research organization that is reporting the aggregated information.

A consistent data source is therefore paramount for this particular study. The SIPRI Institute is one of the leading data sources in the area of defense analysis. SIPRI stands for 'Stockholm International Peace Research Institute' and uses the official NATO definition of military expenditures and the results of their survey are publicly available through the World Bank Webpage. The definition seems fairly straightforward covering military-related personnel cost, O&M, procurement, R&D, construction and donated military aid.[290]

Therefore the SIPRI data, obtained through the World Bank economic database, will be the primary data source for input figures in this study. The sources for data used in this study set clear definitions and guidelines in order to make numbers comparable across nations. However a certain mismatch has to be expected due to the complexity of this task and the possibility that nations intentionally or unintentionally misreport certain numbers. For China, SIPRI uses estimates based on officially reported numbers from the Chinese government with adjustments based on input from analysts and experts in the area.[291] SIPRI lists the missing defense-related research and

[290] see SIPRI, Definition of military expenditures 2013
[291] see SIPRI, China 2013

development as the biggest off-budget item which needs to be added for comparability reasons. This number will be called original or officially reported number going forward. As alternatives this study will also use a low and high level estimate as suggested by the US Department of Defense.[292] Due to the lack of transparency in the Chinese defense budget today, multiple other sources and experts may come up with even different estimates. The focus of this three scenario approach is simply to illustrate how varying spending assumptions can have an impact on the efficiency scoring. For this purpose the used sources fulfill their purpose.

4.2.3 Output Key Performance Indicator

4.2.3.1 Composite Index of National Capabilities Database

The CINC index belongs to the scientific studies of the Correlation of War project. CINC stands for Composite Index of National Capabilities and considers demographic, industrial and military indicators in order to measure the power of nations.[293] The advantage of this indicator for the scope of this study is that the data are available in a consistent way for each year from 1816 to present (2007 as the latest available dataset). Furthermore it uses a basket of indicators and does not purely correlate the power of a nation to a single basic indicator as some of the other commonly used approaches do as described in the prior chapter. The specific datasets of the CINC

[292] see Department of Defense, Military Power 2009, p. 32
[293] see COW Project, National Material Capabilities 2010, p.3

consist of military personnel, military expenditures, total population, urban population, steel consumption and primary energy consumption.

Military personnel considers all troops on active duty and available to a government to use against foreign adversaries. Military expenditures are included to reflect the financial resources that are available to the Armed Forces of a nation. The researchers made these numbers comparable and excluded budgets for civil ministries under military command which some nations officially report within their defense budget.[294] Total population is considered, because a state with a large population can maintain a larger army, can maintain its home industries during war time and absorb losses in wartime more easily than can a small nation.[295] The key source for the data is the report of the United Nations Statistical Office.[296]

The urban population is considered as a further indicator that can be seen as a proxy for measuring intangible demographic factors. The research documentation names the factors educational standard, social organization, life expectancy, industrialization and industrial capacities as advantageous and higher ranked in urbanized areas.[297] This aspect addresses one of the key concerns stated at the beginning of this paper regarding lacking consideration of intangibles in most classical material focused power measures. Steel production is used to reflect the industrial dimension of a nation because it is one of the main ingredients for finished goods (for

[294] see COW Project, National Material Capabilities 2010, p.3
[295] see COW Project, National Material Capabilities 2010, p.23
[296] see COW Project, National Material Capabilities 2010, p.23
[297] see COW Project, National Material Capabilities 2010, p.30

the data up to 1900 actually the nation's iron production was used as the prime factor). As a second indicator for industrial capabilities, energy consumption is used since the greater the energy consumption, the larger the manufacturing base of the economy.[298] Also other authors support the assumption that a strong economy leads to strong military capabilities.[299] One might wonder why steel and energy consumption is used instead of standard economic indicators like GNP. However a study by Beckley suggests that the factors iron and steel production and energy consumption lead to similar results compared to the usage of GNP as the factor of measurement.[300] Therefore an elaborated discussion on this matter is not relevant in context of this study.

The CINC model is showing the relative balance of power and capabilities in the year of measurement. For each factor and nation the fraction of the global total is calculated. The average across each of those scores determines the CINC score for each nation. This implies that performance can only be benchmarked within each year's dataset. The performance of country A in 1995 cannot be compared with the performance of country B in 2000. As part of this study the datasets will therefore be kept and analyzed separately for each year. This shall be noted since alternatively one could achieve a larger pool of data points if one were to put them all in one sample as 'possible' efficiency scores in the military environment in general. Time is relevant as a factor and the global power balance is very dynamic and relative with changes over time. For above reasons the CINC score also does not grow over time in absolute terms

[298] see COW Project, National Material Capabilities 2010, p.42
[299] see Hitch, C./McKean, R.: Defense in the Nuclear Age 1960, p.15
[300] see Beckley, M.: Economic Development and Military Effectiveness 2010, p.67

even though destructive power evolved drastically from bows and arrows to nuclear weapons and stealth bombers.

Only for a specific nation does a year-over-year comparison and changes over time provide meaningful data. In fact it is a great way of gaining additional insight for this study as it actually points out how well the nations adapt to changes within the political environment and when efficiency scores change if this is caused by changes to the output or input factor.

As a caveat it shall be noted that the CINC index has used iron and steel production as a measure for manufacturing and innovation potential of a nation for already quite some years now. These indicators are supposed to represent a proxy for the quality of its military equipment. Today however the integration with information technology is becoming much more important for determining the level of sophistication of products. Tellis (et al) states that any methodology that aspires to evaluate the combat proficiency of Armed Forces should incorporate an assessment of whether a country is integrating, would be interested in integrating or is capable of integrating advanced information-intensive technologies.[301] The RAND organization comes to a similar conclusion and claims that a nation's capability in the Information and Communications sector is a good metric for judging its national power.[302] With growing importance of this industry for the sophistication of military equipment, this factor may

[301] see Tellis, A./Bially, J./Layne, C./McPherson, M., Measuring National Power 2000 p.44
[302] see Tellis, A./Bially, J./Layne, C./McPherson, M., Measuring National Power 2000, p.56

have to be considered in the context of measuring military capabilities at some point going forward as well.

It shall further be underlined that the indicator considers active military personnel only as part of the measurement. Some nations actually maintain an extensive and supposedly very effective reserve force. The US and Israel, which are also two of the focus nations in this paper, shall be mentioned in particular. It does not appear unrealistic to assume that a high focus on reserve units can be financially efficient for a nation. One can think of military functions with corresponding civil occupations such as pilots, policemen, firefighter etc.. People in these occupations could be contributing to the economy at the same time as they are maintaining their skill-sets for a parallel military function. A commercial pilot could fly paying customers instead of an empty military aircraft to get practice time in the air. This example oversimplifies the actual situation a bit, but certain synergies cannot be neglected for jobs that either have a direct corresponding military occupation or an occupation that at least requires similar skill-sets and expertise. Buck provides a great introduction into this topic outlining different models for calculating the costs of reserve units and also outlining the importance of actual utilization of reserve units in order to make them an economical alternative to active units.[303] A detailed analysis of this matter is suggested to the military experts but will not be covered in this analysis.

[303] see Buck, J.: The Cost of the Reserves 2008, pp.175-185

4.2.3.2 Gross National Income Data

Economic KPIs are indicators that have often been used as a single-factor measurement of national power and national capabilities. There are some concerns with regard to using single-factor analyses based on economic output as a measure for power as defined in this paper. The discussion in chapter two has made it clear that national power and military capabilities cannot be bought and pure numbers of troops do not explain superior battlefield performance. Already in 1960 Hitch and McKean anticipated that e.g. technological changes can have major impacts on military capabilities which can outweigh a pure quantitative resource advantage.[304] They actually defined the power term more precisely to accommodate for this by distinguishing a nation's basic national power from specific military capabilities. Accordingly indicators of basic strength (like GNI) are not proportional to potential military capability in their view.[305] A further argument associated with economic KPIs is that an economically advanced and powerful nation has a better-skilled and better-educated population and therefore a larger pool of human resources available for the military itself as well as for the production of sophisticated military equipment. This however does neglect the impact of intangible factors specific for the military such as experience and training. The importance of both besides others has been discussed in Chapter 3.4.2. Dressing a successful manager in camouflage does not automatically make him a good soldier.

---

304 see Hitch, C./McKean, R.: Defense in the Nuclear Age 1960, p.18

305 see Hitch, C./McKean, R.: Defense in the Nuclear Age 1960, p.85

A further lack of this model is the ability to accommodate for organizational changes. The merging of the West German Armed Forces with those of the former German Democratic Republic can illustrate this issue. By merging both nations, the GNI as the output measure increased significantly by 17 percent for Germany.[306] It seems doubtful that the military capabilities increased as much at the same time, given the significant amount of coordination and alignment work required to make these former adversaries work towards a new common goal under one leadership and the fact that for the most part the military assets of the former DDR were actually abolished.[307]

Using GNI as a measure for power has a further interesting implication if an economic perspective is added to this matter. As outlined before, it is not proven whether investments in the military support or limit economic growth. If military expenses were assumed to limit economic growth from a macroeconomic perspective, following this logic, a nation would actually get stronger by spending less or even nothing on weapons.

Besides the criticism regarding the simplification, it shall however be credited that if the term military capability is defined on a high strategic level, the arguments seem to hold together. A prolonged full blown war threatening the soil of a nation will certainly lead to a conversion of most resources into the production of weapons. An economically advanced nation is therefore presumably more capable of affording a long-lasting conflict.

---

[306] see CIA World Factbook 1990

[307] see Schneider, Peter: Die Neuen Kameraden 1994

And even the CINC index which has been identified as the primary indicator for this study has an economic aspect as part of its basket of factors. This underlines the interdependence of economy and military capabilities that is seen by a lot of scientists in international politics.

It shall further be emphasized that this paper will lay out options for the analysis of efficiency. The GNI will be one factor that represents the area of single-variable approaches and results will be available for the reader to draw his or her own conclusions.

4.2.3.3 Qualitative Factors

The single- and multi-input factors listed above provide proxies that are supposed to derive the military capabilities of nations based on publicly available and measurable factors. The issue is that none of them actually determine the actual capabilities of the Armed Forces; they just assume a certain level of capabilities based on external indicators. Presumably these factors do not cover any intangible factors that are specific to military organizations. Military expertise, training, quality of service members and other factors cannot be derived from general economic indicators. Just because a nation can afford to produce sophisticated military assets and have highly-skilled and educated citizens does not mean that the Armed Forces can effectively employ them. A positive correlation is assumed and plausible in the concept of single- and multi-factor approaches as suggested above. However a specific evaluation would be helpful since the military does have characteristics very different from any other organization.

This is where the qualitative factor will help to address the issues identified in the prior chapter. The topic is especially relevant today because modern conflicts are different in nature compared to any conflict in the last century. The acceptance of casualties is very low and a quantity-over-quality approach in terms of military strategy would not be accepted by the majority of citizens in today's industrialized nations. Not just having military assets available but actually their quality and deploying them effectively become important factors.

The current state of research does not provide a lot of public information with regard to an assessment of the quality of Armed Forces. Some studies analyze the Armed Forces of specific countries but those analyses do not provide an aggregated total consistent database that could be used for an FDH Analysis.

However there are a couple of sources that can be accessed. For one there is the www.GlobalFirePower.com Web page that provides a ranking of Armed Forces based on a list of 45 factors that are taken into account. The results used to be a pure ranking. Only recently a power index has been added to the ranking in order to also highlight the distance between the ranked nations on an ordinary scale. The data prior to 2013 are therefore not suitable for a FDH analysis due to the lack of detailed information.

Alternatively Dunnigan provides a score and ranking of nations in his book 'How to make war' and also on the Web page strategypage.com. Dunnigan has extensive experience as an author, military-political analyst, consultant to the US Defense and State departments as well as an author of multiple war games. This underlines the amount of professional expertise that went into creating these ratings. His database is transparent and the ranking is a result of the individual scores which are published in a numerical way. This type of data can therefore be used as an output factor for the FDH Analysis. The Armed Forces database is not maintained on an ongoing basis and provides only an indicator of the quality of troops as of mid-2008.[308] Therefore a sequential analysis is not possible as the output factor remains constant in each scenario and only the input factor changes. The question now becomes how to correlate the 2008 quality ranking to any of the years analyzed in this paper. Since it was outlined that investments in military assets take time to develop and show operational impacts, it will be suggested in this paper to test the data model based on the percentage of GDP defense spending in 1995, 2000 and 2005, reflecting investments in the years prior to the study. The data points will be good references to see to what extent the timing matters. As an example the investments in training for officers in 1995 would in fact have an impact in 2008 to the extent that some of those recruits from 1995 will have reached senior-level positions and become decision makers in the Armed Forces by 2008.

Dunnigan provides explanations for the factors and reasoning for using them on his homepage along with the actual datasets:[309] He points out that his database consists of quantitative values derived from public databases and qualitative scoring based on historic trends and performances of the nation's Armed Forces. Furthermore he points out that the qualitative scoring is subjective to a certain extent and readers

[308] see Strategypage: Database 2008
[309] see Strategypage: Database 2008

may impose their own evaluation. The core of his model is that he is not just quantifying a nation's military assets, but he is actually discounting them based on an efficiency index.[310] This index is derived based on the intangible factors leadership, equipment quantity and quality and experience – combat as well as training, support, mobility and tradition. An index of 100 is reflecting perfectly-efficient Armed Forces from an operational execution perspective. The combination of efficiency factors and physical assets then derive the land combat power per nation. The manpower is evaluated not just by the number of troops, but in combination with an assessment of the officer corps' leadership capabilities. Same applies to the equipment which is evaluated not just by taking account of numbers, but actually respective qualitative assessments of the factors mentioned above. In other words, if two nations have the exact same number of military assets, the nation with the lower scoring on the qualitative factors would be considered a weaker nation as the assets are discounted accordingly. Naval forces are excluded from this analysis given that their purposes are vastly different. Dunnigan points out that each branch of the military fulfills different tasks and naval military assets cannot occupy inland cities just as tanks cannot hunt submarines at sea. His focus is on land forces in this study due to the fact that those are the forces that ultimately transpose the power needed to achieve one's military goals.[311]

This part of the research model is meant to provide a new innovative alternative to the single- and multi-factor models described in prior chapters. It shall be encouraged

[310] Not referring to financial efficiency here.
[311] Naval forces are analyzed by Dunnigan as well, they are just not factored in in terms of the combat power ranking.

that as more studies and data points in the qualitative area become available, further testing should be performed. Given that the military has to fulfill a myriad of tasks, it becomes very difficult to compile the performance level of nations into a single digital number. Further testing in this area could actually extend into an analysis of specific military operations. War games could provide insight into what it takes to achieve a certain military objective. By comparing different options of engagements or approaches taken by different nations, the most economical option could be determined by applying an efficiency analysis like the FDH.

4.2.4 Remarks regarding the Countries analyzed

4.2.4.1 China

China's Armed Forces are called People's Liberation Army or short PLA. The purpose for which they are maintained and which strategic foreign policy goals China has set are fairly difficult to assess. Some official statements allow a glimpse at China's goals and western analysts are working hard to assess the Chinese military capabilities and foreign policy goals.

In 2002 President Jiang Zemin reoriented the military toward what he officially stated as a force that is capable of engaging in local wars under modern high technology conditions.[312] This is a change similar to what most western nations faced after the end of the Cold War. The Chinese government furthermore – at least officially -

[312] see Zemin, J.: On National Defense and Army Building 2002, p.83

states that it does not aspire to a dominating status. According to China's statements, the growth of military expenditures is at the level of the growth of the Chinese economy and China's strategy is characterized by a doctrine of peaceful rise without attempt to threaten neighbors or challenge the power balance of the world.[313] However there are discrepancies that raise questions. For one the Chinese government claims that the increase in military expenditures is mainly devoted to non-threatening expenditures such as better pay for soldiers.[314] Critics however challenge this and claim that China does in fact acquire new power-projection capabilities that influence the regional balance of power.[315] Also, the Chinese military spending is only in line with economic growth if the officially reported numbers are used. External analysts commonly agree that those numbers are vastly under-reporting the actual spending and can only roughly estimate what they truly are. In the year 2009 e.g. the US Department of Defense estimated the defense expenditures of China to be up to $150 billion compared to a more conservative SIPRI estimate of $105 billion.[316] Besides getting budget from the government, the PLA also receives additional income from arms exports and the government actively invests in and subsidizes the military industry with about $3 - $5 billion each year.[317] All numbers are aiming at improving military capabilities but are not considered in the official reports. With regard to China it becomes therefore especially clear that analyzing military capabilities has to go beyond measuring the pure quantity of military equipment and personnel in terms of money allocated for them. The pure

[313] see Zemin, J.: On National Defense and Army Building 2002, p.52
[314] see Chen, S./Feffer, J.: China's Military Spending 2009, p.48
[315] see Chen, S./Feffer, J.: China's Military Spending 2009, p.48
[316] see Annual Report to Congress: China 2009, p.31
[317] see Chen, S./Feffer, J.: China's Military Spending 2009, p.55

number of troops with around 3 million is already a high number, but not necessarily reflective of their actual capabilities. Beckley highlights this point and attributes the number of troops to demographic factors and sees specifically a gap in capabilities in the area of advanced firepower, targeting and communication.[318]

China's focus on matters of national security and national power becomes evident further through recent studies.

Chinese strategists have actually developed a Comprehensive National Power Index short CNP[319] which can be seen in analogy to the CINC as a basket of factors that result in a ranking of nations based on their national power. Furthermore China is in the process of modernizing its military arsenal; but evaluating the success of the transformation is hard to measure since the PLA is untested in modern combat.[320] One further observation has been made by US analysts who claim that China is in process of following the US doctrine of jointness and focus on close collaboration between branches of the military.[321]

All of this information makes it clear that China is aiming at becoming a military power and is in process of modernizing its military assets. Therefore it is important to include China in this analysis even though the data need to be handled with caution.

---

[318] see Beckley, M.: Economic Development and Military Effectiveness 2010, p.74
[319] see Chang, Chin-Lung: A Measure of National Power 2004
[320] see Annual Report to Congress: China 2009, p.10
[321] see Annual Report to Congress: China 2009, p.12

4.2.4.2 Israel

The Israeli Armed Forces are also called IDF – which stands for Israeli Defense Force. Israel is an interesting data point in this study since it is the one and only nation of the six that is facing a realistic threat from immediate neighbor states. It shall be interesting to see if and how this may impact the performance on the efficiency frontier.

As a further interesting characteristic, the IDF relies heavily on conscript soldiers - men and women alike, with some exceptions, are required to serve. Furthermore Israel has an elaborated reserve system with about 3 reserve soldiers for every active duty service member.[322]Israel receives financial aid from the US which is part of Israel's officially reported percentage of GDP defense spending. These grants are of substantial value with USD 1.8 billion in 1995[323], USD 3.1 billion in 2000 and USD 2.2 billion in 2005.[324] Military grants are supposed to be used to transform and modernize military equipment and can also partially be used to support the local arms industry. As a reference point the US report to Congress states that about 26 percentage of the grant is used for procurement of military assets from local suppliers in Israel and the remaining part is to be spent on arms imports from the US accordingly.[325]

Overall the required data for this study are available in a consistent form from SIPRI, World Bank and any of the additional sources that are being used.

---

[322] see Global Firepower: Israel 2013
[323] see Sharp, J.: Report for Congress: Aid to Israel 2010, p.26
[324] see Sharp, J.: Report for Congress: Aid to Israel 2010, p.24
[325] see Sharp, J.: Report for Congress: Aid to Israel 2010, p.5

4.2.4.3 Germany

Germany has recently transitioned from a conscript military to an all voluntary force and in 2011 the last drafted soldiers joined the service. This change is notable since the datasets used in this study will still work with data that reflect the German Bundeswehr in its conscript form. But even more recent data would still not fully reflect the new form of Armed Forces, since structural transformations take time.

The role of the German Armed Forces is described in the document "Verteidigungspolitische Richtlinien" issued by the ministry of defense, which emphasizes the unlikeliness of conventional conflicts and the focus of the Armed Forces on local regional engagements, peacekeeping missions and others.[326] This transfers the Armed Forces to an instrument of foreign policy and presents a major expansion of tasks compared to the prior responsibilities that were defined in the 'Grundgesetz' Art.87a Abs 1 Satz 1 as 'deterrence of threats to the German homeland' which mainly referred to the threat posed by the Warsaw Pact during the Cold War. Notably the defense budget does apparently not back up this expansion of tasks since the defense spending of Germany post-Cold War and reunification is characterized by a decline in absolute terms as well as in percentage compared to other government activities.[327] This budget constraint will actually further accelerate due to a change in accounting methods. As of 2006 pensions for retired service members are supposed to be covered by the Einzelplan 14 as well. The 'Einzelplan 14' represents the section of defense-

---

[326] see BMDg: Verteidigungspolitische Richtlinien 2011, p.1
[327] see Bayer, S.: Der Einzelplan 14 2013, p. 256

related government spending in Germany. This steadily increasing budget item consequently reduces the budget that is available for operational activities and investments. Bayer underlines that increased efficiency is the only available option for the German Armed Forces to cope with the dilemma of facing more responsibilities with fewer resources.[328] Germany is furthermore to some extent benefiting from the US involvement in Europe, since the US maintains a significant amount of facilities and active military units on German soil, which accordingly represents opportunities to share certain costs as well as increases the level of perceived security by their pure presence. As outlined in the alliance section of this paper, Germany benefits as a 'free-rider' from this situation as it has to maintain a lower level of its own assets since it can credibly rely on the support of a foreign nation in times of war.

4.2.4.4 United Kingdom

The United Kingdom is a member of NATO and therefore most data available for this study are pretty straightforward and available in public databases.

The specific tasks defined by the UK Ministry of Defense office are in line with what other western industrialized countries have defined and what has been mentioned in several areas of this analysis already.[329]

One notable addition however is the specifically defined support of overseas territories. The UK still maintains a lot of direct or indirect relationships with former

[328] see Bayer, S.: Der Einzelplan 14 2013, p. 260
[329] see Management of Defense: Mission of Armed Forces 2013

colonies and territories. The Falkland War from 1982 illustrates the implications that this may have. Furthermore the UK joined the US in the war in Iraq which makes its Armed Forces one of those with very recent deployment in actual ground combat.

4.2.4.5 United States of America

In the last decade of the 20th century the US national security policies were focused on waging two concurrent major-theatre wars, one on the Korean peninsula and one in the Middle-East.[330] For the early 21st century however the potential threats have changed and are seen more in the area of terrorism, weapons of mass destruction, cyber warfare, religious fundamentalists, narcocriminals, regional conflicts, failed states, scarce resources, global pandemics and potential future peer competitors.[331] Both national security agendas will be covered by the dataset of this study which include data from the late 20th century as well as early 21st century. These political changes of focus in particular can be seen as a major reason for increasing requirements for an efficient operation. Gansler argues that in order to address these new threats in an effective and affordable way, a fundamental rethinking of military operations is required and specifically political components should be included in order to avoid wars in the first place instead of focusing on pure military actions.[332] Interestingly the current tension with North Korea has put some focus back on traditional forms of ground warfare. And the capabilities in this area, in particular in

[330] see Gansler, J.: Democracy's Arsenal 2011, p.79
[331] see Gansler, J.: Democracy's Arsenal 2011, p.79
[332] see Gansler, J.: Democracy's Arsenal 2011, p.89

combination with the threat of nuclear or chemical weapons, are currently not very well developed as a recent war game of the US Armed Forces surfaced.[333]

In the case of the USA, the military budget does not include most spending related to the nuclear arsenal since this is under the budget of the Department of Energy.[334] This in addition to further, excluded numbers like supplemental payments for the wars in Afghanistan and Iraq, military pensions as well as any military-related contributions made by NASA, NSA and other government departments can add up to about 50 percent of the official number.[335] To get another perspective, Gansler speaks of a reported budget of $441.5 billion in 2005 and estimates an additional $100 billion as supplements for the wars in Iraq and Afghanistan and the nuclear arsenal.[336]

In terms of this study it does actually help that the defense budget of the US excludes the cost for active deployments since it makes the data more comparable to the nations that are not engaged in a current military conflict of similar scope. In reality however it is suspected that making a clear distinction is difficult and some war-related incremental expenses are expected to still be embedded in the 'regular' defense budget for ongoing operations.[337]

---

[333] see Rizzo, J./Tapper, J.: War Game plays out poorly 2013
[334] see Chen, S./Feffer, J.: China's Military Spending 2009, p.55
[335] see Chen, S./Feffer, J.: China's Military Spending 2009, p.55
[336] see Gansler, J.: Democracy's Arsenal 2011, p.18
[337] see Stiglitz, J./Bilmes, L.: The Three Trillion Dollar War 2008, p. 26

4.2.4.6 Russia

Data reports for the Russian Armed Forces are becoming more public and reliable. During the times of the Cold War most data were based on assumptions by leading defense analysts. However specifically for recent years data regarding Russia are included in most public databases. One challenge with Russian defense figures is the significant fluctuation of the value of the Russian currency - the ruble. Specific attention is required in cross-country comparison when data is being used and currency adjustments as well as PPP adjustments have to be considered. The databases used for this study incorporate these and the sources ensure that comparable data are available. Defined tasks and missions are in line with the goals other nations set for their Armed Forces:[338] Security for homeland, just as UN peacekeeping missions and counter terrorism are listed. Notable additions are the clear definition to maintain and ensure readiness of the nuclear arsenal as well as the enforcement of national interests in the territorial waters and global oceans. Given the size of the Russian territory and its shorelines this is a significant task in addition to the potential political ramifications that such statements may have.

[338] see Russian Ministry of Defence: Mission and Objectives 2013

4.3 Free Disposal Hull Analysis

4.3.1 Overview

This chapter will cover the actual application of datasets in a FDH Analysis. Three examples have been chosen in order to analyze the efficiency of Armed Forces. The primary indicator used will be the CINC index, which covers a basket of sub indicators as a proxy for military capabilities. The GNI application to the model is added as a second reference point and a single-factor measure. The third group shall extend the current state of research and add a qualitative measure. The results of the three approaches will be compared. The intention of the comparison is not to map and match results, but rather to test the model based on the application of different output factors. In the end it depends to a certain extent on the context and purpose of an analysis which approach is more appropriate in order to take specific actions for efficiency improvements within each nation.

4.3.2 Composite Index of National Capabilities

4.3.2.1 Overall Results

Applying the CINC score and percentage of GDP defense spending to the data set provides interesting results. Table 1 shows in the left column the scoring range of efficiency in percentage. The columns to the right show how many nations in percentage of the total data population score in the respective efficiency corridors. One initial finding is that the number of countries scoring in the lower sections of the efficiency ranking is high. In the year 1995, 72 percent of nations are below a 40 percent efficiency score, 63 percent in 2000 and 76 percent in 2005. It shall be noted here that this situation is not purely attributable to the development stages of those nations that are compared within one sub sample. Industrialized nations can be found in the lower ranking just as Third World nations are found in the higher scores. In order to accommodate for the varying estimates on defense spending for China, it will be analyzed how the different scenarios impact the results. Table 2 is an extract of the overall dataset and shows the efficiency score of the six focus nations within the overall population of data points. For each year three data points are shown based on the three different assumptions of China's defense spending with the originally reported number per SIPRI (o) and the additional two estimates of higher spend in a low (l) and high (h) estimate scenario.

Efficiency Score in %	1995	2000	2005
81% ≤ 100%	8%	6%	6%
61% ≤ 80%	4%	6%	5%
41% ≤ 60%	16%	26%	13%
21% ≤ 40%	32%	32%	40%
0% ≤ 20%	40%	31%	36%

Table 1: CINC Efficiency Scores Dataset

	1995			2000			2005		
	China o	China l	China h	China o	China l	China h	China o	China l	China h
China	100%	100%	92%	100%	100%	100%	100%	100%	100%
Germany	58%	58%	58%	66%	66%	66%	71%	71%	71%
Israel	7%	7%	7%	7%	7%	7%	6%	6%	6%
Russian Federation	39%	59%	60%	26%	26%	26%	26%	26%	26%
United Kingdom	32%	32%	32%	41%	41%	41%	40%	40%	40%
United States	100%	100%	100%	61%	88%	100%	51%	70%	100%

Table 2: CINC Efficiency Scores Countries

One initial finding suggests that China's efficiency is on a high level no matter which estimate is being used. Interesting is the comparison of the results based on the differences in the underlying assumptions. In the original model as well as the low estimate model, China and USA are both 100 percent efficient and lead the efficiency ranking in different sample sets. Nations are always benchmarked against the DMU on the frontier that produces at least as much output, but with a lower input. Therefore with varying estimates for China's defense spending, its position on the frontier changes accordingly. Different sample sets in the FDH context therefore means that nations are either both on the frontier or their performance is measured against two different DMUs that reside on the frontier.

This situation changes with the assumption of higher defense spending for China. Now China and USA are in one sample set and the US dominates China in 1995. For 2000 and 2005 China is leading the scoring in each scenario and only with the high estimate the US is not as a benchmark in the same sub sample with China and scores 100 percent as well.

Bottom line is that with regard to the efficiency scoring of the US and China, both are relevant for the benchmark, but results vary significantly depending on the assumptions used for China's defense spending. The rankings of Germany, Israel and the UK do not change in the different scenarios, since China is in a different area of the production frontier and not seen as a benchmark DMU. Russia is a benchmark to China only in the 1995 sample set and its efficiency increases accordingly with higher assumptions on defense spending for China for that particular year.

The purpose of this analysis is not necessarily to compare the performance of the six countries among themselves, but rather how the six countries are positioned within the overall sample set. However a look at the structure of domination reveals notable information. Germany dominates Israel and the UK, the UK and Russia dominate Israel, and the US dominates Israel and Russia. Israel is therefore dominated by all five countries that are being analyzed within the overall sample set. This structure also indicates that for each nation a country with similar development status is in the same sub sample as a benchmark and also that it was a valid assumption to use these six countries for a deeper analysis of efficiency drivers, since they are in some way related to one another in terms of the efficiency frontier.

One weakness of the FDH Analysis is that DMUs potentially are efficient by definition. As outlined above this is the case if a nation is on the outside curve of the production frontier and is seen as efficient even though it could actually be more efficient than it currently is. The three scenario approach used for China in this model supports this finding. The officially reported number is the lowest and based on the common understanding of experts is for sure under-reporting the actual spending. Therefore although China is efficient in the scope of the sample set it can presumably be more efficient since with actual spends being higher, China would actually be already efficient at a lower spending level. Same applies to the US for the scenarios with the scores of 100 percent efficiency. In all these cases it is not known if an even higher efficiency would be feasible to achieve. And since the form and shape of the production frontier is not known, these data cannot be modeled or assumed. An actual empirical data point has to prove that this particular input/output relation is in fact feasible. To illustrate the look of the efficiency frontier Figure 14 shows a subset of data points for the year 2005, which is the most recent available data set. Not all data points are labeled in order to make the chart easier to read. The focus is on the frontier and countries around it, not on the illustration of all individual nations. The countries shown are the OECD countries as examples for nations that can be considered developed and industrialized for comparability reasons. Since neither Russia nor China are current OECD members, these two data points were added.

In connection with Table 2 the respective effective percentages are illustrated based on the distance of nations to the frontier. In this data set the US is 70 percent efficient. Accordingly a reduction of defense spend by 30 percent would shift the data point towards the left and therefore onto the frontier. China would still dominate until the US would be able to tie or exceed the Chinese output performance as well.

Japan and China show clearly a superior performance in terms of efficiency over their respective benchmarks. China is shown with the low estimate as a presumably more realistic alternative to the official number as reported by SIPRI. China illustrates the outlier impact as the data point lies way out of the regular scope of data. Same with Israel given that the defense spending in percentage of GDP is that much higher for reasons outlined in other sections of this paper. Also the US is prone to the outlier effect with China being the only benchmark nation in close proximity on the frontier.

Figure 15 shows for better data clarity another subset of data points without the outlier nations. Japan is excluded from the frontier not because there is evidence to question the results, but actually to show the remaining countries on a more comparable basis. Based on this subset of data, Germany would now be one of the nations that is determining the frontier. One challenge with the data points is the comparability of nations. Given that one of the sub indicators determining the CINC score is an economic one, bigger economies like Germany will naturally score higher than smaller nations. Accordingly for smaller economies a higher defense spending is actually required to even produce as high of an output as they do since with higher defense spending they can maintain a higher number of service members offsetting their economic inferiority. Reducing the spending may substantially lower their output as the more specific military factors, such as number of service members, would presumably have to be lowered in the CINC index accordingly.

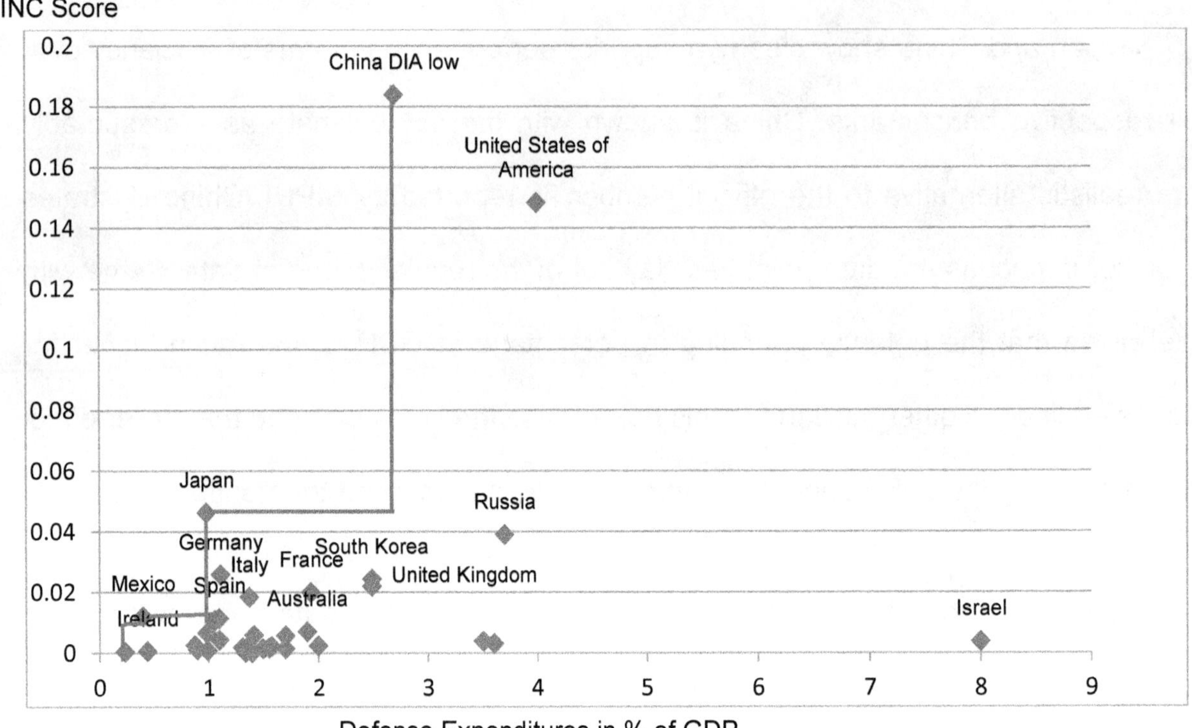

Figure 14: FDH Efficiency Frontier CINC 2005 OECD

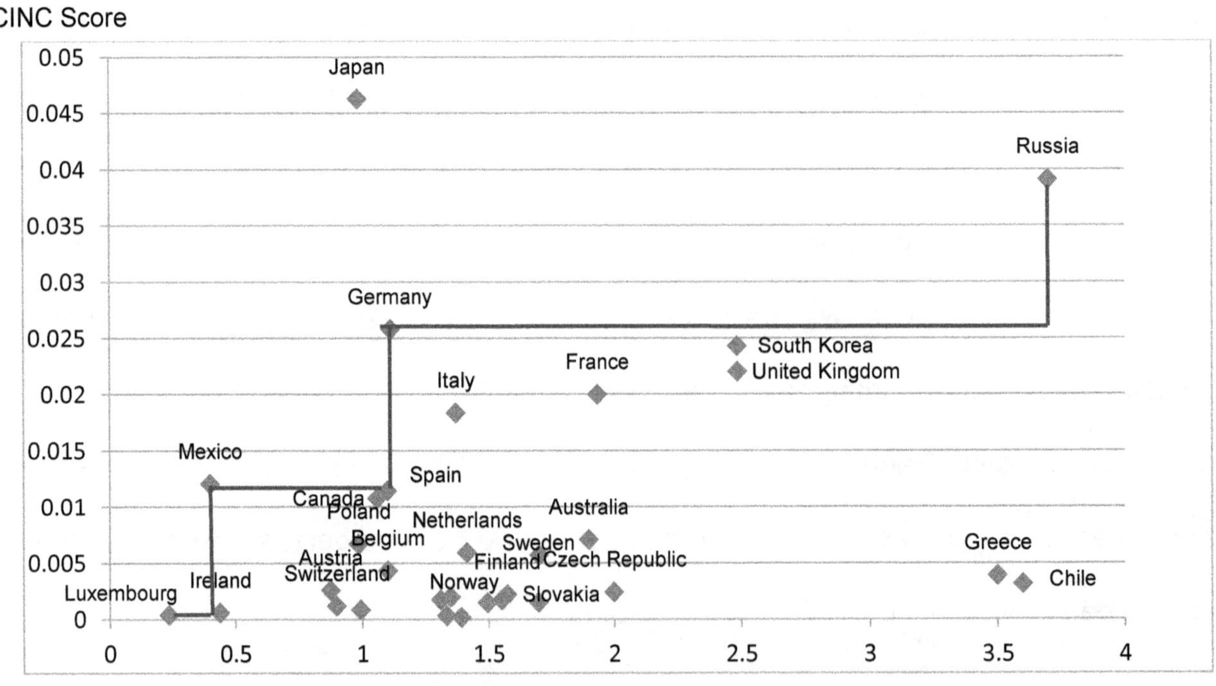

Figure 15: FDH Efficiency Frontier CINC 2005 OECD Outliers adjusted

What the results however show is that this in fact can lead to inefficiencies as those particular nations need to dedicate more resources of their economy to defense, if they aspire to a high level of military capability. For more operational analysis to see if efficiency improvements are feasible for those countries, a comparison with countries of similar size and requirements would be more appropriate.

The frontier furthermore illustrates the weakness of lacking operational factors in the CINC index. Case in point, the UK spends USD 57 billion on defense according to the CINC data base with 205,000 people in arms. Germany spends USD 38 billion with 284,000 people in arms. Germany is a conscript military while the UK maintains an All-Volunteer Force (AVF). Chapter 5 will show that the costs per soldier are in fact higher in an AVF model but also come with substantial operational advantages. Furthermore Chapter 3.6 indicated that the UK in fact maintains a more technology-focused military heavy on capital in terms of military equipment over man power. Any advantage based on the capital military assets maintained is not part of the CINC equation. If the UK in fact maintains sophisticated equipment that could offset or even supersize inferior numbers of military personnel on the battlefield, this would not be reflected by the CINC score. Same applies to the service members. If AVF soldiers are presumed to be more effective then conscript service members, this would not be accounted for in a pure quantitative comparison. The qualitative model in the upcoming Chapter 4.3.4 will try to extend the analysis in that regard.

4.3.2.2 Results of sequential FDH Analysis

As a next step it shall be analyzed how the sequential set-up of the model helps to gain further insight. For this purpose the efficiency development of the nations will be analyzed with the assumption of defense spending for China at the officially reported level. Since the results for the US and China are at a high level anyhow and will not impact the scoring of the other countries as outlined above, this is a pragmatic approach to gain meaningful data in a predefined scope of sample data. As outlined in previous chapters, investments and changes within the military organization take time to take effect. Notably if money is spent on new military assets, the development cycle causes high expenses, while at the same time the capabilities will not increase at the same level due to the time it takes to produce the equipment and implement a doctrine for its operational usage. In order to accommodate for this fact, a five-year timeframe has been chosen.

Table 3 illustrates the changes that can be seen when the efficiency score is being compared. The year 2000 number shows the change over 1995 data and 2005 the change over 2000 data accordingly.

The question now becomes whether those changes are attributable to an increase in output, a decrease in input or other impacts. Other impacts specifically refer to datasets of other nations which improved their scoring and therefore raise the bar to benchmark performance against.[339]

Change Efficiency	2000	2005
China	0.0%	0.0%
Germany	12.7%	7.4%
Israel	4.3%	-23.4%
Russia	-32.0%	-1.5%
United Kingdom	27.9%	-2.3%
United States	-39.3%	-15.5%

Table 3: CINC Efficiency Changes

In order to answer this question the change in efficiency as illustrated above is required, along with the changes in input and output measures for the respective timeframe. These are illustrated in Table 4. The column 2000 represents the change year 2000 over year 1995 and the column 2005, 2005 over 2000 accordingly. Although China is already at a score of 100 percent, this analysis shows that both factors increase over both timeframes, with the output factor CINC actually increasing at a faster pace than the input.

[339] The CINC is a relative power measure. Increases in Defense spending do not automatically translate into increasing CINC scores, as the CINC score is highly depended on actions of other nations. Higher spending may in some cases actually be a requirement to keep the status quo in a year over year comparison.

	change in CINC		change in mil % of GDP	
	2000	**2005**	**2000**	**2005**
China	14.8%	18.1%	7.5%	10.9%
Germany	-14.7%	-8.4%	-8.5%	-7.8%
Israel	2.4%	-6.7%	-8.3%	-2.5%
Russia	-18.9%	-21.1%	-16.2%	0.5%
United Kingdom	-6.2%	-0.4%	-19.4%	1.4%
United States	1.6%	3.7%	-19.8%	31.3%

Table 4: Changes CINC Score and Military Spending

Germany, whose efficiency score increases over both periods, actually shows decreases in both areas with output factors decreasing more than input factors. In absolute Dollar terms Germany spends around USD 30.6 billion in 2000 as well as 2005. The conclusion is that the German GDP actually grew between 2000 and 2005 while the defense spending had been kept flat in absolute terms leading to lower percentages. The decrease in CINC indicates a reduction in relative military capability. Given that efficiency increases, the data indicate that Germany is benefiting from shifts in the overall data set in terms of the efficiency frontier – this lowered the 'bar' to measure up against. One could only speak of initiated efficiency gains if either spending had decreased more than the CINC score or if the output had increased at a higher pace than the input. Since Germany decreased in military capabilities at a higher rate than the input while still improving the efficiency score, this can only be attributable to changes in the dataset and poorer performance of benchmark nations. One further finding is that Germany is compared with reasonable benchmarks. As an illustrative point this will be explained by the data generated for the year 1995 and the DMU Japan. Germany spends about 1.6 percent of GDP on defense with an output score of 0.03. With about 0.95 percent of GDP Japan spend significantly less while producing more output in CINC terms with 0.059. Accordingly Japan dominates Germany with 100 percent efficiency over 58 percent. In absolute Dollar both nations spend about 50 million on defense. This indicates that Japan significantly outperforms Germany as it dedicates fewer resources from its economy and still produces a substantially higher output. While Germany is closing the gap to Japan over time as shown by the increasing efficiency scores in Table 3, Japan still operates significantly more efficiently in 2005 as it is the dominating country for Germany in the sample set with 100 percent efficiency over ~70 percent. The finding that Japan operates efficiently in terms of producing public goods is also supported by other research projects. Afonso (et al) determined the efficiency of the public sector among OECD countries in producing non-monetary goods such as healthcare and education, with Japan actually being the nation with the highest efficiency score.[340]

Israel's data show a clearer correlation. In 2000 the efficiency had increased by 4.3 percent over 1995. This was caused by increased capabilities; CINC is increasing by 2.4 percent and a reduction in military spending as a percentage of GDP of 8.3 percent. As for Germany this change does not necessarily reflect actual cost cuts. In absolute terms the spending in 1995 was around USD 24.5 billion and grew in 2000 to

[340] see Afonso, A./Schuknecht, L./Tanzi, V.: Public Sector 2003, p.17

USD 39.6 billion. In absolute terms the spending almost doubled, but in correlation to the development in capabilities and a decrease in spending as a percentage of GDP this actually led to an increased efficiency score. However the efficiency score increased only by 0.3 percentage points overall, so one could say that besides significant investments in the military, the level of efficiency remained constant in the case of Israel. The score of around 7 percent for 1995 and 2000 however indicates that the efficiency was not high in the first place. In 2005 the score actually drops to around 5 percent with a decrease in the capability scoring of 6.3 percent and a decrease in defense spending of 2.5 percent comparing percentage of GDP. Since the absolute military spend increased further to $ 45.7 billion, the increase in capabilities was not in line with the additional investments. Without going into deep political discussions in this economic paper, it shall be noted that Israel has a lot of actual and perceived threats in the Middle East that can drive decisions to invest in defense despite an inefficient use of resources. The World Values Survey can give one indicator for this. In the year 2001, which is the only data point currently available, 41 percent of Israelites answered that military strength should be the highest priority for the nation. One may argue that this should not matter, since the increasing investments should increase the produced output accordingly. To Israel's credit it shall also be noted that a military in peacetime looks different than one preparing for an extensive war. Modern ammunition e.g. can be useless after being stocked unused for too long. Nations in peacetime can use old ammunition for training exercises and only maintain a certain amount in stock, rotating it out over time. A nation preparing for a war may stock up a significant amount of resources, just to be prepared for the worst.[341]

This fact is certainly not considered as explicitly by the CINC index as a proxy measure for nation's military capabilities. This just proves the point of how difficult it is for Israel to be compared with nations that operate in different political environments.

Furthermore Israel maintains a significant amount of reserve units and reserve units are not considered in the used output measure, which only accounts for active duty personnel. This is one area of extension for future studies once it is better understood how reserve units impact military performance.[342]

Russia shows a decrease in the efficiency score from 39 percent in 1995 to 26 percent in 2000 as well as 2005. The sequential analysis indicates that this change is mainly caused by changes in the output factor. The CINC ranking decreases by 18.9 percent from 1995 to 2000 and further by 21.1 percent from 2000 to 2005. At the same time the spending in percentage of GDP is reduced by 16.2 percent 2000 over 1995 and then remains almost constant 2005 over 2000.

The UK improves its efficiency score from 32.2 percent in 1995 to 41.1 percent in 2000 and shows a slight decrease in 2005 to 40.2 percent. The improvement in the year

[341] One could think of the US being in a similar situation fighting wars in the middle-east. However, these impacts have been eliminated in the datasets used as the US is using a specific separate fund for on-going war efforts. This is good for the study, since it makes numbers more comparable to other industrialized nations.

[342] The challenge with reserve units is that nations maintain them with various degrees of intensity. In some nations they just exist on paper with rare or no training. Other nations like Israel and USA try to maintain them at a readiness status comparable to active units. Since these stages are not evaluated across all nations, the traditional measures exclude reserve units all together.

2000 can be attributed to a lower allocation of defense spending in percentage of GDP. The CINC ranking decreases by 6.2 percent but the decrease in defense spending in percentage of GDP is higher with 19.4 percent. 2005 over 2000 the efficiency ranking is almost constant just as the changes to the input and output factors. Defense spending in absolute terms were at a level of USD 21.7 billion in 1995, increased to USD 23.3 billion in 2000 and increased again to USD 30.3 billion in 2005. The moderate increase in 2000 seems to have positively impacted the efficiency while the increase of 30 percent in absolute terms from 2005 over 2000 did not influence the efficiency significantly. In other words the higher defense spending apparently was used to acquire assets required in order to maintain the status quo in terms of the military capabilities relative to benchmark nations. Efficiency can only improve if the same or more output is achieved with less input. The UK however increased both factors, while maintaining a constant efficiency score. The percentage of GDP allocation is with 1.4 percent change slightly higher than the increase in the CINC score with 0.4 percent, but so did also the efficiency score decrease slightly by 2.3 percent. With regard to the UK, the World Values Survey provides two data points of relevance. The confidence of the British citizens in their Armed Forces has been analyzed in 2005. 28 percent had a 'great deal' of confidence in the Armed Forces and 47.9 percent 'quite a lot'. What this indicates is that the perception of the people shows satisfaction with the service produced by their Armed Forces or, in other words, the level of military capabilities maintained meets their expectations. Therefore from an efficiency perspective it would be interesting to analyze further how the British military could maintain that level of output while reducing the cost basis in order to improve efficiency. The alternative of driving efficiency by increasing the output while maintaining the input would improve the efficiency score as well, but the survey indicates that the citizens are not necessarily interested in higher capabilities since they are already satisfied with the status quo. This is further supported by the question around the importance of defense for the country. Only 11.9 percent saw a strong military as the top priority, which certainly also leads to the expectation that higher investments in the military are not favored. To summarize, the UK maintained constant military capabilities from 2005 over 2000; the citizens are satisfied with that ranking, but at the same time do not see further investments or expansions of capabilities as a priority of the country. Consequently efficiency improvements should focus on maintaining capabilities and lowering costs.

An analysis of the US data provides quite divergent results. While in 1995 the ranking is 100 percent in each scenario, in 1995 and 2000 results vary significantly based on the assumptions for Chinese spending. On the input side the US decreased defense spending by about 20 percent as percentage of GDP from 2000 over 1995. From 2000 to 2005 expenses increase again by about 31 percent. At the same time the CINC index shows increases on the output side for both time periods. 2000 represents a growth of 1.6 percent besides the reduction in spending and 2005 shows an increase of 3.7 percent which is just a fraction of the increase in spending of 31 percent. The reduction in spending in 2000 is again just a reduction of spending allocation as a percentage of GDP, since in absolute Dollar terms the expenses increased by 8.2 percent. The 2005 increase in absolute Dollar terms is 27.1 percent, which is about at the level of increase as percentage of GDP. One conclusion here is that military capabilities increased over the 10-year timeframe, but the increase was significantly below the level of increase in spending as percentage of GDP as well as absolute Dollar terms. In theory, this cost increase cannot be attributed to the costs for ongoing missions, since those deployment costs are excluded from the reported numbers by SIPRI. However it is certainly presumably difficult to truly distinguish incremental costs from deployments from cost caused by regular activities. This issue has already been pointed out in reference to the study by Stiglitz and Bilmes.

From an efficiency perspective the results of the US ranking vary significantly depending on the assumptions used for China. In 1995 the US efficiency is independent from the Chinese numbers since they are in different sub samples of the FDH Analysis. In 2000 the US results are 61 percent based on China's official number, 88 percent based on the low estimate and 100 percent with the high estimate. For 2005 the results are 51 percent, 70 percent and 100 percent respectively. Since China is the only dominating benchmark in the first two scenarios, the respective results are highly dependent on assumptions for China's input. The results from the WVS with regard to the US are shown in Table 5.

Confidence in Armed Forces	1995	1999	2006
A great deal	32.7%	33.8%	34.9%
Quite a lot	51.7%	47.6%	46.5%
Not very much	11.7%	14.6%	13.6%
None at all	2.1%	3.3%	2.2%
Don't know	1.7%	0.8%	0.8%

Table 5: WVS Confidence in Armed Forces US

Positive responses dominate the data set with 84.4 percent in 1995, 81.4 percent in 1999 and 2006. Although the changes are only minimal, the scoring a 'great deal' increases over the time by about 2.2 percentage points. 'Not very much' increases as well by about 1.9 percentage points. 'Quite a lot' decreases about 4.2 percentage points. Over the same time period, 14.4 percent of US citizens ranked 'strong defensive forces' as the first priority for the nation, 15.9 percent in 1999 and 31.5 percent in 2006.

E001.- Aims of country: first choice - Strong defensive force	1995	1999	2006
USA	14.4%	15.9%	31.5%

Table 6: WVS Aims of Country US

The WVS supports the assumption that the capabilities of the US Armed Forces meet the expectation of the US citizens. At the same time they rank military strength with increasing importance over the analyzed timeframe. The data do not necessarily indicate efficiency issues for the Armed Forces, since the scoring is very high. However it has to be noted that the data for the US, due to its dominating size, are in the area of the model that can cause the described issues of outliers. The US can be seen as being efficient by definition due to a lack of sufficient benchmark data. Given that the US citizens rank the military strength high as shown by the WVS potentially makes a discussion around efficiency in this area not necessarily a priority on the political agenda. As a side note, it should certainly be noted that in more recent years the reduction of US military spending is a topic after years of costly wars in the Middle East, a global financial crisis and a continuously challenging economic environment.

The results of the FDH analysis based on the CINC index do support Hypothesis 1.), since efficiency results differ between the nations. It shall be emphasized that in the absence of a known production frontier the scoring measures relative performance scores between nations. They are good data points for comparisons of nations and evaluating potential drivers of efficiency and measures to improve efficiency. However a high scoring does not automatically mean that a nation is operating as efficiently as it could; it simply shows that other nations are less efficient.

4.3.3 Gross National Income - FDH Analysis

The GNI is a factor that is commonly used to determine the military capabilities of nations. As illustrated above this single-factor measure represents the economical capabilities of a nation and is used as a proxy to determine the power that a nation can mobilize in times of war. The results of the FDH analysis with the GNI as a factor are being used here in order to show a complete picture with regard to potential factors that can be used to evaluate the efficiency of Armed Forces. It shall be emphasized that today's military faces a myriad of tasks and the nature of warfare for industrialized nations has changed drastically. Specifically the number of counterterrorism and peace-keeping missions has increased and most nations do not necessarily face the risk of an all-out conventional war anymore. Keeping this context in mind is very important. The conclusion of the FDH Analysis based on GNI as an output factor has to differ from the conclusion drawn in the context of the CINC or qualitative indicators which focus more on actual than potential war fighting capabilities. Furthermore it shall be emphasized that the FDH uses input and output factors for its analysis. The term GNI will be used going forward as a synonym for 'military capabilities' to make clear for the reader how capabilities are measured in these scenarios. This shall not imply that military expenses actually drive the GNI itself. This is the scope of studies in a different context and different economic field and still intensively debated. Tables 7 and 8 illustrate in a snapshot the performance of the six nations. The first table shows the actual efficiency score based on the application of data in the FDH analysis. It will again be a three scenario approach with the added two estimates for China to the original number. In addition the second table will help with the sequential analysis as it shows how input and output factors changed year over year to interpret the changes in efficiency scoring. The 2000 numbers show the changes in percentage over 1995 and 2005 over 2000 accordingly.

		1995			2000			2005	
	China o	**China l**	**China h**	**China o**	**China l**	**China h**	**China o**	**China l**	**China h**
China	100%	100%	100%	100%	100%	69%	100%	100%	100%
Germany	98%	98%	98%	66%	96%	100%	100%	100%	100%
Israel	5%	5%	5%	6%	6%	6%	6%	6%	6%
Russian Federation	53%	53%	53%	72%	72%	72%	73%	73%	73%
United Kingdom	41%	62%	64%	48%	48%	48%	54%	54%	54%
United States	100%	100%	100%	100%	100%	100%	100%	100%	100%
Brazil	91%	91%	91%	100%	100%	100%	100%	100%	100%
France	32%	48%	76%	37%	37%	37%	45%	45%	45%
India	100%	100%	100%	100%	100%	100%	100%	100%	100%
Japan	100%	100%	100%	100%	100%	100%	100%	100%	100%

Table 7: GNI Efficiency Score

	Changes GNI		Changes Mil ex	
	2000	**2005**	**2000**	**2005**
China	66%	80%	61%	93%
Germany	15%	24%	-5%	-7%
Israel	43%	19%	18%	6%
Russian Federation	18%	70%	-12%	49%
United Kingdom	35%	32%	-6%	15%
United States	37%	27%	-4%	47%

Table 8: Changes GNI and Military Expenses

China is scoring at 100 percent efficiency in all scenarios but one; Only in 2000 with the high estimate assumption for China's spending, the efficiency score is 69 percent. A look at the details reveals that China is dominated by Japan in that particular scenario. One question with China is whether we are facing the outlier phenomena, since the size of military expenditures as well as GNI is substantial and may put the nation at the edge of the efficiency curve with not many nations that represent benchmarks. In more recent years that would be even more likely since the growth in GNI and military expenditures for China accelerated substantially further. The data of this study reveal an indication to that trend. In the years 1995 and 2000, China has quite a few benchmark nations with Germany, France, Japan and the United Kingdom. As both input and output factors grow substantially, as shown in Table 8, the DMU moves into different areas of the efficiency frontier. In 2005 China is only benchmarked against France in the 'official' scenarios. The more likely scenarios with higher estimates on defense spending move China into an area without benchmark nations. This in fact makes it difficult, if not impossible, to interpret the results of 2000 and 2005 due to the outlier effect.

Germany is dominated by Japan in the 1995 dataset, for all three scenarios. This is mainly due to the fact that Japan's GNI with USD 2.9 trillion is higher than Germany's with USD 1.8 trillion and military expenses with USD 51 billion for Germany and USD 50 billion for Japan being pretty much equal. In 2000 the estimates for China have a big impact. China becomes a benchmark and Germany's efficiency score increases with increased assumptions for military expenses for China. Germany's score is 66 percent, 96 percent and 100 percent respectively, dominating e.g. France as a benchmark nation. In 2005 Germany is scoring 100 percent and is dominating two other DMUs, the UK and France. So even though the amount of benchmarked nations is small, interestingly the nations can be seen as very relevant from a practical perspective. Germany, France and the UK as fellow EU members and direct neighbors can be likely seen as benchmarks for more detailed analyses to derive operational decisions to improve efficiency. In a sequential view, Germany is actually experiencing an increase in GNI and a decrease in military expenditures in 2000 and 2005. In 2000 the efficiency score does not increase since China is added as a benchmark dominating Germany. In 2005 the increase in output and decrease in input in fact does lead to a higher efficiency scoring over France and the UK.

Israel scores at the lower end of the ranking with 5 percent in 1995 and 6 percent in 2000 and 2005. Changing estimates for China do not impact the efficiency score of Israel at all, indicating that it is either dominated anyways or that both nations are in different areas of the production frontier. Israel is actually not dominating any other DMU in either scenario. Israel is operating under political circumstances that differ drastically from the other five nations. Israel perceives threats from immediate neighbor states, Iran and Syria shall be named in particular. Both nations are benchmarks on the production frontier for Israel in all three years. The results of a direct comparison are shown in Table 9. Syria and Egypt both spend less on defense than Israel with Egypt experiencing almost double the GNI of Israel it scores significantly higher in efficiency accordingly with 64 percent vs. 5 percent in 1995 as an example. Syria scores in between Israel and Egypt with between 14 percent and 24 percent efficiency. The GNI is about half the size of Israel, but military expenditures between USD 1 billion and 2 billion being significantly lower.

GNI/mil ex in billion USD				1995		2000		2005	
	1995	**2000**	**2005**	**GNI**	**mil ex**	**GNI**	**mil ex**	**GNI**	**mil ex**
Israel	5%	6%	6%	95	10	135	12	160	13
Syrian Arab Republic	23%	14%	24%	44	1	51	2	74	2
Egypt, Arab Rep.	64%	51%	43%	177	4	251	4	332	4

Table 9: Comparison Israel with Syria and Egypt

The lower performance of Israel is not necessarily surprising since it was outlined that Israel's population is putting a premium on the ability to defend itself. The discussion about alliances has pointed out that in certain occasions nations can't be seen as isolated DMUs if there are credible beliefs that other nations may stand by in case of a conflict. In Israel's case it may not just perceive a threat from either of the two neighbor states independently, but there is actually the risk that multiple nations have to be opposed. Accordingly Israel can as well – according to official statements from the

US[343] – credibly rely on the support from the US in case of a war, which will impact that power balance in the region. The detailed analysis of the three nations in particular and the factor of alliances is out of scope of this paper. The logic shall just be noted here to reach a common understanding.

Russia's efficiency increases from 53 percent in 1995 to 72 percent in 2000 and 73 percent in 2005. This is mainly caused by higher increases on the output side than on the input side.[344] Interestingly Russia is consistently dominated by two specific DMUs – India and Brazil. Even though they are not necessarily operating under the same political circumstances, both of them are emerging economies with India actually being on the same continent with close proximity to Russia.

The United Kingdom improves efficiency from 32 percent in 1995, to 41 percent in 2000 and 40 percent in 2005. UK's efficiency scoring is only influenced in 1995 by the differing assumptions on defense spending for China. In the years 2000 and 2005 it is dominated by China in all scenarios.

The USA scores 100 percent in the efficiency ranking in all scenarios across the whole timeframe. There are no benchmark nations for the US, since the input and output factors are so much higher over other DMUs that we are faced with the outlier

[343] see Dvorin, T.: We would back Israel 2013

[344] As outlined in prior chapters, all numbers are at constant currency and purchase price adjusted. Fluctuations like these typically indicate exchange rate effects. However, Russia's economic development was characterized by lots of ups and downs in the late 90s leading to these high changes in percent.

effect. The data and scoring for the US are therefore not useful for further analysis based on this scenario.

Overall applying the GNI as the output assumption to the FDH provides a challenge for the interpretation of results. The GNI is an output measure for economic performance of a nation. It has been outlined in the introduction that it is still heavily disputed whether military expenditures support economic growth or have a contradicting effect. Furthermore GNI swings significantly in developing and emerging countries like Israel, Russia and China. So in theory their economy becomes stronger and the potential for wartime production increases, but it seems to be questionable to which degree the military organizations benefit from this progress. Especially because it has also been pointed out, that a major contributor to military capabilities are soft factors such as the skill level and expertise of the members of the Armed Forces and the implementation of doctrines, that support the effective use of military assets.

In terms of the datasets themselves, they however do also support hypothesis 1.), and show that efficiency varies between nations to quite a degree.

4.3.4 Quality of Armed Forces - FDH Analysis

This Chapter will cover the results of the FDH Analysis based on an application of a measure for the quality of a nation's Armed Forces. Dunnigan provides related data in his book 'how to make war' and on the Web page www.strategypage.com. Results are shown as of mid-2008 and are applied on input data from 1995, 2000 and 2005.

Since only one output dataset is available, the results will not be analyzed in a sequential manner as in the prior two chapters. The three scenarios provide alternatives to compare and to a certain extent leave it open for readers to judge whether they feel investments in 1995, 2000 or 2005 would be more appropriate to tie to a quality level of the Armed Forces achieved by mid-2008. It shall be emphasized again that military investments take time to become operationally effective. The approach of this chapter differs from the prior two FDH applications, since external factors as proxies for military capabilities are not used, but an actual capability evaluation at a specific point in time. The data points will be supplemented with findings from the statistical analysis such as number of benchmark DMUs for each nation as well as the naming of notable nations that present benchmarks. Table 10 more generally shows the results for the six focus nations based on each of the three years and scenarios. Figure 16 illustrates the production frontier based on the qualitative factor and the defense spending as a percentage of GDP for 2005.

	1995			2000			2005		
	China o	**China l**	**China h**	**China o**	**China l**	**China h**	**China o**	**China l**	**China h**
China	100%	100%	100%	100%	100%	72%	100%	100%	98%
Germany	100%	100%	100%	100%	100%	100%	100%	100%	100%
Israel	20%	31%	31%	24%	34%	39%	27%	37%	53%
Russian Federation	39%	59%	59%	50%	72%	82%	55%	73%	73%
United Kingdom	58%	88%	88%	78%	100%	100%	85%	100%	100%
United States	100%	100%	100%	100%	100%	100%	100%	100%	100%

Table 10: Efficiency Score - Quality

Comparing the scenarios based on the assumptions for China's spending level shows that results differ, but only slightly. China scores fairly high in each scenario with

100 percent or close to 100 percent. The only exception is in 2000 in the 'high spend' scenario where the score reaches 72 percent. The main reason here is the interdependence with the US. US and China are in the same sub-sample in the 'high spend' scenarios and with increasing spending levels, China becomes dominated by the US in terms of the production frontier. Similar is the case with Israel, Russia and the UK for which efficiency scores increase with increasing assumptions for China's defense spending.

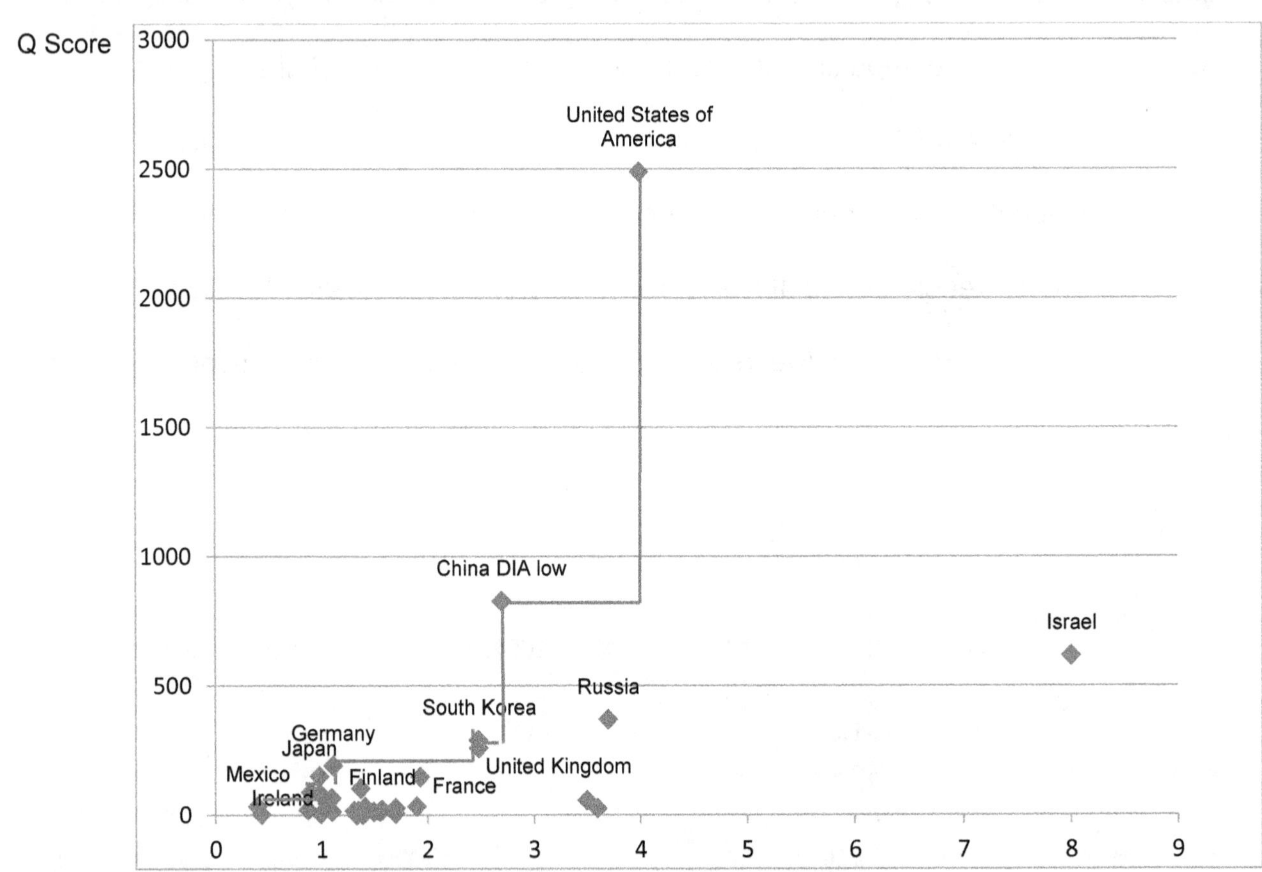

Figure 16: Efficiency Frontier OECD – Quality

UK actually is only in the same sample set with China in the 'official' scenario. Russia just as UK moves into a different section of the efficiency frontier is no benchmark to China in the 'high spend' model. The United Kingdom is in a suitable data pool with 40 or more DMUs in each scenario. The dominated DMUs among many others are nations such as France and Turkey. France in particular can be seen as a good benchmark nation as it operates under similar global political circumstances as a member of the EU and the NATO alliance.

An interesting finding in China's sub-sample is that mostly countries on the same continent are considered benchmark DMUs, which helps with the interpretation of results given the close proximity and similar geographic and geopolitical ramifications. The big economies that one may want to compare against like western industrialized nations or even regional big powers such as Japan and India are however not in the same sample. Comparisons with the US are possible in the 'high' scenario, however are prone to interpretation errors due to the potential outlier effect already described in more detail in several other sections of this paper.

Assessing China's capabilities correctly is certainly essential to derive the correct conclusion. One question obviously is how detailed the existing military assets are evaluated in terms of their capabilities. The US report to Congress on China's military indicated in the year 2009 that the majority of military equipment of China is fairly outdated. This is shown in Figure 17. Even though the report covers only the 2000 number and going forward, the 2000 number already indicates that historically the military assets of China were fairly outdated. Therefore a similar trend can be assumed to be seen for 1995 as well. Since investments in the military sector take time to become operationally effective and the modernization grade is still in 2009 far below 50 percent, it is questionable if estimating China's military capabilities does truly account for this fact. On the one side there is a trend to modernization, which certainly leads to higher outputs based on newer equipment; on the other side still the majority of the equipment is fairly outdated.

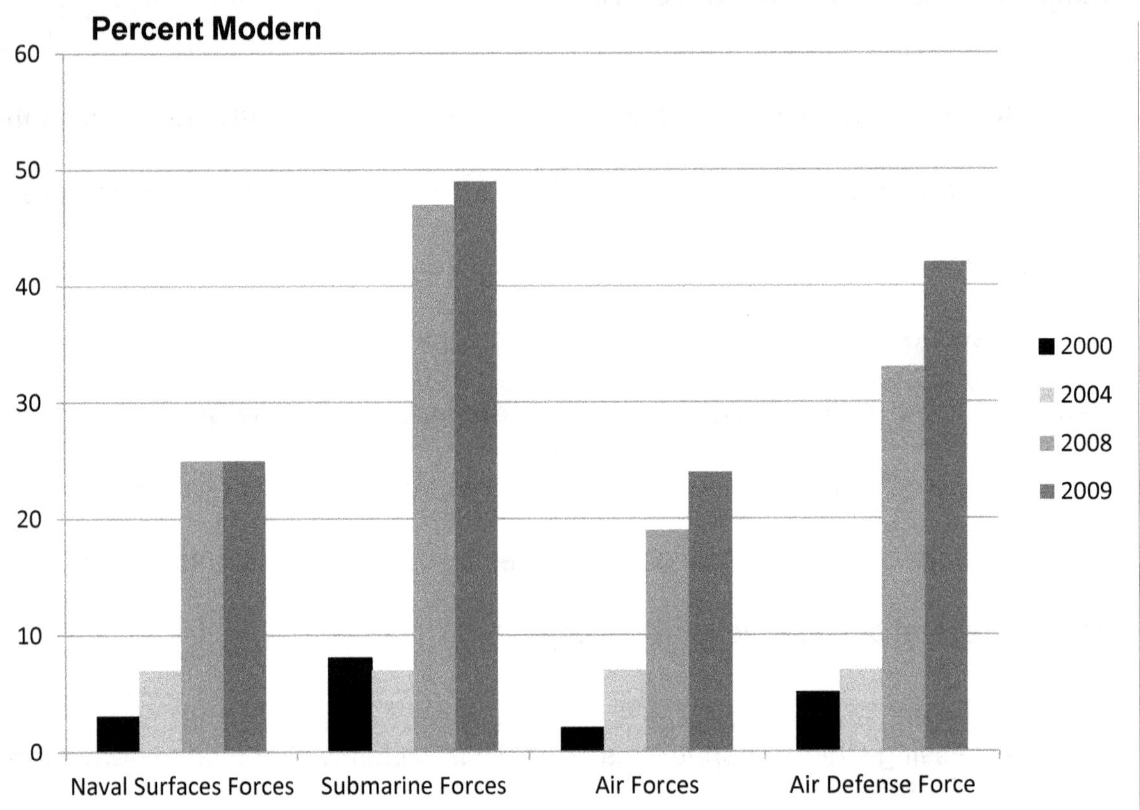

Figure 17: US report to congress China Defense Spending

(see Department of Defense: Military Power 2010, p.45)

Another practical example for the relevance of up to date equipment can be seen in the context of the missions in Afghanistan. McKinsey estimated that from 80 available German aircrafts type CH-53, only 20 would qualify for missions in Afghanistan per technical standards and even of those, only about 10 were mission-ready and deployable.[345]

Assets reported on paper apparently do not necessarily match with assets being available. Nations follow different maintenance patterns and overall, old equipment obviously is more prone to repairs than newer equipment. Implementing brand new equipment however may have its challenges as well, as recent discussions around issues with the US Fighter Jet F-22 have proven.[346] The true status of the equipment can therefore hardly be determined by analyses on the whiteboard and even nations may not know the true readiness status of their arsenal themselves, until it is called upon and tested under realistic conditions on the battlefield.

Germany's results are independent of China and the score is 100 percent, while dominating at least 66 other DMUs including several European neighbors such as Italy, France, Sweden and Portugal. Germany's high efficiency score is presumably driven in majority by the fact that Germany's defense spending is comparably low, as already pointed out in the chapter about alliances, where it is described that other EU and NATO partners challenge the low contribution of Germany in terms of defense spending. Interestingly the efficiency score of Germany is high, so one may argue that even though the spending is lower, the contribution relatively speaking is high. This actually suggests that the historic approach of measuring a nation's contribution to alliances in terms of percentage of GDP spending on military may have to be revised. A

[345] see McKinsey& Company: The Future of European Defense 2013, p.12
[346] Mount,M.: More Problems for F-22 2012

focus on actual material commitments or support of joined missions should have more of a focus and it should be left to the nations to find a way to meet those commitments.[347] This would actually encourage more focus on efficient behavior across the board of all members in an alliance.

Due to Israel's political situation it is spending a fairly high amount of its GDP on defense which brings the nation at the edge of the efficiency frontier with fewer benchmark nations. Israel is dominated by China and the US and is dominating Oman and Saudi Arabia. This makes is difficult to draw conclusions, as China and the US are just questionable benchmarks due to the completely different size and structure of their economy causing the outlier effect. Once again this indicates the relevance and consideration of individual international political circumstances as part of this study, which highly impact the spending level on defense in a given point in time.

Russia's efficiency score is highly impacted by the differing assumptions for China, since its efficiency increases with higher spending assumptions for China. Russia is dominated by the US, India and China, depending on the scenario by either or all three nations at the same time. The global political balance indicates that these are reasonable benchmark nations, since all of them are big players in the current global political arena.

[347] Some nations claim that Germany is not living up to commitments of alliances in terms of actual boots on the ground in support of ongoing peacekeeping missions. Just investing more in military assets will not help the alliance, if they are not actually being deployed and utilized. This is certainly more a political driven discussion and not a focus in this economic paper.

The United States is scoring 100 percent in each scenario and is dominating many other nations. Comparing the options of using either 1995, 2000 or 2005 percent of GDP spending as suitable input impacts the number of benchmark DMUs in the model. 25 DMUs are benchmarks to the US in 1995. With US spending about 2.5 percent of GDP for defense spending. There are 39 benchmarks in the 2000 scenario where the US spending level was at 3 percent of GDP. In 2005 percentage of GDP spend for the US increased further to 4 percent which moves the US into a different section of the efficiency frontier with 15 DMUs. The US is still prone to outlier effects just as all 100 percent scoring DMUs are. There is always the possibility that a lower spending level would already be sufficient to reach the same output, but there is just no DMU that is actually performing at that level to benchmark against. Due to the fact that the production frontier for military output is not known, the free disposal hull variant has been chosen on purpose for this paper and different input levels cannot be simulated as it is simply not known, if they are even feasible. For illustrative purposes Figure 18 shows the efficiency frontier for the OECD countries without the outlier DMU, the USA. Notably Israel scores significantly better compared to the CINC and GNI approach and is (without the US data point) positioned on the frontier. Looking at the data points it becomes clear that the high qualitative ranking assigned to the Israeli defense forces lifts up their efficiency performance. While Israel has substantially less equipment and manpower than Russia, it still scores higher in terms of measured land power. The intangible factors therefore are a force multiplier for Israel, making up for the fewer available military assets. While Russia appears on the frontier in the OECD sub-sample it in fact is also dominated in terms of efficiency by the non-OECD nation India (added for illustration purposes).

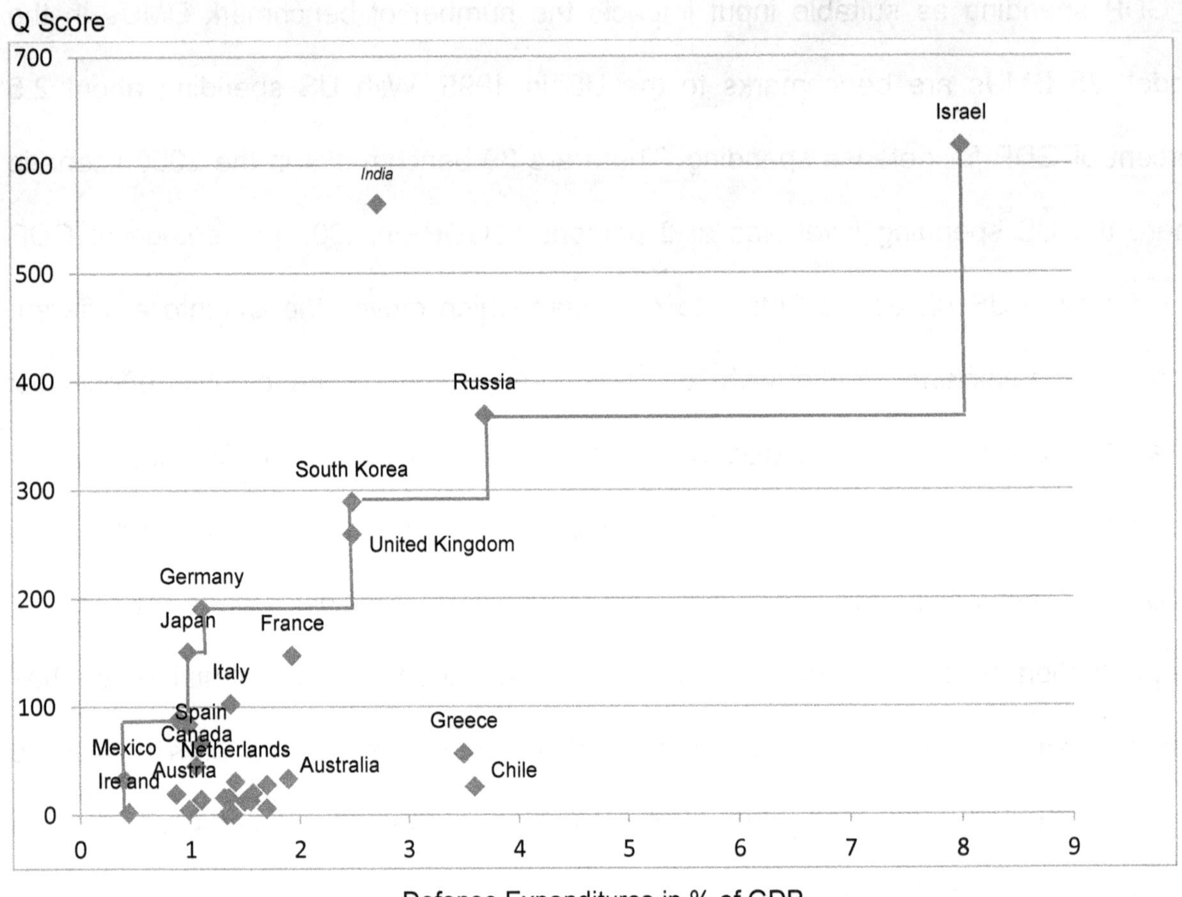

Figure 18: Efficiency Frontier OECD – Quality Outlier Adjusted

The armies of Russia and Israel – even though they are not benchmark nations to one another – apparently do have significantly different structures with Russia focusing on material and Israel on intangible factors such as the quality of its people. While improving the intangibles may at a glance appear to be a financially inexpensive way for improving the output, it shall be noted that it does cost the Armed Forces money as well to develop intangible factors. As outlined before, military training exercises are fairly expensive and Russia may have to sacrifice in quantity of troops if it were to attempt to improve the intangibles through training within its given budget. It may also be open to determine to which extent intangibles in the military environment can in fact even be developed in a training environment. Combat leadership and military tradition are certainly more reliably fostered through live missions, which are certainly not feasible to be conducted in times of peace.

The qualitative assessment of efficiency is providing an interesting extension to the more commonly used indicator-based assessments for military capabilities. It actually supports the assumption that military contribution in alliances should be more measured on outputs achieved, than as input contributed in terms of military spending. The qualitative assessment is certainly subjective to a certain extent as it is mostly based on analytic assessments by individuals rather than by data derived through facts and statistical observations. Dunnigan certainly can be seen as a reliable analyst and expert in this area, but the data only reflect his opinion. It will be interesting to apply other similar output factors going forward as likely similar assessment approaches may become available from different sources at some point in the future.

Hypothesis 1.) can be seen as confirmed by this qualitative measure just as on the prior two scenarios. Efficiency does differ between nations based on the output factors applied in the model.

4.3.5 Comparison of the three Models

One interesting finding reveals the analysis of the total dataset. Table 11 correlates the number of DMUs in a specific efficiency corridor with the respective average defense spending in percentage of GDP or actual military expenses in case of the GNI, for that dataset. For all CINC and Quality scenarios the average percentage of defense spending is high for those countries in the dataset that score low on efficiency. Respectively the percentage of GDP spend is lower in the corridor for countries with a high efficiency score. This seems to indicate that a high spend on defense tends to lead to lower scores on the efficiency frontier. This raises the question if high spending levels themselves lead to wasteful behaviors in Armed Forces and that slimmer militaries are forced to work efficiently due to scarce resources. This would be an interesting area for more extensive research.

The GNI study on the other side shows almost twice as many DMUs in the efficiency range of 80 percent or higher than the CINC study. The spending level in absolute Dollars is however much higher for that sub-sample than for any of the less efficient ones. This underlines why GNI as a power measure may be unsuitable for efficiency studies. Realistically only economically powerful nations can afford high defense spending in the first place. Those nations may simply be able to afford higher military spending than smaller nations and the GNI in itself is driving the output score at the same time. The percentage of GDP measure as input on the other side is a better measure, since it actually puts the spending in proportion of each nation's economy and therefore accounting for the fact that some nations simply have a bigger economy than others. Efficiency itself is not driven by size, but is actually a relative measure. Size would only become relevant in more operational analyses in context of economy of scale and scope in process activities. These certainly have a very relevant impact, but the datasets do not allow for isolation of this factor. The field of science currently does not have a model for assessing the economies of scale and scope in the context of military spending. The results of this study will hopefully trigger discussions in this area to encourage further studies. The overview reveals further, that the number of DMUs in the lower scoring range is fairly high in all three models with more than 50 percent of the DMUs scoring 40 percent or less in efficiency. This supports the claim of this paper that there appears to be a lack of focus on the topic of efficient defense spending.

Table 12 illustrates the comparsion of the three different approaches for each year and each of the six focus countries in particular. The results between the different factors are consistent in some, but different in other areas. To keep it simple, for the pure purpose of comparing results for China only the results based on the officially reported number are listed.

China's results in all three models are 100 percent for all three years. Since only the officially reported numbers are considered, it can be presumed to be slightly lower in reality, depending on which alternative analyst assumption one may trust the most. Germany's score is high in the GNI model which is not necessarily surprising given the high economic output of the nation. Only the year 2000 proves to be an exception due to the significant growth of China's economy as outlined in Chapter 4.3.3.

CINC						
	# DMU			Average % GDP		
Score	1995	2000	2005	1995	2000	2005
80 ≤ 100	11	8	8	1.0	0.7	0.7
60 ≤ 79	6	8	7	1.2	1.4	1.1
40 ≤ 59	22	35	18	1.3	1.2	1.2
20 ≤ 39	45	43	54	2.2	1.9	1.6
0 ≤ 19	55	42	49	4.2	5.3	3.5

GNI						
	# DMU			Average Mil Ex		
Score	1995	2000	2005	1995	2000	2005
80 ≤ 100	27	24	23	21777	21334	33660
60 ≤ 79	13	11	10	4208	8009	8505
40 ≤ 59	19	22	29	5556	6148	5572
20 ≤ 39	43	45	41	2446	3999	3698
0 ≤ 19	34	26	26	3392	3182	3771

Quality				
	# DMU		Average % GDP	
Score	2000	2005	2000	2005
80 ≤ 100	11	15	1.2%	1.3%
60 ≤ 79	12	12	1.4%	1.4%
40 ≤ 59	33	18	1.5%	1.6%
20 ≤ 39	40	34	2.5%	2.2%
0 ≤ 19	31	36	5.7%	6.2%

Table 11: Comparison of all three datasets

	1995			2000			2005		
	GNI	CINC	Q	GNI	CINC	Q	GNI	CINC	Q
China	100%	100%	100%	100%	100%	100%	100%	100%	100%
Germany	98%	58%	100%	66%	66%	100%	100%	71%	100%
Israel	5%	7%	20%	6%	7%	24%	6%	6%	24%
Russian Federation	53%	39%	39%	72%	26%	50%	73%	26%	50%
United Kingdom	41%	32%	58%	48%	41%	78%	54%	40%	78%
United States	100%	100%	100%	100%	61%	100%	100%	51%	100%

Table 12: Overview Efficiency Scores Focus Nations

Also the qualitative approach leads to a 100 percent score under the assumption of either spending level. The capabilities of the German Armed Forces are obviously regarded high even though the spending level is rather low in percentage of GDP compared to other nations. The low spending level is the main driver for keeping the efficiency score on a high level overall. It seems questionable if this is truly sustainable and whether Germany is not saving today at the cost of a drop in future capabilities. Since the qualitative score is available for one timeframe only, it will be interesting to see if the recent drop in military spending will lower the assessed capabilities at some point in the future as updated data become available.

Germany's CINC efficiency performance is increasing from the middle scoring range of 58 percent in 1995 to 71 percent by 2005. This is also mainly driven by the drop in defense spending. The CINC score drops as well from 0.033 to 0.026 in that timeframe indicating a decrease in 'output' produced. This however is compensated for in terms of relatively lower defense spending, which improves the efficiency score accordingly.

Russia has the highest score in the GNI model with 53 percent, 72 percent and 73 percent for the respective three years. The scoring is significantly lower in the qualitative scenario with 39 percent in 1995 and 50 percent for 2000 and 2005. The CINC score is the lowest with 39 percent in 1995 and 26 percent for 2000 and 2005 respectively. Since the CINC index is a basket of indicators and actually shows the lowest score, the expert regards the performance level of the Russian Armed Forces higher than what the basket of financial and social statistics suggests.

The UK is in a similar situation as Russia, only that the qualitative scoring is the highest. 2005 data show a representative pattern with a GNI score of 54 percent, 40 percent for CINC and 78 percent for the qualitative approach. Accordingly the expert regards the 'output' produced by the UK's Armed Forces higher than economic and social indicators suggest.

The US scores 100 percent efficiency for each GNI and Quality, but only about half of that based on the CINC in 2000 and 2005. Since for the reader's convenience and simplicity, only the official China spending is shown above, it shall be noted that this is caused by China dominating the US in those scenarios. The outlier effect and impact of one specific data point on the study with China shades the possibility for interpretation.

The bottom line of these analyses is that there are different options available to analyze the efficiency stage of Armed Forces. The three chosen scenarios cover two dominating approaches used in the science of international politics along with a qualitative assessment as an innovative model in terms of economic studies. The GNI seems to be too superficial as illustrated above. The qualitative model may be open for interpretation and further productive scrutiny. However applying the current proposal of ratings reveals interesting new discoveries for the interpretation of the results. All results appear logic under the outlined assumptions and restrictions. The CINC indicator appears to be the most suitable indicator for further analyses. It follows a balanced approach of considering several indicators as proxies. The qualitative scoring is a good addition, but represents for the most part only the assessment of one single expert and his team. Furthermore only one dataset for a single year is available, which makes more detailed analyses difficult.

The results do prove that Hypothesis 1 stated in this paper appears to be true. The efficiency stage of Armed Forces does differ from nation to nation. The following chapter will now start to address hypothesis 2, to see if there are certain factors that can be seen as having an influence on the efficiency scoring.

5 Analyzing Drivers for Efficiency

5.1 Overview

Based on the efficiency scoring determined in the prior chapters, this chapter will now address potential drivers of efficiency for Armed Forces. Due to the complexity of this topic and the absence of consistent datasets for most drivers, this part of the study is more focused on qualitative assessments. Wherever possbile, this analysis will however use datasets as proxy indicators to complement the arguments. The challenge in this section of research is that the influencing factors can be found in the general economic and political environment, but also very specifically in areas that require military expertise. The scope of this paper will be focused on the economic aspects. However, the research conducted in this paper can certainly be used by Armed Forces to conduct similar analyses in the scope of military operations.

The CINC indicator has been determined to be the most suitable data point in the scope of further analyses of the results. It is more objective and number-driven than the qualitative approach and it uses a variety of data and does not oversimplify the complex phenomenon of military capabilities, as the GNI approach does. The further outlines will therefore use the results of the FDH-Analysis based on the CINC output as supplementing data points to the qualitative assessments.

The introduction to this study already provided a brief outlook regarding indicators that will be analyzed in terms of this paper to evaluate their impact on efficiency of Armed Forces. This chapter will now more specifically name, define and cluster these factors. These indicators will be generally called drivers and will include external factors that influence Armed Forces and the way they operate, but also resources that the Armed Forces actively use to derive military capabilities. These resources in the military context include, but are not limited to, human resources, technical prowess, industrial base, and governmental structures.[348]

One overall scheme that will be found in the sub chapters touches a currently discussed phenomenon called 'Revolution in Military Affairs' or short RMA. Shimko defines RMA as a milestone revolution in the way armed conflicts are being conducted. In the scope of efficiency, RMA means that new technology combined with proper doctrine and organization, can be seen as a force multiplier that allows fewer soldiers with fewer weapons to be equally effective, while at the same time causing less collateral damage and fewer civil casualties.[349] O'Hanlon supports this view and points out that technological change does not make a revolution, but actually catalyzing decisions of policy makers are required to exploit the advantages.[350] Cohen further states:[351] The RMA can be different from country to country and in today's discussion the US is usually in focus. The US based RMA is characterized by the need for power projection, quick wins, low casualties and flexibility. China is working a similar transition of its Armed Forces, but is much more focused on a potential occupation of Taiwan and a domination of the South China Sea. Israel transformed its forces to gain superior

---

[348] see Millet, A./Murray, W./Watman, K., Military Effectiveness 1986, p. 37
[349] see Shimko, K.: The Iraq Wars and America's Military Revolution 2010, p.11
[350] see O'Hanlon, M.: The Science of War 2009, p.179
[351] see Cohen, E.: Transformation in Military Affairs 2004, p.398

capabilities with regard to urban guerilla warfare. Cohen also underlines Shimko's statement with regard to doctrine and organization. Technology alone does not yield transformational change. To him public companies can go out of business if they do not adapt new technology and processes, while Armed Forces can still operate the old way, in particular if there are no real world missions that might prove them wrong.[352] Cohen also states that Armed Forces tend to be more conservative with regard to applying innovations, because the costs of failure are higher in the military than in a commercial environment. However there are also critics to the claim of an ongoing RMA. Cohen summarizes the criticism with RMA supposedly being abstract from geopolitics, too technology-focused and missing consideration of reactions by weaker opponents[353]. The recent missions in Afghanistan and Iraq still keep military personal involved in individual battles with ambushes and house-to-house firefights.[354] This can be seen as similar to combat situations on battlefields of many historic battles.

Discussing the controversy around the RMA is not the scope of this paper, but highlighting the discussions certainly points out that there are significant changes on the way in the military environment. Having described the theory in this overview chapter will set the stage for the further more detailed analysis of certain aspects of this phenomenon. It also highlights the interdependence of factors and that even though the following chapters will try to cluster them, none of them can be seen as completely independent of the others.

[352] see Cohen, E.: Transformation in Military Affairs 2004, p.399
[353] see Cohen, E.: Transformation in Military Affairs 2004, p.396
[354] see Cohen, E.: Transformation in Military Affairs 2004, p.406

5.2 Technological Changes

5.2.1 Weaponology

The modern infantryman is far better equipped and more lethal than any soldier in the past due to equipment of higher sophistication and the availability of modern information technology.[355] This makes innovation a key ingredient for national power and military capabilities. A nation that is capable of producing highly sophisticated weapons can be seen as carrying a competitive advantage over their adversaries. Accordingly it can be argued that a nation with better equipment can operate more efficiently. 'Better' in this case shall not solely refer to pure destructive power. The following outlines will explain how technology can impact the efficient operation of Armed Forces in multiple aspects. Accordingly 'better' equipment refers to a multitude of characteristics, such as longer lifetime, lower maintenance costs, better suitability for a nation's military doctrine and many more.

O'Hanlon suggests a classification of military technology into the areas Sensors, Communication, Main engines and Robotics, Explosives and Weapons and Defense against weapons.[356] For the purpose of this paper a similar, but simplified classification shall be used. This chapter will address weapons technology in general referring to military specific equipment, while the following chapter is dedicated to the improvements

[355] see Cohen, E.: Transformation in Military Affairs 2004, p.406
[356] see O'Hanlon, M.: The Science of War 2009, p. 177

in information technology. All outlines will take the perspective of how innovation in technology may have an impact on the efficiency of military organizations.

Weapon systems are usually classified as Weapons of Mass Destruction (WMD) for nuclear, chemical and biological weapons, major weapon systems for vehicles like Tanks, Aircrafts, Battleships, SALW for Small Arms and Light Weapons and dual use systems that have military as well as civil usage.[357]

New technologies in these areas can drastically change the way of warfare. Some disruptive technologies can create power, like the armors of medieval knights[358], or in modern analogy nuclear weapons. Those technologies increase the strength and power of those who know how to build and use them. Other inventions dispense power by making existing technologies obsolete, like the example of guns, which made most sorts of armors and even fortifications ineffective.[359] Furthermore, technological changes can favor either an attacker or a defender and the respective edge, that one over the other has, changes over time. So while at first the development of the machine gun gave a significant advantage to the defender, the development of tanks shifted the advantage back to the attacker.[360] Some scholars however see technological advantage as dyadic and not systemic; meaning that if one party enjoys technological advantages over the other, it prevails no matter if in an offensive or defensive situation.[361] In the context of modern warfare which requires high mobility, this seems reasonable since

[357] see Smith, R.: Military Economics 2009, p.142
[358] see Smith, R.: Military Economics 2009, p.133
[359] see Smith, R.: Military Economics 2009, p.133
[360] see Biddle, S.: Military Power 2006, p. 15
[361] see Biddle, S.: Military Power 2006, p. 16

even an attacking force may find itself in a defensive position and the knowledge around defensive maneuvers may help the attacker to bypass and prevail in combat. In other words, a nation with innovative military assets can be seen as carrying a competitive advantage. This by itself however does not necessarily translate into efficiency. Developing new technology is expensive, which certainly is reflected by higher cost on the input side of the efficiency model. Furthermore, technology actually has to be introduced and applied successfully in order to even have a positive impact on the output side. Introducing new technology can actually cause quite a few complications. Often new technologies are introduced before the military knows how to use them and how to embed them into effective military doctrines. Self-loading rifles, tanks and nuclear weapons required a long period of learning and organizational restructuring was required until they were able to be efficiently used.[362] Furthermore, a military might initially reject a technical innovation if it sees even higher potential in an even further innovation in the future.[363] Also technologies seen as too disruptive may be rejected if they threaten the status of an existing organization or social environment. This can in fact be seen as a strong indication of operational ineffectiveness if this occurs.[364] Unmanned vehicles, specifically drones, are certainly an example for an innovation that is currently threatening the jobs of air force pilots. This shows that the impact of innovation is two-fold. The defense industry of a nation needs to develop and produce suitable products for the military. However the military also needs to be receptive to change and be creative in thinking about ways to employ those technologies to their

[362] see Smith, R.: Military Economics 2009, p.132
[363] see Millet, A/Murray, W/Watman, K., Military Effectiveness 1986, p. 55
[364] see Millet, A/Murray, W/Watman, K., Military Effectiveness 1986, p. 56

advantage. The discussion around the RMA proves this point. The timeline below illustrates some examples of certain military innovations and shows when they were introduced in history.

Submarines, Radar, Sonar Mobile warfare tactics, Nuclear weapons	Helicopters, Jet Planes	Satellites Ballistic missiles	Cruise missile, Stealth, infrared, Night-vision technology	Precision strikes, rapid Battlefield communication, Modern computing
1940	1950	1960	1970	1980/90

Figure 19: Key Innovations in Military Technology

(see O'Hanlon, M.: The Science of War 2009, p. 175)

Radars, jet planes, satellites and computers have been employed by military organizations for decades and are no recent development. Actually having all these work in concert facilitated by information technology has to be seen as the true revolution. Accordingly, a national defense base that truly understands the needs of its customer can drive efficiency by producing the most suitable products based on the most innovative technologies and operational doctrines.

An even stronger impact on efficiency can be derived from the management of product lifecycles once products have established themselves in the military organization and its doctrines. When it becomes time to replace a military asset it is important to recognize that costs in the military context significantly increase on an annual basis - which on average has been determined to be around 8 percent per year.[365] Besides inflation, this increase considers the factor of technological advancements. Military equipment gets more expensive over time due to technological advancements and a country has to dedicate continuously more resources to stay up-to-date and competitive.[366] So each new generation of weaponry tends to be more expensive than a pure replacement of an older version.[367] Given the increased price per unit, with a given budget less weaponry can be purchased, which also again increases the cost per unit due to the loss of economies of scale.[368] As a practical example, the current US main battle tank M1 costs three times as much as the M60 which it replaced; presumably it is also at least three times as effective due to the embedded technological innovations, but the cost per unit has increased substantially nevertheless.[369] The bigger the equipment, the more impact it may have on the military operation. If an aircraft carrier needs to be replaced and the new one costs as much as three old ones, it either gets very expensive or the mission range of the naval forces has to be reduced, since one single ship likely will not be able to cover the same area at sea as three ships could. This also highlights why the military capability function does not follow a linear trend on the production frontier and why the free disposal hull has been chosen for this study. Reducing the input beyond a certain point may have significant impact on the output, if a threshold is reached that significantly limits the Armed Forces in fulfilling certain tasks. Postponing replacements to avoid these higher costs however is also not

[365] see Smith, R.: Military Economics 2009, p.111
[366] see Smith, R.: Military Economics 2009, p.111
[367] The replacement does not have to be a completely new model; even established production series of military equipment receive updates over time to stay up to date. The B52 Bomber is in service since 1955 and received several significant upgrades increasing the price per unit from est. $ 14 MM at introduction to $ 53 MM for a more recent model.
[368] see Smith, R.: Military Economics 2009, p.112
[369] see Gansler, J.: Democracy's Arsenal 2011, p.26

a good solution in the long run. Old equipment tends to be more expensive to maintain, which over time limits the amount of budget that is available for investments at a later time. And postponing these maintenance activities to avoid further costs can be another trap. Operation and Maintenance (O&M) expenses are a cost position that is often easily cut, but in the end puts the readiness of the military at risk[370] given that equipment may be available on paper only, but not ready to be used on the battlefield. Not investing may therefore potentially help efficiency in the short term, but hurt later on when increasing amounts of budgets have to be allotted to continuously increasing maintenance efforts. It gets even worse when the military assets are not mission-ready in a state of emergency, if these maintenance efforts are also suspended to achieve further savings. Careful product lifecycle planning is therefore essential to ensure efficient use of resources by understanding when it is the more economical option to extend the lifetime of military assets, and when it is time for replacements.

Making the decision to replace an older model with a newer, modern version can have further, broader implications. A nation with qualitatively superior weapons can certainly withstand a quantitatively superior adversary with equipment of less sophistication.[371] However, sophisticated technology requires better trained troops in order to be effectively used.[372] Freedman describes that the stress on high-quality weaponry has reduced the importance of numbers, but at the same time added a

---

[370] see Shalikashvili J.: Keeping the Edge in Joint Operations 2001, p. 34

[371] This so called off-set strategy was actually followed by the NATO members trying to oppose the quantitative superior troops of the Warsaw Pact.

[372] see Shimko, K.: The Iraq Wars and America's Military Revolution 2010, p.38

premium on the quality of troops.[373] This underlines the holistic view that is required to address military efficiency, since technology actually impacts the way service members need to be selected and trained, which will be covered in more detail in Chapter 5.4.

A further product lifecycle-related aspect is the logistical component. According to Naegle, a weapon system's logistical supportability has to be seen as a critical performance parameter.[374] Improved logistic supportability design equals combat power.[375] Logistics is a key business function for any organization and can substantially drive efficiency. If done right, it avoids the wasting of resources by delivering products on time at the lowest cost possible. The costs for logistics can be further kept down if weapon systems are easy to maintain and easily transportable. Given that most modern weapon systems are considerably based on software components, it shall be emphasized that the definition of maintenance not only refers to the repair of hardware, but in these days also includes continuous software upgrades.

While newer equipment is more expensive, it may achieve significant savings in rather unrelated areas. Technological advancements can help to achieve the same goals with fewer required military assets. During the First Gulf War, more targets were defined for engagement in a single day than the Air Force attacked in total in World War II during the 1942/1943 air campaign.[376] Furthermore, while in 1991 during the First Gulf War an Air-Wing unit of about 70-80 aircrafts could be expected to hit 200 targets, this

[373] see Freedman, L.: The Revolution in Strategic Affairs 1998, p.40
[374] see Naegle, B.: Logistics and Sustainment 2008, p.85
[375] see Naegle, B.: Logistics and Sustainment 2008, p.86
[376] see Deptula, D.: Effects based Operation 2001, p.2

number increased drastically by the year 2003 to 700 targets.[377] The cost for a tomahawk strike on a target was estimated to be around $1 million during the Gulf War of 1991; by 2003 technology allowed the upgrade of conventional ammunition to intelligent bombs called JDAM for Joint Direct Attack Munition at a cost of about $20,000.[378] These upgrades were in fact mainly possible due to the utilization of already existing communication devices in the public sector. A specific military-related separate project would have increased the cost to about $68,000 per unit.[379] This intelligent ammunition can significantly decrease the load on the logistical support, since the more accurate projectiles decrease the overall absolute need of a combat unit.[380] As a similar example, more fuel-efficient engines can certainly drive efficiency by less consumption of expensive resources as well as a reduced need for support units providing it. Aside from the financial aspect reduced oil consumption can also save lives as illustrated by a practical example. During the missions in Iraq and Afghanistan one in 24 fuel convoy missions resulted in the death of a soldier due to their high vulnerability to enemy attacks.[381]

As an outlook to the future, further areas of science may continue to change the way war is being fought. Especially the areas of biology and medicine may have a significant impact in the near-term. Current articles in the field of biology and security specifically mention cognitive enhancements for military personnel, as well as new non-

[377] see Hettena, S.: Nimitz Deployment 2003
[378] see Woodall, P.: Military-industrial Complexities 2003, p.55
[379] see Smith, R.: Military Economics 2009, p.136
[380] see O'Hanlon, M.: The Science of War 2009, p. 183
[381] see Chow, E.: A lean, green fighting machine, 2013

lethal tactics, such as directed energy weapons as realistic scenarios.[382] High-energy laser weapons are also seen as a realistic scenario as well as non-lethal microwave devices for deterrence.[383] And finally, advances in nanotechnology can help create things like highly resistible, but light weighted body armor or recognizance vehicles so small that they can barely be seen with the human eye.[384] Armed Forces pursue an interest in this field of science to expand potential performance of their own troops and diminish the performance of their enemies.[385]

To summarize the outlines above, there are indications that weapon systems do have an impact on the efficiency of Armed Forces. These impacts are positive, since with better technology potentially more can be achieved with a lower quantity of assets. Due to the technological advancements, these military assets get however more expensive over time, which is offsetting some of the presumed savings. Furthermore, adversaries are often innovating as well, which means going with time in terms of innovative equipment is often a necessity to even maintain the status quo. As the FDH analysis showed, power balance is relative and several nations showed increases in defense spending, but were not necessarily achieving a higher measured output. As a further takeaway, postponing necessary replacements does not always achieve the goal of saving money. Increasing O&M expenses offset presumed savings from delayed investments. Determining an economically efficient equipment replacement plan can help manage this situation and ensure economic use of defense Dollars.

---

[382] see Lin, P.: The Ethics of Biologically Enhancing Soldiers 2012
[383] see Gansler, J.: Democracy's Arsenal 2011, p.102
[384] see Gansler, J.: Democracy's Arsenal 2011, p.102
[385] see Royal Society: Brain Waves Module 3: Neuroscience 2012, p.1

5.2.2 Information Technology

A report of the RAND Corporation states that the most potent and flexible conventional war fighting capabilities require information technologies in their various forms, and a country's combat proficiency can be assessed by understanding whether a nation is capable of integrating information-intensive technologies into its Armed Forces.[386] While this statement in particular references the positive impact on capabilities, technological change also directly influences the productivity and efficiency of an organization. An obvious impact would be the improvements in back-office functions like data management processes, e.g. SAP, and general logistic management improvements. In terms of products this topic gets more diversified, as information technology can help Armed Forces in several areas.

Fog of War was a term originated by von Clausewitz and describes a situation in which essential information is either not available in the first place, or is not able to be provided in an adequate timely fashion[387] - a common issue on the battlefield. Although improvements in weapon systems are more easily visible, the improvements in information technology are addressing both elements of the Fog of War problem by enhancing the information flow and therefore potentially providing the greatest contribution to today's military arsenal.[388] Usage of stealth technology such as

[386] see Tellis, A./Bially, J./Layne, C./McPherson, M., Measuring National Power 2000, p.44
[387] see Shimko, K.: The Iraq Wars and America's Military Revolution 2010, p.40
[388] see Shimko, K.: The Iraq Wars and America's Military Revolution 2010, p.41

embedded in the B-2 or F-117 bombers also impacts the information flow, as it reduces the amount of information that is made available to the enemy.[389]

A good example for the tremendous impact of quick information flow is the so-called sensor-to-shooter cycle. This process describes how long it takes from spotting a target until it can be engaged. During the first Gulf War in 1991, this time was evaluated as 3 days - with improvements in information technology this time was cut to 40 minutes by the start of the missions in Afghanistan.[390] This new approach of expedited information exchange between units on the battlefield is also called Network Centric Warfare.[391] According to Citino the 1991 Iraq conflict revealed a quantum leap in the quick flow of information, which is always considered the thorniest issue with regard to command and control matters.[392]

While Network Centric Warfare has improved the overall battlefield awareness, traditional soldiering skills are also still required in reality. Despite satellite and radar support, ground troops still had to apply the traditional and dangerous 'movement to contact' approach in the recent conflicts in the Middle East. This describes the tactic of maneuvering troops until they make contact in order to identify the position of hostile forces.[393] O'Hanlon underlines this and points out that despite significant progress in sensor technologies, their usage is very limited especially in close combat and urban

---

[389] see Shimko, K.: The Iraq Wars and America's Military Revolution 2010, p.45
[390] see Kober, : Change in Warfare? 2005, p.121
[391] see O'Hanlon, M.: The Science of War 2009, p. 179
[392] see Citino, R.: Blitzkrieg to Desert Storm 2004, p 290
[393] see Boot, M.: War Made New 2006, p.398

environments.[394] This is supported by an observation from the Iraq War, where the majority of friendly casualties were caused by misdirected friendly fire.[395] This can be explained by the fact that the military equipment is able to detect enemy military equipment, but not enemy soldiers that blend into the population in cities and therefore essentially cannot be detected before they start firing.[396]

Regarding the state of innovativeness, O'Hanlon argues that given the peak in military innovations reached in recent years, the US Armed Forces will potentially advance at a slower pace going forward, while main competitors like China are catching up to their standard.[397]

IT equipment shows in particular that military innovations are leveraging more and more commercial technologies. As an example, the US has developed a Land Warrior System, more recently called Land Soldier System, based on IT equipment for individual soldiers that collects data from the troops on the ground in order to provide a full battlefield view of the positions of friendly and enemy forces.[398] This system has mainly been made possible and affordable by the significant improvements in commercial sensor techniques[399] like cameras, GPS receivers, displays and server systems that are capable of handling the immense data stream that is produced by soldiers on the ground.

---

394 see O'Hanlon, M.: The Science of War 2009, p. 179
395 see Shimko, K.: The Iraq Wars and America's Military Revolution 2010, p.169
396 see Shimko, K.: The Iraq Wars and America's Military Revolution 2010, p.170
397 see O'Hanlon, M.: The Science of War 2009, p. 184
398 see Gansler, J.: Democracy's Arsenal 2011, p.93
399 see Gansler, J.: Democracy's Arsenal 2011, p.93

Within the area of IT, software in particular becomes a driver for innovation. In most system innovations today, software represents the enabler of the new innovation to a much bigger extent than hardware.[400] Besides the already-noted use of IT in weapon systems, commercial software can also potentially significantly improve the efficiency of internal communication, processes and resource management in the military environment. Public companies have generated significant efficiencies by applying innovative hardware and software applications that support their internal processes. The same advantages can also be applied to the military context with similar impacts on efficiency.[401] Specifically product-tracking methods in transportation systems have enabled an effective analysis of complex supply chains to improve productivity and lower cost.[402] Enterprise resource planning systems (ERP) in particular enabled organizations to share information across all functions.

Researchers from RAND support the importance of information and state that the ability of nations to conduct effective warfare relies heavily on their ability to develop and implement information technology, and operations will increasingly be dependent on how well the military can master information-dominant operations.[403] Improved information technology can be used to better predict the needs of the troops in the field regarding ammunition and supplies. An optimal supply chain, from factory to foxhole[404], can therefore provide a great impact on productivity and efficiency.

---

[400] see Naegle, B.: Logistics and Sustainment 2008, p.90
[401] see DeMarines, V.: Exploiting the Internet Revolution 2001, p. 61
[402] see Naegle, B.: Logistics and Sustainment 2008, p.104
[403] see Tellis, A./Bially, J./Layne, C./McPherson, M., Measuring National Power p.43
[404] see Shalikashvili J.: Keeping the Edge in Joint Operations 2001, p. 51

Just as in the prior chapter regarding weapon systems the conclusion from these outlines is two-fold. Armed forces need to understand and manage the product lifecycle of their IT equipment. Furthermore a strong defense industry can help Armed Forces to operate efficiently by considering the latest in information technology to produce the right equipment and produce it efficiently at the lowest cost.

5.2.3 Defense Industry

The defense industry represents the link between the technological innovations as described above and the Armed Forces. Whether a technology is specifically developed for the Armed Forces or commercial technology is simply applied in a military context – the defense industry will be tasked with delivering the final product. These products can either be weapon systems or information technologies, or a combination of both as outlined in the prior two chapters. The hypothesis to be tested in this chapter is whether a strong national defense industry can plausibly have a beneficial impact on the efficient operation of Armed Forces. In order to address this question, notable characteristics of the defense industry will be described in the upcoming outlines as well as a working concept defined of how the strength of the defense industry could actually be measured in context of this study.

The defense industry has some unique aspects compared to industries that are serving the private sector. Poast lists the following characteristics:[405] First of all the market for defense goods is typically a monopsony, as the government is the only

[405] see Poast P.: The Economics of War, p.105

customer of the industry. This derives from the fact that a nation's security is a public good and even though every member of the nation has an interest and benefit from the good, the government acts as a single organization on their behalf to provide it.[406] Second, the market is typically oligopolistic as there are only a few, sometimes even just one supplier with the capabilities to provide the service or product. In 2005, the US government had spent 85 percent of its R&D budget and 74 percent of the hardware procurement budget just with the top five suppliers.[407] Third, the price is often not the main factor in the negotiations, but the technical capabilities of the product are focal points. This leads to the fourth criteria, that the competition is often limited to a technical and political rivalry between the suppliers. Fifth, the cost of projects are often high and just a very limited amount of projects can be funded simultaneously. Sixth, the government might select a company for a contract, but in order to ensure that the other companies remain in business and do not supply adversary forces, there are certain outside benefits the government grants to them as well. Alternatively, the government might encourage two companies to team up and share a contract, so that both can stay in business. This can come with a high price literally speaking, since competition is eliminated and a monopoly is created.[408] And the last factor is that as a result of the above characteristics, within the arms industry regulations and pervasive government involvements are higher than in any other industry. Based on these characteristics of a market with limited competition, it can be a challenge for Armed Forces to obtain good and fair prices for the product they purchase, as the following outlines will show.

[406] see Bish, R./ODonoghue, P.: The Monopsony Problem 1970, p.1370
[407] see Gansler, J.: Democracy's Arsenal 2011, p.129
[408] see Gansler, J.: Democracy's Arsenal 2011, p.168

Not just the market situation, but also the types of business transactions have some unique conditions in the area of defense. Contracts in the defense industry are often classified as projects, since each transaction is unique and temporary in nature.[409] The military typically does not buy already existing products; it aspires to gain access to new capabilities and contracts defense companies to develop those. There are no 'off the shelf' shops for aircraft carriers or long range bombers. The acquisition of a new aircraft carrier e.g. represents a project while in contrast its regular ongoing maintenance is considered a routine business operation.[410]

While projects occur in the civil commercial sector as well, they tend to be more complex within the market of defense goods. Rendon and Snider summarize these characteristics as follows:[411] Projects taking place in a military environment can make a difference in life and death situations and matters of national security. They also incorporate in most cases highly advanced technology and require a high skillset in the area of research and development. Furthermore in democratic countries, these projects are funded by public funds and managed by public officials, which makes those projects part of the public political decision-making process. This high level of interdisciplinary complexity makes it difficult to exactly measure costs, schedules and performance.

The arms industry of a nation is often called the defense industrial base. Just as with public companies, the military has the option to buy from domestic companies or to

[409] see Rendon, R./Snider, K.: Project Management 2008, p.2
[410] see Rendon, R./Snider, K.: Project Management 2008, p.2
[411] see Rendon, R./Snider, K.: Project Management 2008, p.13

import internationally as Smith outlines: [412] One of the trade-off seems to be on the one hand that importing is often the cheaper solution, given that a competitive market drives the prices, but a risk is faced in case of a conflict when the supply might be cut off by the foreign supplier. On the other hand if a nation decides to purchase domestically, the national arms industry might become a strong political actor enabled by the increased dependencies.

The setup of the Defense Industry today differs significantly from the time of the World Wars, when military equipment was mainly produced by converted commercial production facilities.[413] In practice, today's defense Industry is to a certain extent internationalized:[414] EADS is a consortium of companies from the UK, Germany, Spain and France. BAE has its headquarters in the UK, but produces and delivers goods to multiple countries around the world. The F-16 Fighter Jet is produced by the US-based company Boeing, although effectively multiple pieces of the aircraft are being manufactured in countries around the world. The pressure to internationalize and export goods seems to be higher for European companies than for US companies. US companies export about one fourth of their production, while European companies export three-quarters of their output.[415]

This increasing openness of the defense industry has also further implications. Carter emphasizes that while in the past superior technology was often exclusively developed by and for the military, in the future it matters more if and how nations are

[412] see Smith, R.: Military Economics 2009, p.138
[413] see Gansler, J.: Democracy's Arsenal 2011, p.10
[414] see Smith, R.: Military Economics 2009, p.140
[415] see Defense Science Board: Report 1999, p. 9

able to adapt commercially-developed technology into military functionality along with the implementation of effective strategies and doctrines.[416] This is mainly due to the fact that new defense systems are developed by defense companies through leveraging increasing portions of commercially-developed technology components into weapon systems.[417] The reason for this trend is that the government-focused R&D efforts become less and less profitable for the industry. In the 1980s one Dollar spent on contracted research was followed by three dollars worth of equipment procurement - In 2001 this ratio is only half of that making it less and less lucrative for defense companies to actually focus on defense-related research.[418] This trend is also reflected in the R&D budget of the US Department of Defense, which increasingly focuses on the development component instead of research.[419]

Gansler also points out that specifically the extreme cyclical swings in defense procurement activities over the centuries created significant inefficiencies.[420] This can have a severe impact on the national security. In times of war, which often come unpredictably, the need for military equipment can peek considerably. While the defense industry is often flexible enough to react and potentially produce the required assets, in reality there is a shortage on the market of raw materials like titanium or nickel, which are often imported from abroad and can lead to significant delays in the

[416] see Carter, A./White, J.: Keeping the Edge 2001, p. 11
[417] see Carter, A.: Keeping the Technological Edge 2001, p.134
[418] see Carter, A.: Keeping the Technological Edge 2001, p.139
[419] see Carter, A.: Keeping the Technological Edge 2001, p.135
[420] see Gansler, J.: Democracy's Arsenal 2011, p.11

production cycle.[421] Accordingly, it is a balancing act for a government weighting the benefits of increased competition against the risks of losing control.

The defense market is also an area in which politicians may impose a strong influence to drive political agenda items that do not necessarily have much to do with the Armed Forces themselves. Arms exports can be a tool for foreign policy and investments in military equipment can be seen in certain political views as a method for stimulating the economy.

The outlines show that the structure of a nation's Defense Industry is rarely, if at all, set up under conditions of free competitive markets. It can be prone to inefficiencies due to limited pricing competition as well as influence from external parties and politicians.

The defense industry however can also be seen as a potential driver for efficiency of Armed Forces. The hypothesis here is that a strong local industry provides better goods that fit the specific needs of the local Armed Forces. As Beckley states, military effectiveness cannot be bought, it has to be developed.[422] Accordingly a nation could import the military material, but not the expertise and learning curve that come with it. Hence, a military will be better off influencing the production of equipment and being directly linked to the development process. Accordingly, the products will better meet the individual requirements of the nation's Armed Forces and increase their capabilities along with enabling efficiency gains. The efficiency gains can presumably

---

[421] see Gansler, J.: Democracy's Arsenal 2011, p.133

[422] see Beckley, M.: Economic Development and Military Effectiveness 2010, p.74

be even higher, if the local defense industry serves Armed Forces of other nations due to economies of scale and scope based on higher production volumes. The efficiency gains are therefore potentially two-fold with an increased efficiency by helping the local Armed Forces achieve a higher 'output' due to better suited equipment and through lower prices, based on higher production volume in terms of export of goods. As a limiting factor the strong dependence with the political decision-making process shall be emphasized. It is fairly common that governments restrict their arms industry from exports in general, exports to certain countries, or in some cases they even decide on a case-by-case basis.

In order to measure the strength of the defense industry this study will build a volume indicator. The more output the industry of a nation produces, presumably the stronger it is. The total output of the defense industry in monetary terms however is not available in any economic statistical database due to the confidentiality of data and the fact that a lot of defense companies are not publicly listed companies. As an alternative, a proxy indicator will be used that is based on a quantification of import and export data in terms of arms trades.

A country that imports a lot of arms can be considered as having a weak arms industry, since apparently not all the required equipment can be produced locally. At the same time a high export indicates an attractive and powerful local arms industry. By calculating the share of export transactions in percent of total transactions, an indication is given whether more goods are exported or imported. A further advantage of using a balance is that it eliminates to some degree the impact of trade restrictions. Absolute export volumes may be skewed due to restrictions that governments put on the arms market. The balance however is a relative measurement. If a nation has a highly restricted arms market and still imports more arms than it exports, the lack of local capabilities can be seen as even higher, since the Armed Forces had to be much more convincing in the process of getting the import approved through the acquisition process.

	1995	2000	2005
China	61.2%	26.5%	13.1%
Germany	77.8%	86.6%	90.4%
Israel	23.3%	28.9%	44.8%
Russian Federation	98.2%	100%	100%
United Kingdom	62.1%	72.4%	64.3%
United States	94.1%	96.7%	91.9%

Table 13: Indicator Strength of Arms Industry

Table 13 illustrates the results of this analysis. The underlying import and export data have been derived for this study from the SIPRI Arms Transfer database. This database uses publicly available data, news and reports to collect the required information in a compiled way. The underlying transaction volume does not represent the actual sales price of weapon systems, but uses a Trade Value Indicator (TVI) which represents the value of the equipment based on production costs.[423] For used equipment a respective discount factor is considered to reflect the decrease in value.[424] This process is intended to make arms transfers more consistently comparable on a global basis. Given that only official data sources are used, it is implied and also clearly

[423] see SIPRI Import/Export (2012)

[424] SIPRI uses 40% of the TVI value for used equipment being sold as is and 60% of the TVI for used products that actually have been refurbished prior to sale.

stated by SIPRI that a challenge can be faced with transactions that are not publicly communicated or only published with a delay in time. The database covers all major weapon systems and excludes the value of technology transfers, small arms and military non-weapon equipment. Since arms transactions have significant values and do not occur in each year, the data points in Table 13 represent an average of transactions over the five prior years. For the scope of this paper, the analysis is conducted for the six nations that were considered for a more detailed analysis. This is due to the fact that a broader and global analysis is a complex endeavor which would be worth a detailed study itself. The scope of this paper will be to take a glance at the situation to determine, if a respective relationship of the defense industry and efficiency of Armed Forces is a plausible hypothesis. The example of Israel in particular will show why a general statistical analysis is not feasible in this context and rather more qualitative factors need to be considered as part of the interpretation on a country-by-country basis.

The percentages express how much of all cross-border arms transfers for a nation present an export of goods. Based on the outlined logic a high percentage, notable greater than 50 percent, presumes a competitive local arms industry in scope of this paper, since more weapons are exported than imported. In order to put the data into perspective, it is helpful to also look at the development of arms transactions for the nation overall, which is illustrated in Table 14. Again a five-year average is used for the comparison.

	1995	2000	2005
China	-6%	-8%	104%
Germany	25%	-26%	-21%
Israel	48%	-23%	12%
Russian Federation		12%	71%
United Kingdom	-16%	0%	-25%
United States	8%	-8%	-48%

Table 14: Development of Indicator for Strength of Arms Industry

For China in 1995 around 61 percent of arms transfers were exports. The percentage drops to 26.5 percent in 2000 and 13 percent in 2005 respectively. Even by using five-year average data, the seasonality of defense transactions becomes obvious looking at these major swings.

The absolute transactions decreased by 6 percent in 1995, 8 percent in 2000 and increases significantly in 2005 by 104 percent. Comparing the data points, this indicates that while exports shrink in double-digit percentage points, the actual total transfers shrink only slightly in 1995 and 2000 and actually double in 2005. The arms transfers are therefore over the 20-year timeframe very active and are showing a strong trend toward significantly higher arms imports with a peak in 2005. Accordingly the local industry appears to be relatively weak, since China is importing much more military goods than it exports.[425]

For Germany the export rate is high for all timeframes. In 1995 the aggregated total of exports is 77.8 percent of overall transactions. In 2000 it is 86.6 percent and 90

[425] Information around Chinas Defense Industry and its programs are not publically available. The only notable examples are an aircraft carrier and new stealth fighter, for both of which no actual performance data, production numbers or market introduction dates are available at the time of this study.

percent in 2005. This indicates a strong arms industry. The continuously increasing trend toward exports however also leads to the plausible conclusion that the local Armed Forces are not acquiring much new equipment. This may cause problems in the long-term for the national arms industry, since exporting weapons is much more complex and riskier than producing for the local market. Political barriers and bureaucratic efforts involved in weapons export may make it at some point unprofitable for German manufacturers to stay in business, especially if companies rely on production volumes that go beyond the local demand.

Israel's exports make up 23.3 percent of transactions in 1995, 28.9 percent in 2000 and around 44 percent in 2005. The imports are therefore much higher than the exports, respectively, indicating a relatively weak local arms industry. However, 2005 marks a change in trend since the export portion of total transactions increased significantly. This assumption of improvements in the Israeli defense industry is backed up by studies of the US Congress. The US grants military aid to Israel and expects about one quarter of that aid each year to be spent with local defense suppliers.[426] These investments are supposed to develop the local arms market in Israel by increasing its economies of scale and helping to develop highly sophisticated equipment for niche markets.[427] However Israel still procures most of its equipment from the US, which forces the suppliers to focus on exports. In order to stay profitable it is estimated that the Israeli defense industry needs to sell as much as 75 percent of products

[426] see Sharp, J.: Report for Congress: Aid to Israel 2010, p.5
[427] see Sharp, J.: Report for Congress: Aid to Israel 2010, p.5

abroad.[428] Even though this background seems to contradict with the findings above, it still shows that the Israeli defense industry would be comparably weak without the US grants, specifically since the balance still shows that most of the equipment is purchased from foreign suppliers, notably the US. Furthermore the US maintains a veto power when it comes to weapons exports that may contain US technology, and Israel claims to lose export business occasionally due to competition from US defense manufacturers.[429] Given the high interdependence with the US, the data for Israel are shaded and not easy to analyze.

Russia's arms transfers prove to be very strong, specifically on the export side. For the whole timeframe the export portion of total transfers is around 99 percent to 100 percent. From a global perspective Gansler reports figures that show Russia as the global number two with regard to arms sales in absolute Dollars.[430] Respectively it appears that Russia has a strong defense industry. In terms of volume, 2005 represents a peak year, since total transactions grew by 71 percent over the average in prior years.

The US show a strong arms export over the whole timeframe with 94.1 percent in 1995, 96.7 percent in 2000 and 91.1 percent in 2005. Total transactions are pretty stable in 1995 and 2000 and decrease significantly 2005 over 2000 by 48 percent. The volume change is quite volatile, but due to the high export rates overall across the years the arms industry appears to be fairly strong. Overall, the data in table 15 show some support for the assumption that a strong arms industry has an impact on efficiency.

[428] see Reuters: Pentagon says Israel improves arms-export control 2007
[429] see Sharp, J.: Report for Congress: Aid to Israel 2010, p.7
[430] see Gansler, J.: Democracy's Arsenal 2011, p.150

Average 95-05		
	Defense Industry	**Efficiency Score**
China	34%	100%
Germany	85%	64%
Israel	32%	6%
Russian Federation	98%	30%
United Kingdom	66%	38%
United States	94%	71%

Table 15: Average Efficiency Score and Defense Industry Strength

Germany and the US have the strongest arms industries and both score fairly high in the efficiency ratings based on the CINC model (China official). UK and Israel score in that order less on efficiency with a lower defense industry strength indicator. The odd outs are China and Russia, with Russia indicating a strong arms industry but low efficiency, and China with a high efficiency, but a low scoring in the defense industry. China respectively is modernizing its Armed Forces as explained in Chapter 4.3.4. For this matter it in fact may import more equipment simply to catch up with the status quo of other nations. The established nations with rather constant governmental and economic structures may represent better indications.

As a caveat it shall be mentioned that this analysis provides a snapshot and proxy indication. A valuable extension in this area could be a more detailed analysis of the arms industry of each nation based on specific product demands of the Armed Forces and whether they could be fulfilled locally. Also, an analysis of the specific government restrictions and a potential incorporation of an analysis of how allied countries exchange arms would be helpful. Specifically the last area could be of interest. Let's presume country A is an ally of country B. If country A is good at producing fighter planes and exports most of them to country B, and country B is good at producing tanks and exports them to A, this would be an interesting finding in terms of burden-sharing and benefits in alliances. However this would not be reflected in an analysis as shown above, since imports and exports for both countries would be high, while at the same time there is in fact a significant level of sophistication in the arms industry of both countries and they take advantage of their respective competitive advantages. However again, one could also argue that exports overall for both countries would be higher than their imports since third nations may have an interest in purchasing those products as well. Bottom line is that the figures above seem to fulfill their purpose as a proxy for this study, but certainly leave room for further and more detailed analyses.

5.3 Government Policy and Financial Management

5.3.1 Policy

The organization Armed Forces is in western industrialized nations part of the public governing process and as such embedded in related policies and procedures. More specifically, the government influences the military through the aspects of financial support, a sufficient industrial base, sufficient quantity and quality of manpower and the conversion of those resources into military capabilities.[431] Efficiency in the government is hereby aiming at making a positive contribution to the productivity of public

[431] see Millet, A./Murray, W./Watman, K., Military Effectiveness 1986, p. 37

organizations and the economy as a whole.[432] Accordingly efficient government processes formulated through policies can impact the efficiency of the Armed Forces as a public organization directly as well as indirectly by creating favorable conditions for conducting business for any supplying companies in the private sector.

A challenge in this area is that on the operational side governmental organizations usually do not have a built-in mechanism that fosters efficiency like a price mechanism or competition - both factors that could run inefficient private companies out of business and therefore provide an incentive to innovate and drive efficiency.[433] Accordingly, a government needs to actively look for and identify inefficient processes and put policies in place to improve them.

Government policies can essentially impact Armed Forces in three areas. They define and formulate their purpose and funding, they set the rules and conditions for how they have to operate as a public organization and they influence the economy and therefore any private company that interacts with Armed Forces as suppliers. The following outlines will explain how these influences can specifically drive efficiency.

First of all, the government of a nation in general has the authority to decide how the available money is allocated and how much budget contributes to which area of the public sector. In this view specifically marginal costs need to be considered; they reflect how much benefit an increase of the defense budget has and what the trade-offs are

[432] see Jones, L./McCaffery, J.: Financial Management 2007, p.32
[433] see Hitch, C./McKean, R.: Defense in the Nuclear Age 1960, p.105

based on the fact that this money is not available to be spent for other purposes.[434] The decision regarding the funding level is accordingly reflected in policies and annual budget documents.

More specifically, the government can also have a direct influence on the spending within each of the governmental sectors, such as the Armed Forces. In the US for example, the Congress has the ability to influence military investment decisions and can even decide on matters like the closing of specific military bases.[435] As a further example, a former British policy was to maintain a naval fleet at least the size of the next two largest fleets combined.[436] The later example implies a certain focus on naval forces, no matter what the military leadership may think would be required to face current threats.

Also, the specific political environment has to be considered when it comes to formulating policies around funding for the military. There is a significant difference between maintaining Armed Forces in peacetime as compared to during wartime. As a practical example, the US Humvee vehicle is expected to be replaced after 13 years of regular service, but had to be replaced due to heavy wear already after two years of service during the operations in Iraq.[437] So even without additional force build-up, it needs to be recognized by policy makers that deployed troops are tremendously more expensive and missions can not necessarily be funded at a peacetime budget level.

---

[434] see Smith, R.: Military Economics 2009, p.88
[435] see Smith, R.: Military Economics 2009, p.27
[436] see Smith, R.: Military Economics 2009, p.85
[437] see Smith, R.: Military Economics 2009, p.114

Most western nations furthermore set the expectations and goals for their Armed Forces through public policies as well as by way of their constitution or other government papers. These responsibilities set important perimeters and influence the potential of Armed Forces to operate efficiently. If the scope of responsibilities is defined very broadly, the military has to maintain immense capabilities to be ready for just about anything, which can produce inefficient excess capacities and the issue of being able to do many things, but none of them effectively. If the definition is too narrow while in fact the missions are much broader in nature, not enough funds may be provided to the Armed Forces in order to enable them to actually operate under the conditions of reality. Bayer indicates that the German Bundeswehr is facing a respective challenge, since the German security policy lists a very diverse list of tasks and missions, supposedly without adequate support in budgetary terms.[438] Even though Germany scores high with 100 percent in some years of the CINC model, this indicates that the model has to be interpreted in the right context. The CINC output suggests a generic theoretical capability level of Germany's Armed Forces, but does not indicate whether the Armed Forces are actually capable of conducting the specific tasks and missions they are facing in reality.

For the most part, the tasks of Armed Forces certainly focus on providing defense to the homeland, but can go far beyond that. A nation e.g. might decide to use Armed Forces as a tool of foreign policy. The US government made extensive use of its military resources for many years to foster relationships with foreign countries through

---

[438] see Bayer, S.: Der Einzelplan 14 2013, p. 254

humanitarian support, peacekeeping or just peacetime cooperation between military forces.[439] This is very relevant given that in the year 2002 it was estimated that every deployed US soldier in Iraq costs incremental $ 500,000.[440] While these are the costs for a deployment in a war zone, it can be assumed that any deployment of troops in foreign countries comes at a significant price tag. Therefore, these activities are difficult to efficiently plan for, since they may come up at rather short notice and may not have been considered when the annual budget has been set for the Department of Defense.

Based on the outlines above it appears plausible, that a clear definition of tasks along with adequate funding supports the Armed Forces' abilities to operate efficiently. However, it does not ensure efficiency automatically, since the tasks and funding are external factors provided to the Armed Forces and they still need to ensure to execute in an efficient way.

Government policies further influence the way the defense budget is being administrated. Given the long-term nature of military investments the US DoD actually provides, besides a budget for the current year, a very specific three-year outlook and a rough five-year outlook of its budget.[441] Furthermore, it distinguishes between outlays and budget, which allows in fact a transfer of activities from one fiscal period to the next - opposing the habit commonly found in public finances that tie budget to current fiscal periods. The US approach certainly provides a significantly higher incentive for efficient budget management than the 'spend it or lose it' mentality of other governments.

---

[439] see Sherwood-Randall, E.: International Relations, p.239
[440] see O'Hanlon, M.: The Science of War 2009, p. 17
[441] see O'Hanlon, M.: The Science of War 2009, p. 11

Government policies can also have an impact on efficiency from a different angle. Besides setting the objectives for the organization Armed Forces, the government also influences the environment in which they operate. In the US, the Constitution states that all decisions with regard to the acquisition of equipment and infrastructure for the Armed Forces are under the authority of the Congress. And these policy decisions are under a strong influence of political developments and not always rational, coherent and stable.[442] This can be explained by the fact that defense-related spending and objectives can also be driven for economic and social purposes, which are under political influence and might contradict with a prospective efficient operation.

Policies in the governmental environment typically arise for one of three reasons according to Rendon and Snider:[443] First, a policy maker may have a specific agenda for solving a specific problem or issue. Second, a specific event may be a trigger for high awareness to a problem that requires immediate changes. The USA e.g. reacted to the high casualty rate in Iraq caused by improvised explosive devices with an expedited acquisition process to provide suitable equipment for the operational forces.[444] And third, each administration may pass down general guidelines to its departments, which point out the respective strategy and general guidance regarding new political priorities for the nation.

Some of these governmental policies may actually contradict with efficient operations. A common restriction for Armed Forces is that national suppliers have to be

[442] see Snider, K.: Defense Acquisition 2008, p.18
[443] see Snider, K.: Defense Acquisition 2008, p.24
[444] This certainly indicates that the specific battlefield conditions were not estimated correctly at an earlier stage – otherwise there wouldn't have been a lack of suitable gear in the first place.

preferred or sometimes have to be exclusively used. This in fact limits the ability of military leaders to have access to potentially lower priced goods from abroad or the possibility to outsource certain activities. As a further example, potential closing decisions regarding military bases can be listed as well. The closing of a military base might make sense operationally and financially for the military, but politicians might still push for maintaining them as a contributor to the local economy in their district.

A practical example that illustrates some of the issues of these policies is the Berry Amendment, which was enacted in 1941 by the US Congress. This act was supposed to protect the nation's industrial base in wartime and is a policy that strictly prefers local sourcing.[445] The US Army enacted in the year 2000 that all soldiers shall wear a black beret with their uniform. Given that the local suppliers were not able to supply all required berets, a Chinese company was contracted.[446] After political resistance aroused, $6.5 million worth of Chinese-manufactured berets were actually disposed. With regard to weapon systems, in the US the restrictions are even higher as a result of the 1920-issued Arsenal Act, which states that defense equipment has to be made within the domestic arsenal exclusively.[447] In reality this regulation only refers to the final product and to some extent the arms manufacturers still source a lot of their spare parts from companies abroad. Interestingly mostly not because of lower prices, but actually superior performance of those parts manufactured abroad.[448]

[445] see Snider, K.: Defense Acquisition 2008, p.19
[446] see Snider, K.: Defense Acquisition 2008, p.19
[447] see Snider, K.: Defense Acquisition 2008, p.30
[448] see Gansler, J.: Democracy's Arsenal 2011, p.41

This takes the discussion to the third area – the interaction of the government with its defense suppliers. The defense market is an oligopoly market with ramifications that differ quite a bit from a competitive commercial market. One of the significant differences is that the competition is very limited and actions may be required by the government to enable 'fair' transactions. According to Gansler, a structural planning of the defense industrial base can achieve greater efficiency and effectiveness.[449] A government may achieve this by issuing policies that determine the required number of firms and steer competition and the right mix of government and private ownership as well as workforce.[450] The success of such a planning exercise certainly depends on the ability and skillset of civil servants to fully understand the optimal set-up of the industry and steer it accordingly.

There is empirical evidence which proves that some of the aspects explained above in fact help governments to operate efficiently. Mandl (et al) summarize the results of a study among OECD countries in three key aspects:[451] Flexible fiscal rules, modern management practices and the use of market instruments in the provision of public services can beneficially impact the efficient operation of the public sector. Other researchers draw similar conclusions, attributing beneficial impacts to result orientation in the budgeting phases, increased flexibility in allocating funds between departments

[449] see Gansler, J.: Democracy's Arsenal 2011, p.11
[450] see Gansler, J.: Democracy's Arsenal 2011, p.11
[451] Mandl, U./Dierx, A./ Ilzkovitz, F.: Efficency of the Public Sector 2008, p.16

and fiscal periods, an increase in competitive pressure through privatization etc. and a high quality of the work force.[452]

Given that Armed Forces are in fact part of the public sector, these aspects certainly can be considered beneficial as well. Carter actually underlines this from a US perspective and points out, that the Department of Defense should educate program managers and acquisition policy makers with regard to commercial management and financial practices to gain the advantages of the private sector and successfully implement commercial practices in the governmental environment.[453]

To sum up the statements above, there are extensive studies around efficient government processes and how they help achieve a higher output with less input. There is no reason to assume that any of the findings from the OECD or other economic institutions do not apply to the military decision-making process. There are potentially two exceptions. Number one, the defense industry interacts with the government in a rather unique oligopoly situation seldom found in other areas. Second, privatization in the context of Armed Forces certainly has very different implications when it comes to specific military tasks that involve forceful actions. This is the reason why both aspects will be addressed in two dedicated chapters of this paper in more detail.

[452] Curristine, T./Lonti, Z./Joumard, I.: Improving Public Sector Efficiency, p.9
[453] see Carter, A.: Keeping the Technological Edge 2001, p.153

5.3.2 Purchasing Process

5.3.2.1 Armed Forces as a Buyer

The purchasing of products and services to fulfill public purposes is a key activity for government officials. In the case of Armed Forces this process is fairly regulated and controlled through government policies. Due to the rather unique conditions of national security, the following outlines will try to determine if and to what extent efficiency can be gained or lost in the acquisition process in the defense sector.

Armed Forces typically act on the market to acquire new military assets for one of two reasons according to Snider:[454] First, the defense environment indicates a gap between the capabilities of the Armed Forces and what they need to achieve in a particular mission or function. Second, a new technology emerges that provides new or enhanced operational capability.

In the first scenario, the Armed Forces act as an innovation enabler and request research and development services leading to a new product fulfilling their specific need. In the second scenario, they identify beneficial aspects in a technology that actually is already available and originated in the commercial sector. The second approach is fairly common and even military-specific innovations can have their technological origin in the commercial environment. Stealth technology e.g. is based on innovative manufacturing and design technologies that reside in the commercial sector

[454] see Snider, K.: Initiate Defense Acquisition 2008, p.35

and the Aegis Class Cruiser is an example of a military asset that is heavily built around commercial equipment.[455]

From a purchasing perspective, efficiency can be driven from a pure cost perspective, simply if Armed Forces have access to high-quality products at a low price. This can be quite difficult to be achieved under the rather unique market conditions in the defense sector. The military is often buying products that do not exist and have to be developed by the supplier.[456] Even if the technology originated in the commercial sector, a specific military product will still need to be designed and manufactured by a defense supplier.

Furthermore, typically only a handful or sometimes just one company is able to provide the product and the government is therefore negotiating the price rather than taking a price the competitive market has produced.[457] And even if multiple companies do exist on a global scale, governmental policies often require the Armed Forces to source from a local supplier to ensure independence from other countries, or in order to support the local defense industry.[458] So even if the global defense market is competitive, nations may be restricted to source in a local, monopolistic environment. The implications of a monopolistic situation of a market can be outlined based on a basic supply-and-demand curve as follows.

[455] see Samuels, R.: Rich Nation, Strong Army 1994, p. 26
[456] see Poast P.: The Economics of War, p.107
[457] see Poast P.: The Economics of War, p.107
[458] see Singer, P. W.: Corporate Warrior 2007, p. 152

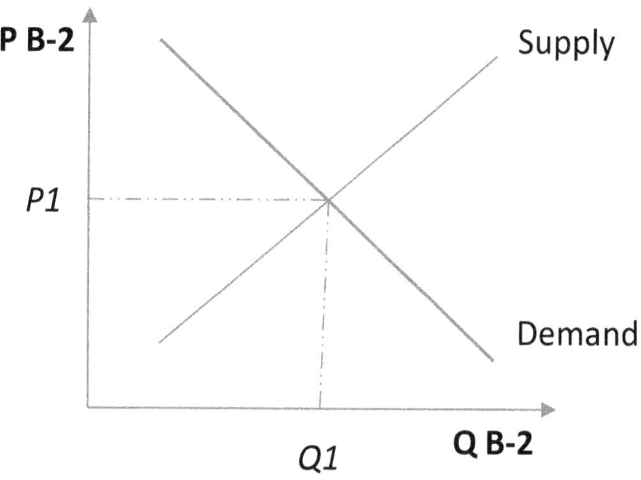

Figure 20: Competitive Arms Market
(see Poast P.: The Economics of War, p.106)

Figure 20 illustrates a perfectly competitive arms market with the example of a B-2 Bomber. Demand is a downward sloping line, illustrating that with increasing prices the demand for the good decreases. Supply is an upward sloping line, given that with an increase in price, the B-2 producer is willing to produce and sell more aircrafts. Assuming a perfectly competitive market, the price for one aircraft will be reflected in the competitive equilibrium where the two lines intersect. However, as a next step it shall be shown now how the single buyer situation, also called monopsony, increases the marginal cost that a government has to bear with the purchase of any additional piece of good. Let's say a government decides to buy nine B-2 bombers. It will have to pay the price that is shown where S and D intersect. If the government now decides to purchase just one additional aircraft more, it will have to pay a higher price for each of them, given that the upward sloping supply curve pushes the equilibrium up to a higher price level.[459] The supplying company would charge the same higher price for each

[459] see Poast P.: The Economics of War, p.107

aircraft and therefore, with increasing demand the marginal cost per aircraft increase for the government.[460] From an efficiency perspective this macroeconomic situation is a very important one, considering the high cost of military equipment and the impact these investments have on the defense budget. For a given budget in this situation, it has to be considered that increasing purchase volumes increase the economies of scale, but at the same time also increase the price per good. To summarize, in monopsonistic markets the single buyer determines the demand curve and with that has to pay higher prices as the quantity demanded increases. The higher demand pushes the market equilibrium where supply and demand intersect to a higher price point which then applies to each single quantity purchased.[461]

And on the other hand, backing out of an existing contract might not effectively lead to respective savings, due to the fact that the price was initially set based on a higher market demand. Lower purchasing volumes cause therefore a loss of economies of scale with resulting higher prices per unit. Not to speak of potential penalty payments from a contractual perspective. Stopping an ongoing project or reducing the aspired amount of equipment purchased is therefore often just a political statement as the savings can in reality never be realized to the full extent.

In the US, the governmental acquisition process is under strict supervision of the Congress and further political institutions. The so-called Nunn-McCurdy Amendment represents a law in the US, which states that each project that exceeds the estimated

[460] see Poast P.: The Economics of War, p.107
[461] see Parkin, M./King, D.: Economics, p.385

budget by 25 percent or more is to be cancelled, unless an exception is requested by the Secretary of Defense.[462] Since defense-related projects are often difficult to estimate, this law adds more focus on accurate budgeting on the one hand, but on the other hand it also adds a lot of bureaucratic effort in case the budget is exceeded. This can certainly happen often, even if all parties involved do their due diligence and start the project with their best intentions. From a management perspective, a law like this seems to provide a reasonable incentive toward accurate project planning, but at the same time can potentially cause a significant amount of additional paperwork.

The product lifecycle of military equipment tends to be very long and investments in the beginning that support reliability can generate big savings later on as described by Smith:[463] The UK calls this cycle CADMID for concept, assessment, demonstration, manufacture, in-service and disposal. For big projects this cycle can last up to half a century. The project Typhoon/Eurofighter was started in 1980 and it is expected that the aircraft will remain in service at least until 2030. Also the B-52 Bomber is still in use and has already exceeded its 50-year service mark within the US Air Force.

Figure 21 illustrates a typical product lifecycle and shows that the operation and support phase is significantly longer and higher in cost than e.g. the investment phase.

---

[462] see Snider, K.: Defense Acquisition 2008, p.25
[463] see Smith, R.: Military Economics 2009, p.129

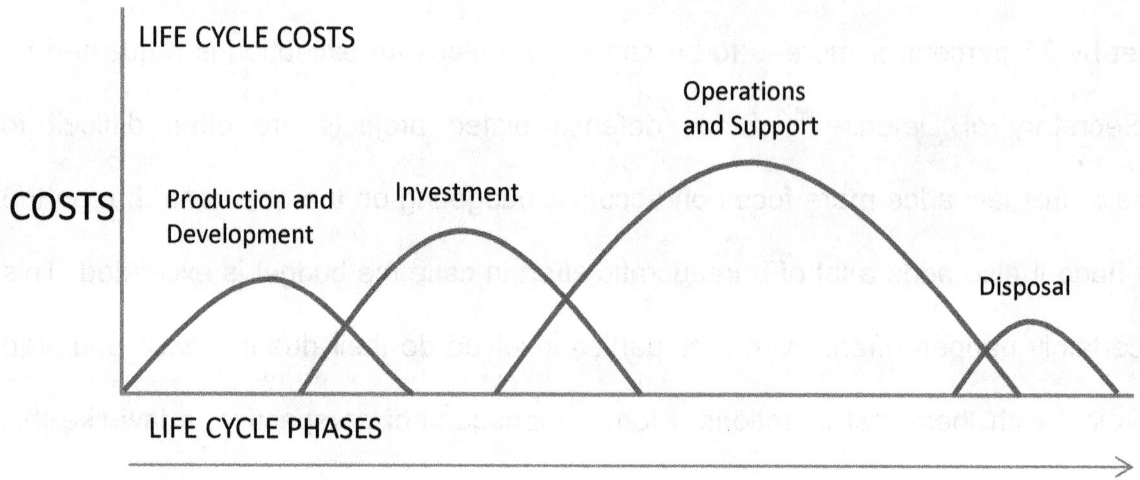

Figure 21: Lifecycle cost of DoD acquisition programs
(see OSD Cost Analysis Group: Cost Estimating Guide 1992)

There are two examples that highlight this fact. Two percent of the lifetime costs of the F-16 Fighter plane arise in the R&D phase, 20 percent in the investment and 78 percent during operation and service.[464] With regard to the M-2 Bradley Fighting Vehicle, the Operation and Service phase even makes up 84 percent of the total cost.[465] This illustrates that not just the cost of purchasing a piece of military equipment should be the focus, but actually the total ownership cost (TOC) has to be considered. Especially since these types of investments already pre-commit spending in O&S in future years. Also, given that a lot of maintenance activities and services are contracted from private companies, an evaluation of the general support concept for a product becomes important.[466] Along those lines the cost of fuel becomes an important factor. While consumers are already struggling with prices of between \$3 and \$4 per gallon, a science board has determined that one gallon of fuel costs the military around \$400 if

[464] see OSD Cost Analysis Group: Cost Estimating Guide 1992
[465] see OSD Cost Analysis Group: Cost Estimating Guide 1992
[466] see Naegle, B.: Logistics and Sustainment 2008, p.105

the actual delivery costs are taken into account for fuel supply trucks, airborne tankers and fuel-supply ships.[467] Needless to say those military vehicles do not have the fuel efficiency of a family van. The introduction indicated that the theory of a revolution in military affairs is based on significant improvements in information technology. In fact, recent trends in the defense sector support this view. Figure 22 illustrates how the software component significantly increased in recent years as a percentage of total system costs. Naegle argues that this trend will continue and emphasizes, that for software components there is very rarely an industry standard available and as part of the design phase an engineer relies on much more input from the customer with regard to expected inter-operability and interface requirements.[468]

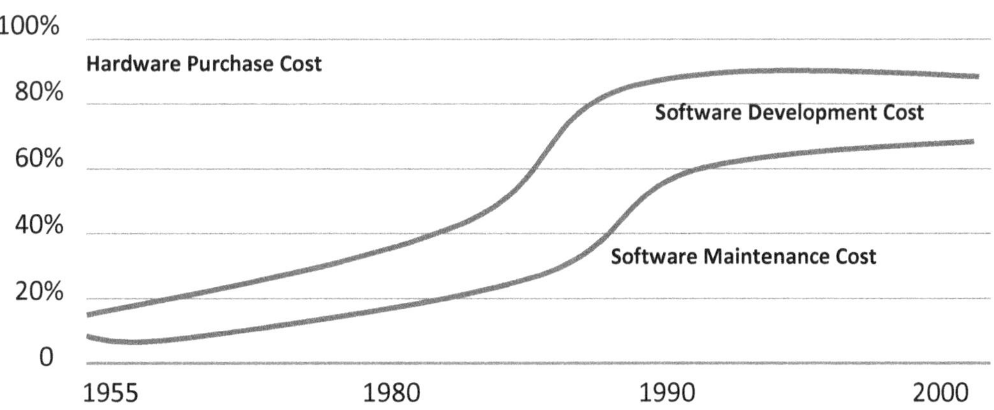

Figure 22: Development of Software and Hardware Cost

(see Osmundson, John S.: Software Project Management 2008, p 65)

When it comes to sophisticated military communication software, there are no off-the-shelf solutions and an engineer requires very specific input as to which devices

[467] see Gansler, J.: Democracy's Arsenal 2011, p.105
[468] see Naegle, B.: Logistics and Sustainment 2008, p.97

need to be connected, at which standard and which potential future systems might require to exchange data in the same standard as well.

Furthermore, software outdates fast and can lose its effectiveness quicker than any of the other components and the need for continued maintenance support starts from the beginning of the deployment of the system.[469] This consequently makes the software maintenance a critical factor in the overall product lifecycle and a major determining factor for the expected total ownership costs.

The unique market conditions make it a challenge to precisely formulate all aspects of the transaction in a contract. Ideally, a federal contract results in a win-win situation and the government receives a high quality product in scheduled time and the contractor receives a fair and reasonable compensation.[470] There are two basic models that are used for federal transactions. Additional contract terms are commonly used, but are built around these two basic variants. One is the fixed cost method and a second one is the cost plus method. Based on the fixed cost method, a supplier is selected and a price per piece of equipment is negotiated.[471] Following the cost plus method, the equipment is specified and the supplier receives a reimbursement for the production cost and in addition an agreed profit margin is applied.[472] The cost plus method provides a challenge, given that instead of having a market drive efficiency and cost improvement that are passed on to the supplier, the supplying company in a cost plus scenario has an incentive, to increase costs because this will increase its profit margin

469 see Naegle, B.: Logistics and Sustainment 2008, p.90
470 see Snider, K.: Defense Acquisition 2008, p.31
471 see Smith, R.: Military Economics 2009, p.128
472 see Smith, R.: Military Economics 2009, p.128

accordingly.[473] Other authors also argue that the fixed price method encourages the buy-in of subcontractors, unwarranted optimism by project managers and other pathological behaviors.[474] The US Congress actually restricted the use of fixed-price contracts for R&D projects in 1988[475] to avoid the potential problems caused by this contract type. In addition to the two general contract types two further, more specialized contract methods exist. Incentive contracts provide an award or extra fee, if certain performance objectives are reached at a higher-defined level.[476] Furthermore, indefinite delivery contracts can be used for products or services that are acquired on an ongoing basis over a certain period of time.[477]

Overall, it is in the interest of the government as well as suppliers to arrange conditions for fair transactions in a market with limited competition. Carter points out that making investments in defense-related products profitable for a company supports their need and also their interest to innovate.[478]

More from a qualitative point of view there are indications that show how nations could align their policies and purchasing procedures to leverage benefits through pooling and sharing of resources. A recent McKinsey study suggests that pooling of resources among European countries could improve long-term productivity at 30 percent of total procurement value.[479] Pooling would consolidate the arms industry and

[473] See Garret, G.: Opportunity and Risk Management 2007, p.185
[474] see Snider, K.: Defense Acquisition 2008, p.32
[475] see Snider, K.: Defense Acquisition 2008, p.32
[476] see Rendon, R.: Contract Management 2008, p.169
[477] see Rendon, R.: Contract Management 2008, p.169
[478] see Carter, A./White, J.: Keeping the Edge 2001, p. 12
[479] see McKinsey& Company: The Future of European Defense 2013, p.8

with fewer companies the production costs per unit decrease due to economies of scale.[480] European nations should further reduce the number of platforms that are currently used. According to McKinsey, European countries maintain 6 times the number of weapon systems of the US, but only spend about 40% as much in monetary volume.[481]

Sharing accordingly would go a step further as some nations could give up certain capabilities all together. It is estimated that 28 percent of Europe's forces are deployable, but only 4 percent are in fact deployed.[482] With a sharing model, the number of unutilized assets can be reduced and furthermore according to the competitive advantage, benefits could be leveraged by having each nation provide what they can produce best.

To summarize the outlined findings, one can say that today's military equipment tends to be more focused around software. Software is more complex to design and maintain than hardware. Furthermore, the operations and support phase is the longest and most cost-intensive in general when it comes to military equipment. Consequently, as part of an acquisition process it is important to focus on effective and efficient project management with regard to the software components in particular. In addition, the consideration of total cost of ownership over the system's lifetime is paramount. Consequently, if a nation manages an effective acquisition process for military assets, it can enhance the efficiency of its Armed Forces. Since the acquisition process is part of

---

[480] see McKinsey& Company: The Future of European Defense 2013, p.15
[481] see McKinsey& Company: The Future of European Defense 2013, p.9
[482] see McKinsey& Company: The Future of European Defense 2013, p.18

the governmental institution, the government effectiveness and efficiency can influence the scoring of nations in the FDH Analysis of this study. Chapter 5.2.3 will aspire to supplement these qualitative statements with empirical data.

5.3.2.2 Privatization

Privatization is a special form of purchasing, since not a product but actually the delivery of a service, is handed over to a private enterprise. The Armed Forces just as private companies are facing the basic economic trade-off of make-or-buy. This means either the good is produced by one's own resources or outsourced and acquired from a third party. The basic monetary trade-off is the comparison of total cost that the organization would incur producing in-house versus the price that a third party would charge for providing the same service. It has to be noted, that in this calculation the transaction costs have to be considered. Transaction costs are costs that occur when an organization enters a transaction with outside parties and reflects the efforts an organization spends on negotiating and enforcing the outside contract.[483] In the in-house view respective managerial and supervision costs have to be considered that arise from the fact that managers have to supervise and control the production process.[484] One of the main reasons for considering an outsourcing of services is to take advantage of a competitive marketplace, which is seen in the context of higher quality, lower cost and stronger firms.[485] Especially with regard to maintenance and support functions the use of contractors is fairly common in the military. In certain

[483] see Fredland, E./Kendry, A.: Privatisation of Military Force 1999, p.151
[484] see Fredland, E./Kendry, A.: Privatisation of Military Force 1999, p.151
[485] see Snider, K.: Defense Acquisition 2008, p.30

cases, civil personnel are even on board of warships or embedded with the operational units to provide the necessary services.[486] Naegle argues that this is caused by the fact that in today's software-intensive systems, it is not feasible from a cost perspective to train and maintain staff within the military that is able to provide this respective support and the trend toward contracting will continue to increase.[487] Leasing is another form for transferring services to the private sector and is currently used as an option by nations. The UK e.g. made the decision to lease tanker capabilities from civil operators rather than purchasing the aircrafts.[488] The aspired advantage is that costs are being decreased due to the fact that the civil operator can increase the utilization of the aircrafts outside of its military usage.[489]

There are risks associated with the outsourcing of military activities. A significant challenge of privatization is the consideration of which extent the contracting companies may also support the Armed Forces of their adversaries. Singer has identified this situation with regard to private military companies, which provided products and services to both sides during conflicts in Africa.[490] Furthermore, outsourced functions might break down if imminent threats occur and private employees flee the dangers. Civil employees that abandon their workplace can only be prosecuted in civilian terms

---

[486] see Naegle, B.: Logistics and Sustainment 2008, p.105
[487] see Naegle, B.: Logistics and Sustainment 2008, p.105
[488] see Smith, R.: Military Economics 2009, p.115
[489] see Smith, R.: Military Economics 2009, p.115
[490] see Singer, P.W.: Corporate Warrior 2007, p.158

for breaking the contract and do not face the significant punishment a member of Armed Forces faces as a deserter.[491]

The privatization of certain capabilities can also increase the strict dependence on the third party in the long-term. If an own organization gives up the skill-set to perform a certain task, it can be very difficult to perform the task in-house again later on if the relationship with the supplier turns bad; this situation furthermore increases the risk of increasing prices if the supplier is aware of the dependency.[492]

Furthermore, civil personnel are bound to fulfill the contracted tasks and not much else. This can provide a challenge in intense battle situations, as the Armed Forces in reality have often relied on the military training of support personnel. Commanders are able to put support personnel in arms when their fighting capability is more important than their support function as a cook, driver, mechanic or secretary.[493]

It has to be pointed out that privatization does not necessarily have to exclude governmental involvement all together. The pure opening of bidding to the private sector can already increase the pressure to drive efficiency for the governmental organization, as it is now competing with private companies to win a contract under conditions of a free and competitive market. According to Gansler, the market forces of privatization enable significant savings, with 20 percent cost reduction if a governmental organization

[491] see Singer, P.W.: Corporate Warrior 2007, p.159
[492] see Singer, P.W.: Corporate Warrior 2007, p.160
[493] see Singer, P.W.: Corporate Warrior 2007, p.163

wins the contract under market conditions and actually 40 percent when the private sector wins.[494]

Overall, the make-or-buy decision seems to be a much more difficult one in the military context. Fredland and Kendry state as follows:[495] The cost-saving argument is much weaker when it comes to defense outputs. The defense environment contains a lot of unforeseeable contingencies, which make it very difficult to create contracts with a private party that describe the scope of responsibilities and the pricing. And even if a contract agreement would have been reached initially, any change of circumstances over time, like a ramp-up of adversary forces, adjustment of objectives, etc. would imply an ongoing renegotiation of contract terms and increase the transaction costs significantly.

The challenge with privatization is that the impact on efficiency is difficult to estimate. Studies show that privatization tends to lead to lower prices, which would be positively reflected on the input side of the FDH Analysis. However, the negative impacts of unreliable support of private firms in war zones or other subtle issues in delivered services may only occur during military operations. It is not always known if and to what extent this may cause problems. Therefore, no definite general answer can be given at this point to which extent privatization actually impacts the efficient operation of Armed Forces. This can only be evaluated on a case-by-case basis by nations as a trade-off of expected benefits and issues based on their individual specific processes.

494 see Gansler, Jacques S.: Defense Industrial Structure, speech 2000
495 see Fredland, E./Kendry, A.: Privatisation of Military Force 1999, p.154

5.3.3 Evaluating the Impact on Efficiency

The question now becomes how the operations of the government can be evaluated and correlated with the efficiency scoring in order to determine, whether a correlation is plausible or not. The challenge obviously is to find a proper indicator to measure this.

Measuring government efficiency is a complex endeavor. The WorldBank Development Research Group has combined an analysis of datasets with a survey of experts in this area to develop Worldwide Governance Indicators. These indicators measure six dimensions of governance: Voice and Accountability, Political Stability and Absence of Violence/Terrorism, Government Effectiveness, Regulatory Quality, Rule of Law and Control of Corruption in the scope of 212 countries and territories for 1996, 1998, 2000 and 2002 through 2008.[496] The individual ranking and scores are available for each of the sub-indicators. This is helpful, since not all indicators are relevant for the efficiency of Armed Forces under the assumptions and circumstances stated above. The two most relevant indicators for this research are Government Effectiveness and Regulatory Quality.

Government Effectiveness [is] capturing perceptions of the quality of public services, the quality of the civil service and the degree of its independence from political pressures, the quality of policy formulation and implementation and the credibility of the

[496] see Kaufmann, D./Kraay, A./Mastruzzi, M.: Governance Matters VIII 2009, p.2

government's commitment to such policies.[497] This links to the outlined qualitative assumptions that government processes and procedures of high quality and efficiency also promote efficiency on the level of the Armed Forces. Lean purchasing processes and independence of pressure from political lobbies would be two examples that are explicitly covered by this indicator.

Regulatory Quality (RQ) [is] capturing perceptions of the ability of the government to formulate and implement sound policies and regulations that permit and promote private sector development.[498] This indicator can be interpreted as a measure for the skill and expertise of governments to understand the requirements of the market. It can also directly link to the defense industry, since the defense industry is in fact a party of the private sector that serves the government in particular and in some countries exclusively.

Both indicators give nations a score in each category. The authors of the study caution users to use data for cross-country comparison due to the fact that rankings are subjective to some extent and particularly a comparison of countries in different development stages can be problematic.[499] However, they emphasize the usage of the data to monitor developments over time for specific nations. The frontier approach of this study limits the ability to statistically correlate the indicators with the efficiency score. All efficiency scores are relative performances to benchmark nations on the frontier. Even nations with weak Government Effectiveness can score high on efficiency

[497] Kaufmann, D./Kraay, A./Mastruzzi, M.: Governance Matters VIII 2009, p.6
[498] Kaufmann, D./Kraay, A./Mastruzzi, M.: Governance Matters VIII 2009, p.6
[499] Kaufmann, D./Kraay, A./Mastruzzi, M.: Governance Matters VIII 2009, p.9

if the benchmark nation's governments are of equal or weaker effectiveness. If e.g. the three lowest scoring nations all appear in one sub-sample as benchmarks, the best performing one will score 100 percent in efficiency, just as a nation in another area of the frontier in comparison with nations in higher rankings of effectiveness. However, the data can still prove to be useful as a proxy to see if a linkage is plausible on a country-by-country basis.

Table 16 shows the analysis for each nation and for each year with a comparison to the CINC efficiency according to the results of Chapter 4 and corresponding Government Effectiveness and Regulatory Quality ranking according to the WorldBank. Table 17 shows the year-over-year variance in the score to illustrate whether changes in GE and RQ are in accordance with changes to the efficiency score. The numbers do not show a clear picture. China interestingly has a high efficiency ranking while government effectiveness and regulatory quality are ranked very low. China's unique single party state government might provide a challenge for the interpretation of the data. Two important perimeters are independence of government from political pressure and formulation and implementation of sound policies. The definition of the above criteria is certainly a much different one for the Chinese form of government versus a democracy. A policy may not have to be as clearly defined to be equally effective in a government form that controls most activities single-handedly anyway. Without judging it might be possible to still operate efficiently e.g. due to faster decision-making processes. However, efficiency at the cost of less political freedom is something a modern western democracy may not even aspire to achieve. For Germany, the UK and Israel a trend can actually be seen. The CINC efficiency scores increase or decrease in accordance with the development of the Government Effectiveness and Regulatory Quality indicator. The UK in 1995 is one exception where CINC efficiency did increase substantially at 28 percent while both government indicators actually decreased.

Russian data are not covered in the Worldbank study. The US with a score of 100 percent cannot be analyzed, since no variation is visible in the observed data statistic.

These data sets offer only a glimpse at further deeper analyses that are required in this area, specifically within a broader data set. The findings for Germany, UK and Israel however do support the qualitative assessment made in the prior chapter, that government behavior and process and procedures are plausible to impact the efficiency of Armed Forces.

	Indicator	1995	2000	2005
China	CINC Eff	100%	100%	100%
	Gov Eff	-0.298	-0.089	-0.166
	RQ Eff	-0.077	-0.326	-0.135
Germany	CINC Eff	58%	66%	71%
	Gov Eff	1.837	1.985	1.547
	RQ Eff	1.46	1.612	1.499
Israel	CINC Eff	7%	7%	6%
	Gov Eff	0.992	1.184	1.056
	RQ Eff	1.092	1.187	0.884
United Kingdom	CINC Eff	32%	41%	40%
	Gov Eff	1.881	1.833	1.750
	RQ Eff	2.035	1.749	1.607
United States	CINC Eff	100%	61%	51%
	Gov Eff	1.702	1.856	1.561
	RQ Eff	1.631	1.688	1.614

Table 16: Government Efficiency and Regulatory Quality

	Indicator	2000	2005
China	CINC Eff	0%	0%
	Gov Eff	-70%	87%
	RQ Eff	324%	-59%
Germany	CINC Eff	13%	7%
	Gov Eff	8%	-22%
	RQ Eff	10%	-7%
Israel	CINC Eff	4%	-23%
	Gov Eff	19%	-11%
	RQ Eff	9%	-25%
United Kingdom	CINC Eff	28%	-2%
	Gov Eff	-3%	-5%
	RQ Eff	-14%	-8%
United States	CINC Eff	-39%	-15%
	Gov Eff	9%	-16%
	RQ Eff	4%	-4%

Table 17: Changes Government Efficiency and Regulatory Quality

5.4 All Volunteer Force vs. Conscript

There are two basic models a nation can consider, to recruit and maintain its stock of military labor. An All-Volunteer Force, short AVF, is a recruitment system in which the military must use pay and provide benefits in order to incentivize people to serve. The conscript model is a mandatory military service, which is also known as a draft. It has to be noted, that countries with a conscript military in most cases still use the volunteer model to fill their officer or non-commissioned officer positions which makes it truly a mixed model.

In order to determine which model is ideal for a country, the costs/benefits of both models have to be considered. The basic economic supply-and-demand curve can be used to illustrate this as shown in Figure 23. The government will hire more people for military service if wages are low and less if they are high, all things being equal.[500] This is represented by the downward sloping line. People will be more likely joining the service if the wages are rising compared to the alternative in the civilian environment.[501]- Shown by the upward sloping line in the figure. In a competitive labor market, the model balances where supply and demand intersect.

The conscript model is illustrated as a vertical bar in the market model; the government can draft as much labor supply as required independent of the wage level. In the scenario shown below, the government pays significantly less wages when it can enforce a mandatory draft for a given demand level L Draft. The competitive market equilibrium for the same number of soldiers would actually require the government to pay wages at level *w'*. Or in other words, if the government lifted the draft, it had to increase the wages from *w* to *w'* in order to obtain the same level of labor supply under competitive market conditions.

[500] see Poast P.: The Economics of War, p.80
[501] see Poast P.: The Economics of War, p.81

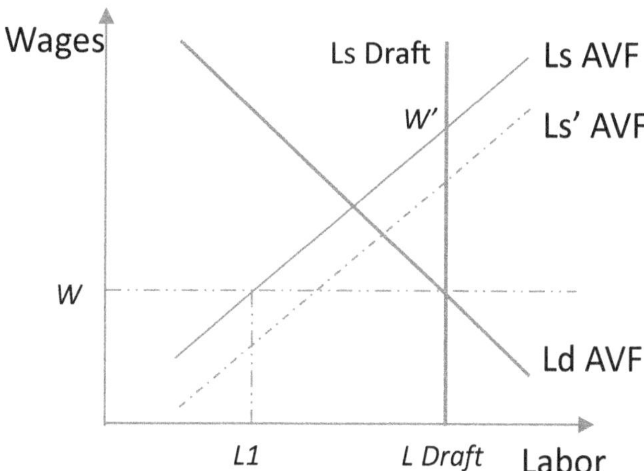

Figure 23: Market Model Draft vs. Conscript

(see Poast P.: The Economics of War, p.82)

In reality though, even in a draft model there is still a certain pool of the workforce willing to join the service at the lower wage level. In this model, if in an AVF scenario the wages are set at *w,* the difference between L1 and L Draft would reflect the gap in military personnel that voluntarily join versus the required total force which consequently has to be filled through a draft.[502]

The second implication of the model is the price of labor relative to other resources. The government equips the military typically with the two resources labor (soldiers) and capital (military equipment). If the labor component becomes more expensive relative to capital in an AVF scenario, the government would then tend to establish a more capital-intensive military.[503]

---

[502] see Poast P.: The Economics of War, p.82
[503] see Poast P.: The Economics of War, p.82

The economic model can also be used to determine the willingness of people to join the service through the labor supply curve. The supply curve in the model is an upward sloping line, so the more motivated people are to join, the fewer wages will be required to actually motivate them to join.[504] Warner and Asch actually add the component of the military lifestyle to the wages that are required to hire someone for the military service.[505] People to whom the military lifestyle appeals would join the military at lower wages than a comparable civilian job would pay. And people, who see the rather strict military lifestyle as a burden, would join the service only if the wages are higher compared to a civilian alternative. This represents the economic aspects of opportunity costs for individuals. In a market model this is reflected by a shift of the supply curve. If people are more motivated to join the service, the supply curve shifts to the right and at each wage level *w* the supply of labor increases - shown as LS'. If people are less motivated, this has the opposite effect and the supply curve shifts to the left.

The selection of either an AVF or conscription also has relevance for a nation's economy overall and certain benefits and disadvantages are associated with both models.

On the conscript side it is being argued that the conscript model provides benefits for the society by contributing training and socialization for young people.[506]

[504] see Poast P.: The Economics of War, p.85
[505] see Warner, J./Asch, B.: All-volunteer Military 2001, p.171
[506] see Smith, R.: Military Economics 2009, p.121

Furthermore conscript service is supposed to provide a link between the society and the military which contributes to a better integration of the Armed Forces.[507]

The economic literature however mostly favors the all-volunteer model. Smith e.g. refers to conscript services as a hidden tax, given that drafted citizens lose the pay and benefit they would have otherwise received in a civil occupation.[508]

From a macroeconomic perspective Brauer also claims that the conscript service burdens a nation with high economic costs, given that all drafted citizens are not available for other productive tasks in the economy and furthermore people are forced into a specific occupation that might not fit best to their skill-set.[509] In the volunteer model the market forces regulate who joins under which conditions the Armed Forces and ensures that only people who see the military as the best available option would join.[510]

This macroeconomic perspective adds some complexity to the research topic. In scope of this paper we use military capabilities on the output side. However since the AVF vs. conscript discussion impacts the economy overall, a nation with an 'inefficient' sourcing model for labor for the military may still use the most efficient one for the overall economy.

---

507 see Smith, R.: Military Economics 2009, p.121
508 see Smith, R.: Military Economics 2009, p.120
509 see Brauer, J.: Economic Perspective on Mercenaries 1999, p. 141
510 see Brauer, J.: Economic Perspective on Mercenaries 1999, p. 141

One view positions the Armed Forces in the conscript model as the more efficient alternative. The logic follows the basic model of market equilibrium.[511] In the AVF scenario the government is forced to pay the market wages as determined by the market equilibrium at the supply-demand intersect. In the conscript model the government can set the wages below that equilibrium and simply determine how many people are drafted. Hence the military pays lower wages in this model then it would have in the AVF scenario.

There are alternative views that consider broader aspects of the labor market and come to a different conclusion in favor of the AVF model. Training people to use weapons and military equipment takes a long time, so that a big portion of the conscript service time has to be dedicated to training and the soldier's expertise cannot be utilized for long.[512] A citizen who becomes a soldier for life or at least for some time of his or her professional career remains for a longer time in a military role and the training efforts can be utilized over a longer time. An AVF military could therefore effectively get the same job done with fewer resources than a conscript force could, due to better training and higher expertise.[513] There also seems to be evidence that the decision around the set-up of the Armed Forces has to be viewed in interdependence with other factors as well. Cohen for example claims that the modern technology requires the personnel of the Armed Forces to be smaller and more professional[514] which mandates a shift from the conscript model to a volunteer military. Cohen actually states that despite the

[511] see Poast P.: The Economics of War, p.85
[512] see Smith, R.: Military Economics 2009, p.121
[513] see Smith, R.: Military Economics 2009, p.121
[514] see Cohen, E.: Transformation in Military Affairs 2004, p.400

example of Israel, Armed Forces today are mostly a volunteer force, as a conscript military is simply too expensive to be good.[515]

The economics of AVF versus conscript are worth detailed research of their own specifically with respect to efficiency. However in terms of this study it will at least be commented on the respective model chosen by the analyzed nations to see if a common pattern is identifiable which might be worthy of further research. For this comparison it will be analyzed how the average efficiency score of nations fitting in one category compares to the scoring of nations in the other category. The sample sets consist of 73 nations and each nation is classified as either AVF or conscript depending on the model applicable in the respective point in time. Notably Germany is still a conscript nation in the timeframe of this research. Some nations actually changed the model during the timeframe, e.g. France and the Netherlands which went from a conscript to AVF in 2001 and 1997, respectively. The used data reflect this change accordingly. It shall be noted that a change from a conscript model to AVF certainly provides a fundamental change to the way Armed Forces operate. These changes take time and some nations may need longer than others to adapt. Some countries may prepare their organization beforehand; others may start reorganizing only after their constitution has changed. A nation announcing a change in 2000 e.g. may still be in fact a conscript military in that particular year since presumably a last round of draftees is still in service. The majority of changes though occurred within European countries and of those mostly after the timeframe that is in scope of this study. The impact of these

[515] see Cohen, E.: Transformation in Military Affairs 2004, p.404 – see also Poutvaara, P. and Wagener, A.: Ending Military Conscription 2011, p.37

shifts from one model to the other should therefore be fairly minimal. For the datasets the by now familiar three scenario approach will be applied with results as shown in Figure 18 based on the CINC efficiency score as computed in this study.

		1995	2000	2005
China O	AVF	33.5%	41.6%	34.2%
	Conscript	32.2%	33.9%	31.4%
	Average	32.6%	36.4%	32.6%
	AVF above Ave	2.6%	11.5%	5.0%
China l	AVF	34.8%	42.6%	35.6%
	Conscript	32.2%	33.9%	31.4%
	Average	33.1%	37.1%	33.2%
	AVF above Ave	5.2%	14.6%	7.3%
China h	AVF	34.9%	43.5%	36.6%
	Conscript	32.0%	33.9%	31.4%
	Average	33.0%	37.5%	33.6%
	AVF above Ave	5.7%	16.1%	8.9%

Table 18: Efficiency Score and Conscription

All data sets show a higher scoring for the nations following the AVF model. In the scenario with China at its officially reported number, the score is 33.5 percent, 40.6 percent and 34.2 percent respectively for each year. The conscript nations score below that with 32.2 percent, 33.9 percent and 31.4 percent respectively.

The difference increases with increasing assumptions for China's defense spending. Since China has a conscript military, the higher defense spending on the input side lowers the efficiency scoring accordingly in those respective scenarios relative to the AVF nations. The score for AVF nations turn out to be between 1 percent and 3 percent higher for the low and high spend scenarios for China. Since the official numbers are presumably understated, the truth can be found somewhere between the low and high level spending model.

Looking at the data, one may draw the conclusion that there is a trend toward improved efficiency in the conscript model due to the increase in efficiency by 2 percent for the conscript nations in 2000 over 1995 as well as the drop in efficiency for AVF nations in 2005 over 2000 by 6 percent. This however is in fact caused by changes in the dataset itself and not because the conscript nations are catching up with their efficiency score. To prove this point, average efficiency scores and deviations from that average will be analyzed as a next step. The last two rows of each scenario show the average for each timeframe and how much the AVF nations score above that average. This reveals that the increase in efficiency score of conscript nations is in fact caused by an overall efficiency increase of the whole sample set and not because the conscript model becomes a relatively more attractive option. To the contrary, the AVF model actually becomes an even more superior choice over the conscript with a score of 11.5 percent above average (14.6 percent and 16.1 percent for the low and high scenarios).

The significance of the advantage AVF has over conscript varies quite a bit between the three scenarios. The use of three data points helps to ensure that not one random data point is used for the final determination but rather a few data points over time. The average advantage of AVF over conscript across all three years for the three scenarios is 6.4 percent (o), 9.1 percent (l) and 10.2 percent (h) (not shown in the table).

Since all datasets show nations utilizing AVF scoring higher, it appears plausible that this model is in economic terms more efficient from the perspective of Armed Forces. And this does not yet factor in the benefits for the overall economy by eliminating the 'hidden' tax caused by a draft model.[516]

[516] As outlined previously we are taking the perspective of the armed forces in this case. The general implications for the overall economy are not considered in this study and actual results may differ if the 'social' benefit of a conscript military would prove to outweigh the financial benefits of the AVF model.

6 Outlook

The prior chapter has provided a first glance at the analysis of factors that can reasonably be assumed to influence the efficiency of Armed Forces. In all cases, literature and data points were available to actually approach the topic to evaluate if and how an influence on efficiency of Armed Forces is plausible. The list of factors is certainly not limited to those identified for this study. In the course of this study two major further factors have been identified that seem to have a significant impact. These two factors are Force Planning and the usage of Private Military Forces. Both factors are not necessarily part of the field of economics nor are compelling studies available at this point in time to feed them into an economic study. Since they are nevertheless important, the following two chapters provide an outlook as to how this efficiency study could be enhanced by further studies and shall also provide some food for thought for senior leaders in the military and defense departments of nations around the globe.

6.1 Force Planning

Troxell defines force planning as the process that involves an evaluation of the threats to the national interest, the establishment of military requirements within given constraint, and finally an assessment of the risk of failure.[517] It is an iterative process of modifying the ends, adjusting the ways or changing the means to maximize the ability to

[517] see Troxell, J.: Force Planning 2001, p.157

protect and further the national goals.[518] Efficiency can have important relevance at each of these planning stages.

The process of force planning can use two different methodologies to define the goal and purpose of the Armed Forces. The first one is called threat-based planning and is an approach in which the defense policy is specifically aimed at opposing an actual or perceived danger.[519] During the Cold War for example the US defense policy was created around fighting a global war against the Soviet Union as a specific threat. This scenario was seen as pretty straightforward with regard to its requirements and was also called a "classic" force planning approach.[520] The second methodology is more generic and called capability-based planning. In this approach not a specific threat is opposed but the Armed Forces are determined by their capabilities to conduct potential future missions and achieve specific objectives.[521] Specifically in the 1990s the budget constraint became a focus in Force Planning and the US created a Base Force Concept that tried to operate under minimum force requirements to fulfill a limited scope of prospective future missions.[522] Efficiency can support both approaches from different angles. In times of scarce budgets, efficient operations can help the military to get more capabilities out of the allotted budget. On the other side thorough force planning can also drive efficiency if the scope is clearly defined and the military knows exactly what type of capabilities are required to avoid maintaining unused excess resources. Troxell highlights that force structure today should be based on an affordable defense

[518] see Bartlett, H/Holman P./Somes, T.: Art of Strategy 1995, p.114
[519] see Troxell, J.: Force Planning 2001, p.158
[520] see Davis, P.: Planning Under Uncertainty 1994, p.16
[521] see Troxell, J.: Force Planning 2001, p.158
[522] see Troxell, J.: Force Planning 2001, p.162

program.[523] Also Kaufmann underlines the economic component, stating that military leaders cannot ask the congress for a blank check, but have to outline what potential future threats they see on the horizon and which capabilities are required at which costs to actually face them.[524]

After setting the goals, nations need to define how they want to achieve them. According to Smith the military has a lot of similarities to the economic value chain of a private company. Efficiency in the private sector can be achieved by readjusting the value chain of a company and in the same manner the military strategist can gain advantages through an optimal set-up of the military value chain.[525] Following this analogy, a productive set-up of the value chain would lead to a better input-output ratio and therefore also help to achieve higher efficiency. In the military, budgets are used to acquire troops and weapons which are then used to compete against adversaries.[526] If this input-to-output ratio can be achieved at the lowest possible cost, it would indicate a high efficiency of the military organization. Nations should look at the threats that they are potentially facing, determine the forces necessary to withstand them, calculate the military capabilities necessary and match the costs required to the available budget.[527] The importance of efficiency in the operational planning process has been recognized by at least some nations. The US has implemented a process in the 1960s under the acronym PPBS, for Program, Planning, Budgeting System, which is supposed to make

[523] see Troxell, J.: Force Planning 2001, p.172
[524] see Kaufmann, W.: Assessing the Base Force 1992, p. 27
[525] see Smith, R.: Military Economics 2009, p.25
[526] see Smith, R.: Military Economics 2009, p.24
[527] see Smith, R.: Military Economics 2009, p.26

sure potential threats can be opposed with respective military capabilities.[528] Secretary of Defense McNamara implemented this system to optimize the link between spending and strategy.[529] However according to Smith this process is rarely applied to the defense budget in total due to the challenge of actually measuring threats and the difficulty of foreseeing potential interdependencies within those assumptions.[530] And given that an objective can be reached in different ways and that the actual situations are hard to predict, different states would assess the capability of the same force very differently.[531]

Furthermore, force planning usually takes place in peacetime without detailed knowledge around specific combat situations and it has to include estimates regarding the capabilities of potential adversaries.[532] And these capabilities can differ quite a bit whether Armed Forces are assessed from an attacker or defender perspective: Biddle suggests defining offensive capability as the capacity to destroy the largest possible defensive force over the largest possible territory with the least attacker casualties in the shortest time.[533] Accordingly defensive capability is defined as preserving the largest possible defensive force over the largest possible territory with the greatest attacker casualties for the longest time.[534] Military strategists traditionally consider the attacker-defender force ratio as an indicator for the potential success of an operation. A commonly used rule of thumb suggests that the attacker forces need to have at least

[528] see Smith, R.: Military Economics 2009, p.26
[529] see Shalikashvili J.: Keeping the Edge in Joint Operations 2001, p. 38
[530] see Smith, R.: Military Economics 2009, p.26
[531] see Millet, A./Murray, W./Watman, K., Military Effectiveness 1986, p. 37
[532] see Pugh, G./Mayberry, J.: Effectiveness General-Purpose Military 1973, p 868
[533] see Biddle, S.: Military Power 2006, p. 6
[534] see Biddle, S.: Military Power 2006, p. 6

three times as much combat power as the defender at the point of attack.[535] This approach is focused on the pure number of troops to determine the necessary resources to be effective with the execution of a mission. The stage of military technology however matters quite a bit. In recent years, especially during the Second Gulf War, speed has been seen as a potential substitute for pure mass and was therefore the basis for the strategy applied during the invasion of Iraq.[536] US Secretary of Defense Rumsfeld based this approach on the experiences in Afghanistan and also General Franks considered the 'Speed Kills' approach in his plans for the invasion.[537] The simple calculation of ratios therefore seems to be outdated or at least should be used with caution.

A common approach to actually conduct force planning follows a three-step process as stated by Kaufmann as follows:[538] As a first step, the national wartime goals and objectives are derived from related peacetime goals. As a second step, respective combat goals are derived that can help to achieve the overall wartime goal. And in a third step, based on game-solution techniques it is evaluated what would be required in order to achieve the defined combat objectives. While steps two and three certainly fit into the responsibility of the military leadership, step one is relevant in the scope of this paper since it links the nation's defense policy with regard to force and budget planning to effectiveness and efficiency. However, also steps two and three underline that there should be strong alignment between the military leaders and the civil servants who are

---

[535] see Dunnigan, J.: How to make war 2003, p.5
[536] see Shimko, K.: The Iraq Wars and America's Military Revolution 2010, p.147
[537] see Ricks, T.: Fiasco 2006, p.75
[538] see Kaufmann, W.: Assessing the Base Force 1992, p. 27

involved in the process of setting the nation's security goals and budgets since both are interdependent. Specifically the war-gaming component may be an interesting area where the results of this study can be connected with military expertise. If in a war game different sets of approaches lead to the same aspired result of the mission, picking the least expensive one would automatically drive efficiency.

Force planning is a very important component in order to ensure efficient use of resources. Otherwise a lot of money is either spent on excess capacities or the wrong assets will actually never be used or see action in combat.A general problem of force planning is that it focuses on combat proficiency relating to the capability of the Armed Forces to act on the battlefield. This expertise is out of scope of this analysis and military specialists should determine indicators that are suitable for empirical research and could be used for a cross-country comparison. However, it becomes clear that civil servants can ensure that force planning becomes an efficient process by setting proper expectations and by encouraging an efficient usage of the defense budget. In the end the civil government officials set the goals, framework and national security policies for the Armed Forces. Therefore Armed Forces can more effectively and efficiently plan with clear expectations.

6.2 Private Military Force

6.2.1 Definition and Overview

The terms Private Military Force and Private Military Firm, or short PMF are used to describe the business sector in which private companies take over military tasks. This differs from the privatization or outsourcing as defined in Chapter 5 given that not just tasks with parallels to the civil sector are contracted but actually tasks and responsibilities that one could see as forceful actions usually provided by the Armed Forces of a nation. Accordingly, there is some controversy around the legitimacy of PMF but also parallels to cost and benefits analyses in terms of efficiency. In the end it is a special form of privatization and privatization of government tasks is very much in scope of efficiency analyses.

In recent years, the number of private forces serving in combat operations has significantly increased. The media is using the term mercenary frequently and mostly to give the topic a negative touch. This is not accurate as the term has a distinct meaning. Singer provides a definition which helps to distinguish mercenaries from PMFs and from regular national Armed Forces. According to him mercenaries are individuals who fight in a war driven by personal and financial gains.[539] More precisely he lists six criteria which are shown in Figure 24:

---

[539] see Singer, P. W.: Corporate Warrior 2007, p. 43

Foreign	A mercenary is not a citizen or resident of the state in which he or she is fighting
Independence	Mercenaries are not integrated into national force and are only bound through an employment contract
Motivation	Mercenaries fight for economic short-term reward, not for political or religious goals
Recruitment	Mercenaries are brought in by oblique and circuitous ways to avoid legal prosecution
Organization	Mercenary units are temporary and ad-hoc groupings
Services	Mercenaries focus on combat service for single clients

Figure 24: Characteristics of a Mercenary

(see Singer, P.: Corporate Warrior 2004, p. 43)

Singer further proposes to define PMFs as the corporatization of military services.[540] The term MF describes the overall phenomenon of outsourced military services, while the equally often-used term Private Military Company describes just one sector within this industry.[541] The skill-set of those companies includes combat operations, strategic planning, intelligence, risk assessment, operational support, training and technical skills.[542] In broader definition, these are all firms that provide international services that are traditionally provided by the national military.[543]

540 see Singer, P. W.: Corporate Warrior 2007, p. 45
541 see Spicer, T. : An unorthodox soldier 1999, p. 15
542 see Singer, P. W.: Corporate Warrior 2007, p. 8
543 see Adebajo, A./Sriram, C.: Messiahs or Mercenaries? 2000, p. 2

The Private Military Companies, short PMC, within this group of companies provide direct military services to a government or nation, while the Private Security Companies or PSCs provide passive security services to private companies that operate in high-risk environments.[544] However Fredland points out that separating combat from non-combat tasks can often be difficult. Those who provide transportation for troops and supplies to and from the battlefield are certainly supposed to be considered part of the combat mission, just as those who provide consultancy services regarding force design.[545] Furthermore companies that provide security in high-risk regions have to expect to eventually end up in combat situations.[546]

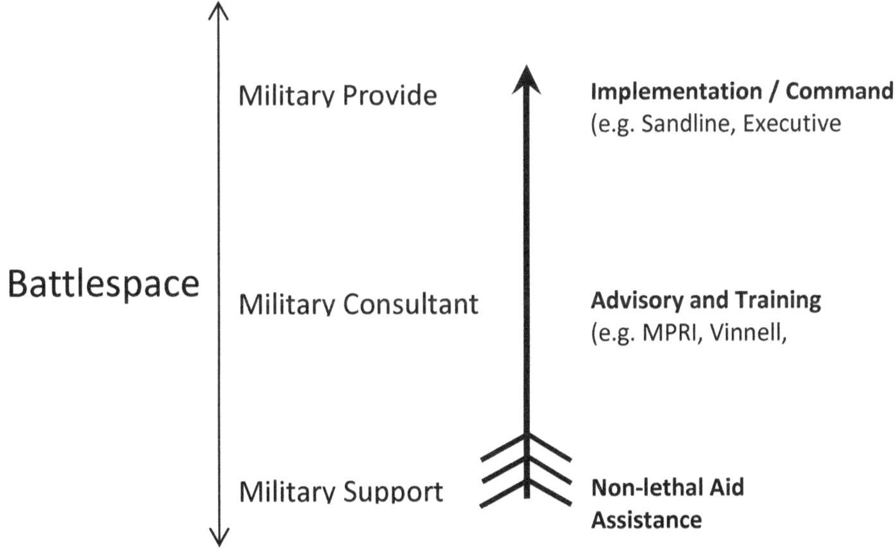

Figure 25: Tip of the Spear Typology

(see Singer, P. W.: Corporate Warrior 2007, p. 93)

[544] see Adebajo, A./Sriram, C.: Messiahs or Mercenaries? 2000, p. 2
[545] see Fredland, E.: Outsourcing Military Force 2004, p. 208
[546] see Fredland, E.: Outsourcing Military Force 2004, p. 208

Singer suggests using the tip of the spear typology to further define the PMF industry.[547] The method can be seen in an analogy to private enterprises classifying outsourcing activities and basically shows in which area of the value chain the external company takes over tasks and responsibilities.

Figure 25 applies the tip of the spear concept on specific military tasks and also shows examples of companies that over time have taken over respective tasks of military operations.

6.2.2 Growth of Private Military Industry

Adebajo and Sriram claim that very specific reasons have caused the rapid growth of the industry specifically since the end of the Cold War:[548] Military demobilization around the world freed up a lot of military talent that was seeking opportunities in the private sector. Furthermore the amount of conflicts globally increased in numbers while it decreased in scope leading to a higher demand for military resources. This was further accelerated by the fact that a lot of countries which are rich in natural resources are in regions of conflicts. Accordingly private companies running their business there contract security services from PMFs. As an example, in 2008 it was estimated that in Iraq alone around 10,000 security personnel of this kind were employed for this purpose.[549]

---

[547] see Singer, P.W.: Corporate Warrior 2007, p.91
[548] see Adebajo, A./Sriram, C.: Messiahs or Mercenaries? 2000, p. 8
[549] see Gaston, E.: Mercenarism 2.0 2008, p. 223

According to Singer the industry around PMFs is characterized by a low entry barrier, given that it is not very capital-intensive and an extensive labor pool is easily and inexpensively available.[550] This makes branding and reputation the key success factor for the industry.[551] Singer furthermore states:[552] Employees are typically hired on the market of ex-military members who bring in a lot of expertise and training which they gathered at the expense of a nation's Armed Forces during their time of regular military service. Another factor that outlines the professionalism that some PMF can obtain is that PMFs can select their employees based on their prior military training and expertise as well as performance evaluation as part of their service record in the regular Armed Forces. As an example, the US Army recruits soldiers trusting to make at least some of them elite warriors within the Green Berets - the PMFs however already know when they hire an ex-Green Beret that that person has endured an extensive qualification process and received high quality military training. Another aspect of PMF is that military resources can be easily obtained and even countries with comparably low population, like a lot of Gulf States, can maintain Armed Forces that are bigger in numbers than would be possible otherwise.[553]

The privatization of military tasks is a growing and very real phenomenon. The global conditions are fairly favorable for companies in this industry to be successful. The next chapter will now outline how this trend could potentially impact the efficiency of Armed Forces.

---

[550] see Singer, P. W.: Corporate Warrior 2007, p. 74
[551] see Singer, P. W.: Corporate Warrior 2007, p. 74
[552] see Singer, P. W.: Corporate Warrior 2007, p. 77
[553] see Singer, P. W.: Corporate Warrior 2007, p. 172

6.2.3 Impact on efficiency of Armed Forces

Nations need to assess the risks and opportunities posed by a privatization of governmental services - in this case military force or certain military tasks. Fredland and Kendry list efficiency and innovation as the two major reasons for the decision to privatize activities.[554] The literature indicates that PMFs are in fact more innovative, more flexible and less expensive.[555] This results from the fact that they are able to source personnel and equipment specifically suited to the mission, while governments have to maintain a broader staff of personnel and equipment to be available for almost any circumstances.[556] This is supported by a practical example: A peacekeeping mission in Sierra Leone was estimated to cost the South African company Executive Outcomes around $36 million while an official UN mission is estimated at cost beyond $90 million.[557] Also Fredland sees significant savings potential resulting from the utilization of private companies for military tasks:[558] According to him, these cost savings have multiple dimensions. First of all Armed Forces are expensive to maintain, while their actual need is rather infrequent. Furthermore, those resources that are being trained and maintained for military contingencies are not available elsewhere in the economy of a nation to produce economic output. In addition to these factors, the private company acts in a competitive environment and has to drive efficiency in order to sustain itself in the market. Furthermore, it can be assumed that private companies can generate economies of scale, given that they utilize their resources on an ongoing

---

[554] see Fredland, E./Kendry, A.: Privatisation of Military Force 1999, p.150
[555] see Adebajo, A./Sriram, C.: Messiahs or Mercenaries? 2000, p. 5
[556] see Adebajo, A./Sriram, C.: Messiahs or Mercenaries? 2000, p. 5
[557] see Adebajo, A./Sriram, C.: Messiahs or Mercenaries? 2000, p. 6
[558] see Fredland, E.: Outsourcing Military Force 2004, p. 212

basis with different customers and overhead costs can therefore be significantly decreased.[559]

It was already stated that PMFs offer significantly higher wages than the Armed Forces of nations. Although the real numbers certainly depend on the job, deployment country and employer according to one source the pay in the private sector of $15,000 per month is significantly higher than the corresponding payment of $50,000 per year in the regular Armed Forces.[560] The question arises why private companies can offer much higher wages and still operate more efficiently than regular Armed Forces. Poast lists four main reasons for this which he summarizes under the concept of efficiency wages:[561] These wages are set above the point where the market balances and still provide an advantage to the hiring company. Higher wages ensure that employees have an incentive to work harder, because they wouldn't find a lot of other job opportunities where they get paid above market level.[562] These highly skilled and motivated workers achieve results in less time. Second, good pay decreases the turnover of personnel which saves the company money on the recruiting side. The third reason is that the company hires already-trained employees which attended military training in the regular Armed Forces.[563] And the forth reason is that PMFs hire employee on a contract basis

[559] see Fredland, E.: Outsourcing Military Force 2004, p. 212
[560] see Poast P.: The Economics of War, p.98
[561] see Poast P.: The Economics of War, p.99
[562] see Poast P.: The Economics of War, p.99
[563] see Poast P.: The Economics of War, p.100

so they do not have a multiple, year-long or even lifetime commitment to their employees.[564]

The use of private military force however can also pose substantial risks. The basis for privatization is a contract between the civil supplier and the government over the delivery of certain services against an agreed upon price. This can be a big challenge in the context of military services. Von Clausewitz already described that war is a series of unique situations, limited by numerous ambiguities.[565] Fredland further states:[566] Military actions in general are characterized by ongoing changes to the circumstances and are interdependent with the actions of the opposing forces. These uncertainties make it difficult to define an exact content and price for this kind of service. Fredland illustrates this with the example of the contract between the US based Sandline Corporation and the government of Papua New Guinea. The goals of the missions are defined on a high level only and a lot of caveats are added to enable flexible renegotiations and price adjustments if conditions of the mission change.

A further risk is posed by unintended external impacts. One example is that another nation is contracting a firm from the national private military industry to perform certain military actions. The consequences for the home nation can be positive or negative. If the scope of the contract and the company's actions are in line with its home country's political interest, the nation's military might not have to act itself and thus cost

[564] see Poast P.: The Economics of War, p.100
[565] see von Clausewitz.: On War 1831, translated by Peter Paret 1976, p. 199
[566] see Fredland, E.: Outsourcing Military Force 2004, p. 211

savings can occur.[567] It is a very different story if the company is hired to act against the political interests of the home country.[568]

National values have been cited as one limitation of this study since some actions and decisions can be seen as immoral in one but acceptable in another nation. This can be seen in the context of a nation's openness toward utilizing PMFs in general but also with which purpose they are being used. PMFs can become an alternative to use force, if political considerations make the deployment of national Armed Forces difficult or even impossible. In other words, a nation could use PMFs as an agent to act upon own interests by either using them to take actions or influence national PMFs if they are employed by another country.[569] Some may see this as a positive aspect. Singer takes a different notion on the same subject. In his view the PMFs might be used as a front company for covert operations of a government and would be in those instances not even truly in business of an open competitive market environment.[570]

Also Brauer analyzed the phenomenon of PMFs from an economic perspective. He points out that efficiency from an economic perspective is a key determining factor for a nation which is influenced by decisions around which elements of the production of security are produced internally and which are to be privatized.[571] With regard to privatization he further states that privatization itself is very straightforward in today's society, given that the public approach of providing certain services is often not

[567] see Fredland, E.: Outsourcing Military Force 2004, p. 212
[568] see Fredland, E.: Outsourcing Military Force 2004, p. 212
[569] see Fredland, E.: Outsourcing Military Force 2004, p. 212
[570] see Singer, P. W.: Corporate Warrior 2007, p. 48
[571] see Brauer, J.: Economic Perspective on Mercenaries 1999, p. 134

necessarily the least expensive option.[572] To him the discussion is therefore not focused on efficiency but actually around legitimacy, authority, authorization and delegation of force.[573]

There are further negative implications to the use of privatized military force. If certain activities are given in the hand of PMFs, turning back is often difficult due to the fact that skills and expertise for that outsourced task get lost and therefore the dependency on the external firm increases.[574] Another factor is that PMFs compete with governments over the same labor force and both aspire to recruit the best soldiers. In addition it was already outlined that PMFs recruit trained soldiers from the Armed Forces, which means accordingly that the government pays for the training of labor force that the PMF can eventually acquire.[575] And on top of that, governments need to increase their pay in order to minimize the incentive of their soldiers to leave the service and switch into private employment.[576]

However the advantage of lower costs through privatization of military actions seems to be a valid argument. While using private forces as part of the regular Armed Forces of a country proves challenging due to the risks outlined above, there are certain areas where outsourcing should be considered as an option. In 1994 the UN decided to intervene in the homicide happening in Rwanda. A private firm made the proposal to conduct the mission of fighting the rebels and reestablishing the new regime. Executive

---

572 see Brauer, J.: Economic Perspective on Mercenaries 1999, p. 135
573 see Brauer, J.: Economic Perspective on Mercenaries 1999, p. 135
574 see Singer, P. W.: Corporate Warrior 2007, p. 79
575 see Poast P.: The Economics of War, p.101
576 see Poast P.: The Economics of War, p.101

outcomes quoted the mission at total costs of $150 million[577]; the actual conducted mission of the UN forces ended up to be more than five times more expensive.[578] Overall the market is unfortunately dominated by non-public companies and transparency is very limited in terms of datasets being available for economic analysis. This chapter has highlighted the context and potential implications for efficiency. However due to the lack of information, no application to the FDH analysis will be possible. However as studies become available that provide some insight into the actual utilization of PMFs across different countries, this will be a valuable addition to studies around military efficiency.

577 see Brauer, J.: Economic Perspective on Mercenaries 1999, p. 185
578 see Brauer, J.: Economic Perspective on Mercenaries 1999, p. 186

7 Conclusion

The results of the FDH Analyses conducted in this study vary depending on the output factor chosen. As pointed out the qualitiative indicator gives to a certain extend insight into the specific capabilities of Armed Forces at a given point in time, while the GNI and CINC are more general measures of military capabilities that also consider the more broadly defined warfighting potential that a nation rather theoretically could bear to arm. This distinction is actually supported by a study conducted by Biddle. Biddle analyzed the outcomes of war in the timeframe 1900-1992 and analyzed to which degree the nations with higher GNP or higher CINC score won.[579] He compares the results to a coin toss since only in around 60 percent of the cases the nation with the higher score won the war. This does not question the concept of the CINC in general, it just points out that military capabilities are more broadly defined than just winning a war and also that for an ad-hoc analysis of military capabilities a qualitative index would be more meaningful. It also indicates the validity of the argument that even if a nation has a high warfighting potential it does not mean it can actually leverage it in cases of a specific war. A balance of both factors seems to be important in order to understand what the state of potential capabilities of a nation really is at a given point in time. In terms of an unexpected war in the short term, a nation may find that the potential is there, but has difficulties to convert this potential into actual warfighing capabilities to fight and win the imminent war. In times of imminent threats it can be worth it for a nation to put a premium on national security and trade efficiency for predominant capabilities as the figures for Israel indicate. However at the same time having a close

[579] see Biddle, S.: Military Power 2006, p. 21

look at the efficiency in the broader scope measured by factors such as CINC or GNI might be a helpful reference point to determine appropriate investment levels for defense in the mid-to long-term.

In addition the worldvaluesurvey has proven to be very helpful for interpreting the results. The UK as an example has shown that actually a reduction in spending is in the best interest of the taxpayer if current capability levels could be maintained at lower cost. In terms of the overall social welfare of the economy, the Armed Forces currently fulfill their purpose in the view of the citizens. Given that the efficiency score shows room for improvement, efficiency drivers should focus on the input side to free up more money to be spent in other areas of the society.

When specific actions to improve efficiency are being defined, it is very important to tailor the discussion to the specific audience that is addressed. As outlined above, some external factors cannot be influenced by any actor, some are under the influence of a nation's government and some are influenced by the senior officers of the Armed Forces. Respectively, different measures for efficiency improvement have to be addressed by different actors. A senior officer cannot be blamed for inefficiencies in the defense industry, just like he or she cannot be blamed for inefficiencies in the political decision-making process. However he is responsible for economic use of the defense budget and the implementation of internal processes that drive efficiency within the military organization.

In terms of drivers for efficiency this study has shown that indicators suggest that an efficient government process can help leverage efficiency in the administration of the

Armed Forces and the procurement process for military assets. Notably the pooling and sharing between allies appear to bear the biggest potential and should be strongly suggested to nations in strong military alliances.

The all-volunteer force has also been proven to be more advantageous over the conscript model resulting in on average about 10 percent higher efficiency scoring of those nations that maintain an AVF model.

Making a qualified decision around the impact of technology has been challenging since the study shows that advanced equipment tends to be more capable but also more expensive than old equipment. Overall delaying overdue replacements to generate short-term savings seems to undermine the purpose since steadily increasing maintenance costs become a significant burden that actually makes it even harder in the mid- to long-term to have sufficient funding once new investments are inevitable. A careful product lifecycle management of military assets can be seen as the most predominant measure to improve efficiency. The strength of the arms industry as defined in this study furthermore indicates favorable relationship since high export rates indicate competitive products while also enabling companies to leverage higher economies of scale and therefore achieve lower prices per unit. Furthermore a nation can better influence what is being developed and produced and that those products fulfill its needs. The data produced in this study show inconsistent results for Russia and China, which however could be caused by very specific circumstances and may not represent a typical arms industry business cycle. Russia tends to sell out excessive stocks of old equipment leading to increased export rates and for China it is not truly known how much the local industries produce – even less than in the case of other western nations where defense companies also do not publish in detail their production volume. Given that China has a high demand for new equipment, exporting may not even be required and possible for those local suppliers hence negatively impacting the export balance as calculated for this study.

This study has also revealed areas that require further research and collection of data; notably the extension of military output and connection to specific security goals would be helpful. The indicators used in this paper are proxies for general military power. For a nation it would be a great addition to understand how the capabilities match the security goals and if there are any excess capabilities that are currently being paid for but which may not be required. At the same time it would be interesting to compare countries with comparable security goals to see if some nations are able to meet those at lower costs in order to derive best practices across all nations.

Also as an addition to this specific study it would be helpful to better understand and define the specific position the nations are in, in terms of international politics. As outlined above the security situation of nations has a major impact on how much capabilities are required and a high-level macroeconomic analysis like the FDH Analysis of this paper may not account for that. One author for example claims that the IDF should continue to focus on efficiency measures but at the same time the high Israeli defense spending should be seen in the context of Israel's situation with higher needs for security capabilities.[580]

Further notable studies should be conducted in the area of Force Planning and military organizations should not just evaluate which doctrine works the best in a given scenario, but should also add an economic component to evaluate the underlying costs. If several approaches lead to the same results, why not pick the one that comes at the lowest price tag for the taxpayer.

Furthermore the private military industry has become a growing and broadly used paradigm but the financials and use of these services are rather shaded and not very transparent. Some studies are available attempting to analyze the structure in the US market but for broader evaluations in terms of efficiency studies more information is required. This study has indicated that an impact seems plausible since it is another specific form of privatization of government services; however it cannot be analyzed yet how material the impact is and whether it is overall a positive or negative trend in terms of helping nations drive efficiency.

In the end the results of this study have shown that both hypotheses stated in the introduction can be confirmed based on the data applied to the various FDH models. Efficiency does differ between the Armed Forces of the studied nations and the results are plausible. The interpretation is somehow limited since only existing nations are analyzed and a true objective production frontier cannot be derived at this point. From

---

[580] see Evan,S.: Israel's defense expenditure 2010, p.51

that perspective the results have to be seen as a relative comparison and efficiency rankings shall not be taken literally. Even for a nation scoring 100 percent there may still be extensive room for improvement as it is simply operating most efficiently among its benchmarks. And these improvements again shall not automatically mean a cut of the defense budget, understanding that efficiency can help Armed Forces to get more capabilities out of the defense budget that is made available to them.

As Hitch and McKean state specifically with regard to efficiency in military decisions - an improved understanding of an issue can already help to foster meaningful actions even if it is based on a rather qualitative and intuitive basis.[581] This analysis has expanded upon this rationale and attempted to support the statement above with real data to help nations manage their Armed Forces and defense budgets more efficiently in the interest of improving the overall welfare of their citizens.

[581] see Hitch, C./McKean, R.: Defense in the nuclear age 1960, p.107

References

Adams, Thomas K. [The Army after Next 2008]: The Army after Next: The First Postindustrial Army, Stanford 2008

Afonso, Antonio/Schuknecht, Ludger/Tanzi, Vito [Public Sector 2003]: Public Sector Efficiency - An International Comparison, Working Paper No 242, European Central Bank, July 2003

Baran, Paul A./Sweezy, Paul M. [Monopoly Capital 1966]: Monopoly Capital: An Essay on the American Economic and Social Order, Monthly Review Press, New York 1966

Barrett, Ted/Cohen, Tom [Spending Cuts 2013]: Senate Democrats offer plan to avoid mandatory cuts, CNN: February 15, 2013 http://www.cnn.com/2013/02/14/politics/congress-spending-cuts/index.html?hpt=po_c1, accessed 25.03.2014

Bartlett, Henry C./Holman G. Paul/Somes, Timothy E. [The Art of Strategy 1995]: The Art of Strategy and Force Planning, Naval War College Review, Spring 1995

Bayer, Stefan [Der Einzelplan 14 2013]: Der Einzelplam 14: Theoretische Bestimmungsgruende und praktische Ausgestalung des Verteidigungshaushaltes, In: Deutsche Verteidigungspolitik, Wiesner, Ina (Ed.), Baden-Baden 2013, pp. 239-263

Bayer, Stefan [Nutzen und Kosten von Auslandseinsaetzen 2009]: Nutzen und Kosten von Auslandseinsaetzen – Eine Oekonomische Perspektive, In: Auslandseinsaetze der Bundeswehr, Sozialwissenschaftliche Analysen, Diagnosen und Perspektiven, Sozialwissenschaftliche Schriften, Heft 47, Berlin 2009, pp. 235-254

Bayer, Stefan [Generation Adjusted Discounting 2004]: Nachhaltigkeitskonforme Diskontierung – Das Konzept des “Generation Adjusted Discounting”, In: Vierteljahreshefte zur Wirtschaftsforschung 73, 01 Berlin 2004, pp. 142-157

Bayer, Stefan [Ecological Damages 2003]: Possibilities and limitations of Economically Valuating Ecological Damages, Tuebinger Diskussionsbeitrag Nr. 254, February 2003
http://nbn-resolving.de/urn:nbn:de:bsz:21-opus-18823, 2003, accessed 25.03.2014

BBC News [Poland seeks Iraqi oil stake 2003]: BBC News, Poland seeks Iraqi oil stake
http://news.bbc.co.uk/2/hi/europe/3043330.stm, 3 July 2003, accessed 25.03.2014

Beckley, Michael [Economic Development and Military Effectiveness 2010]: Economic Development and Military Effectiveness, In: Journal of Strategic Studies 33:1, 2010, pp. 43-79

Bessent, Authella M./Bessent, E. Wailand [Efficiency of Schools 1980]: "Determining the Comparative Efficiency of Schools through Data Envelopment Analysis.", In: Educational Administration Quarterly 1: pp. 57-75., Connecticut 1980

Biddle, Stephen D. [Afghanistan and the Future of Warfare 2002]: Afghanistan and the Future of Warfare: Implications for Army and Defense Policy, Carlisle PA 2002

Biddle, Stephen D. [Victory Misunderstood 1996]: Victory misunderstood: What the gulf war tells us about the future of conflict, In: International security Vol. 21, No 2, Cambridge 1992, pp. 139-179

Bish, Robert L./O'Donoghue, Patrick D. [The Monopsony Problem 1970]: A neglected issue in public-goods theory: The monopsony problem, In: The Journal of Political Economy, Vol. 78 No.6, Chicago 1970 pp.1367-1371

Blackaby, Frank [The Military Sector and Economy 1983]: The Military Sector and the Economy, Introduction to Ball, N. and Leitenberg M., The Structure of the Defense Industry, An International Survey, London and Canberra 1983

BMVg [Verteidigungsausgaben 2013]: Der Verteidigungshaushalt – Einzelplan 14 des Bundeshaushalts – ist der finanzielle Rahmen der Bundeswehr
http://www.bmvg.de/portal/a/bmvg/!ut/p/c4/Nck9DoAgDEDhs3gBSkxc3LyFu

pCiDTb8aKDg9WUxL9_0YIdewsYOhe-EAVbYDp7tq2xsTkVOXIQy16gaZSE-2dXkyoW1C2JGrSd1UjbopVIIZP4Fj1-GD5nD8bI!/, accessed 25.03.2014

BMVg [Verteidigungspolitische Richtlinien 2011]: Bundesministerium der Verteidigung, Verteidigungspolitische Richtlinien, Berlin 27.05.2011

Boot, Max [War Made New 2006]: War Made New: Technology, Warfare and the Course of History: 1500 to today, 1. Ed. New York 2006

Brauer, Juergen [Economic Perspective on Mercenaries 1999]: An Economic Perspective on Mercenaries, Military Companies, and the Privatisation of Force, In: Cambridge Review of International Affairs, Vol. 13 No. 1, 1999, pp. 130 – 146

Brooks, Risa A./Stanley, Elizabeth A. [Creating Military Power 2007]: Creating Military Power – The Sources of Military Effectiveness, Stanford 2007

Brooks, Risa A. [Making Military Might 2003]: Making Military Might: Why do States Fail and Succeed?, In: International Security, Volume 28, Number 2, Fall 2003, pp. 149-191

Buck, Jennifer C [The Cost of the Reserves 2008]: The Cost of the Reserves, In: The New Guard and Reserve, 1st Ed. San Ramo, USA 2008 pp.175-185

Budiansky, Stephen [Air Power 2004]: Air Power: The Men, Machines, and Ideas That Revolutionized War, from Kitty Hawk to Gulf War II,
1st Ed. New York 2004

Burgess, James F./Wilson, Paul W. [Veterans Administration Hospitals 1993]: Technical Efficiency in Veterans Administration Hospitals, In: The Measurement of Productive Efficiency – Techniques and Applications, New York 1993, pp. 335 - 351

Burnes, Nicholos [Berlin's stance on Libya 2011]: Berlin's stance on Libya has isolated Germany in NATO, Interview in Deutsche Welle 13.04.2011, http://www.dw.de/berlins-stance-on-libya-has-isolated-germany-in-nato/a-14985036-0, accessed 25.03.2014

Candreva, Philip J. [Financial Management 2008]: Financial Management, In: Management of Defense Acquisition Projects, American Institute of Aeronautics and Astronautics, Virginia 2008

Cansier, Dieter/Bayer, Stefan [Finanzwissenschaft 2003]: Einführung in die Finanzwissenschaft, München/Wien 2003

Carter, Ashton/White, John [Keeping the Edge 2001]: Keeping the Edge, Managing Defense for the Future, Cambridge 2001

Carter, Ashton [Keeping the Technological Edge 2001] Keeping the Technological Edge, in Keeping the Edge, Managing Defense for the Future, Cambridge 2001, pp.129 - 163

Cebrowski, Arthur [Battle Plan under Fire 2004]: PBS Nova: Battle Plan under Fire, Interview:

www.pbs.org/wgbh/nova/wartech/transform.html

Accessed 25.03.2014

Chen, Sean/Feffer, John [China's Military Spending 2009]: China's Military Spending: Soft Rise or Hard Threat?, In: Asian Perspective, Vol. 33 No. 4 2009, pp.44-67

Chairman of the Joint Chief of Staff [Instruction 3170.01F 2007], Washington DC 2007

http://www.dtic.mil/futurejointwarfare/strategic/cjcsi3170_01g.pdf accessed 25.03.2014

Chang, Chin-Lung [A Measure of National Power 2004]: A Measure of National Power, Paper presented at National University of Malaysia 16-17 February 2004, in Bangi Malaysia

Charnes, Abraham/ Cooper, William W./Rhodes, Edwardo L. [Efficiency of DMU's 1978]: Measuring the efficiency of decision making units, In: European Journal of Operational Research Vol. 2, Issue 6 November 1978, pp. 429-444

Chote, Robert/Emmerson, Carl/Simpson, Helen [Public Sector Efficiency 2004]: Measuring Public Sector Efficiency, In: IFS Green Budget Report 2003, http://www.politiquessociales.net/IMG/pdf/gb2003.pdf, accessed 16.03.2011

Chow, Eugene K. [A lean, green fighting machine 2013]: Why the military is becoming a lean, green fighting machine, The Week 02.12.2013 http://theweek.com/article/index/253455/why-the-military-is-becoming-a-lean-green-fighting-machine, accessed 26.03.2014

CIA World Factbook [GNP 1990]: CIA World Factbook Country data, http://www.theodora.com/wfb/1990/index.html, accessed 26.03.2014

Citino, Robert [Blitzkrieg to Desert Storm 2004]: Blitzkrieg to Desert Storm: The Evolution of Operational Warfare, Kansas City 2004

Coelli, Tim/Perelman, Sergio [Parametric and Non-Parametric Distance 1999]: A Comparison of Parametric and Non-parametric Distance functions: with application to European Railways, In: European Journal of Operational Research, Vol. 117 No.2 1999, pp. 326-339

Cohen, Eliot [Transformation in Military Affairs 2004]: Change and Transformation in Military Affairs, in: The Journal of Strategic Studies 2004, Vol. 27 No. 3, Abingdon 2004

Cornes, Richard/Sandler, Todd [Public Goods 1996]: The Theory of Externalities, Public Goods and Club Goods, 2nd Ed., Cambridge 1996

COW [NMC Documentation V.4.0 2010]: Correlates of War Project, National Material Capabilities Data Documentation, Version 4.0, updated June 2010, accessible: http://www.correlatesofwar.org/COW2%20Data/Capabilities/NMC_Codebook_4_0.pdf (03/26/2014)

Curristine, Teresa/Lonti, Zsuzsanna/Joumard, Isabelle [Improving Public Sector Efficiency 2007] Improving Public Sector Efficiency: Challenges and Opportunities, In OECD Journal on Budgeting Vol.7, No.1 2007, pp. 161 - 201

Davis, Kingsley [National power 1954]: The demographic foundations of national power, In: Freedom and Control in Modern Society, New York 1994, pp. 206-242

Defense Science Board [Report 1999]: Task Force on Globalization and Security, December 1999, Department of Defense, Office of the Under Secretary of Defense for Acquisition and Technology, Washington D.C.

Department of Defense [Military Power 2010]: Department of Defense, Annual Report to Congress, Military Power of the People's Republic of China, 2010

Department of Defense [Military Power 2009]: Department of Defense, Annual Report to Congress, Military Power of the People's Republic of China, 2009

Deptula, David [Effects-based Operation 2001]: Effects-Based Operations: Change in the Nature of Warfare, Arlington 2001

Dunne, J. Paul/Smith, Ron [Employment in the OECD 1990] Military Expenditure and Employment in the OECD, Defence Economics Vol. 1 UK 1990, pp. 57–73

Dunnigan, James F [Special Forces 2009]: Unleashing Special Forces in Afghanistan, http://www.strategypage.com/dls/articles/Unleashing-Special-Forces-In-Afghanistan--6-28-2009.asp, accessed: 25.03.2014

Dunnigan, James F [How to make war 2003]: How to make war – a comprehensive guide to modern warfare in the 21st century, 4th ed. New York 2003

Dunnigan, James F./Nofi, Albert A. [Shooting Blanks 1991]: Shooting Blanks – War making that doesn't work, New York 1991

Dvorin, Tova [We would back Israel]: US Military Chief: We would back Israel in Event of Iran Strike, Israel National News 19.11.2013, http://www.israelnationalnews.com/News/News.aspx/174200#.Up5XPelljlw, accessed 25.03.2014

Eeckaut, Philippe Vanden/Tulkens, Henry/Jamar, Marie-Astrid [Belgian Municipalities 1993]: Cost Efficiency in Belgian Municipalities, In: The

Measurement of Productive Efficiency – Techniques and Applications, New York 1993, pp. 300 – 334

EUNAFOR Somalia [Mission 2013]: EU Naval Forces Somalia, mission statement Operation Atalanta
http://eunavfor.eu/mission/, accessed 25.03.2014

Evan, Shmuel [Israel's defense expenditure 2010]: Israel's defense expenditure, In: Strategic Assessment, Vol.12 No.4, February 2010

Faere, Rolf/Grosskopf, Shawna/Weber William L. [School Performance 1989]: Measuring School District Performance, Public Finance Review October 1989, Vol. 17 No. 4, pp. 409-428

Farrell, M.J. [The Measurement of Productive Efficiency 1957]: The Measurement of Productive Efficiency, In: Journal of the Royal Statistical Society, Series A, General 120 III, pp. 253 - 290

Finlan, Alastair [The Gulf War, 1991]: The Gulf War, New York 2003

Forsund, Finn R. [Productivity Growth in Norwegian Ferries 1993]: Productivity in Norwegian Ferries, In: The Measurement of Productive Efficiency – Techniques and Applications, New York 1993, pp. 352 - 373

Freedman, Lawrence [The Revolution in Strategic Affairs 1998]: The Revolution in Strategic Affairs, 1st ed. UK 1998

Friedman, Georg [America's Secret War 2004]: America's Secret War: Inside the hidden worldwide struggle between America and its enemies,
New York 2004

Fucks, Wilhelm [Formeln zur Macht 1965]: Formeln zur Macht: Prognose ueber Voelker, Wirtschaft Potentiale, Sachsen Anhalt 1965

Gansler, Jacques S. [Democracy's Arsenal 2011]: Democracy's Arsenal, Creating a twenty-first century defense industry, MIT Press, Cambridge 2011

Gansler, Jacques S. [Defense Industrial Structure, speech 2000]: "The Defense Industrial Structure in the Twenty-first Century", speech to the American Institute of Aeronautics and Astronautics (AIAA) Acquisition Reform Conference, January 27, 2000

Cited from Lippitz, Michael J. , Sean O'Keefe, and John P. White with John Brown. "Advancing the Revolution in Business Affairs." Chap. 7, In: *Keeping the Edge: Managing Defense for the Future*. Cambridge, Mass.: Preventive Defense Project, Belfer Center for Science and International Affairs, Harvard Kennedy School, September 2000

Gareis, Sven B./Haltiner, Karl/Klein, Paul [Organisationsmerkmale von Streitkräften 2006]: Strukturprinzipien und Organisationsmerkmale von Streitkräften, In: Handbuch Militär und Sozialwissenschaft, 2nd ed. Wiesbaden 2006, pp. 14-25

Garret, Gregory A [Opportunity and Risk Management 2007]: Opportunity and Risk Management in the Defense Industry – Processes and Tools, In: U.S. Military Program Management – Lessons Learned & Best Practices, Vienna VA USA 2007, pp. 157-189

Gaston, Erika L. [Mercenarism 2.0? 2008]: Mercenarism 2.0? The Rise of the Modern Private Security Industry and Its Implications for International Humanitarian Law Enforcement, Harvard International Law Journal Vol. 49 No.1, 2008, pp. 241 - 248

German, F. Clifford [Evaluation of World Power 1960]: A Tentative Evaluation of World Power, Journal of Conflict Resolution Vol. 4 1960, pp.138-144

Gholz, Eugene [Military Efficiency 2003]: Military Efficiency, Military Effectiveness, and Military Formats, Paper presented at the annual meeting of the American Political Science Association, Philadelphia Marriott Hotel, Philadelphia, PA, Aug 27, 2003 http://citation.allacademic.com/meta/p_mla_apa_research_citation/0/6/4/5/2/pages64526/p64526-1.php 25.03.2014

Global Firepower [Israel 2013]: Israel Military Strength, Ongoing regional threats have powered the Israeli War Machine for decades, 11.05.2012 http://www.globalfirepower.com/country-military-strength-detail.asp?country_id=Israel, accessed 25.03.2014

Global Security [World Defense Spending 2012]: http://www.globalsecurity.org/military/world/spending.htm, accessed: 25.03.2014

Greenwald, Glenn/MacAskill, Ewan [Target List for Cyber-Attacks 2013]: Obama order US to draw up overseas target list for cyber-attacks, The Guardian June 7th 2013, http://www.theguardian.com/world/2013/jun/07/obama-china-targets-cyber-overseas, accessed 25.03.2014

Gombert, David C./Kugler, Richard L/Libicki, Martin c. [Mind the Gap 1999]: Mind the Gap: Promoting a Transatlantic Revolution in Military Affairs, Washington D.C. 1999

Hall, Bronwyn/Mairesse, Jacques/Mohnen, Pierre [Measuring the Returns to R&D 2009]: Measuring the Returns to R&D, NATIONAL BUREAU OF ECONOMIC RESEARCH, Cambridge, MA 02138 2009

Hallion, Richard P [Storm over Iraq 1997]: Storm over Iraq: Air Power and the Gulf War, Washington DC 1997

Hettena, Seth [Nimitz Deployment, 2003]: Nimitz Deployment brings unprecedented firepower to Middle East http://www.globalsecurity.org/org/news/2003/030301-nimitz01.htm, accessed 25.03.2014

Hildebrandt, Gregory G. [Military Capital 1980]: The Economics of Military Capital, Rand Corporation, 1980 R-2665 AF

Hill, Wilhelm./Fehlbaum, Raymond./Ulrich, Peter [Organizational Theory 1974]: Organisationslehre 1, Ziele, Instrumente und Bedingungen der Organisation sozialer Systeme, Bern, Stuttgart 1974

Hirshleifer, Jack [The Paradox of Power 1991]: The Paradox of Power, In: Economics and Politics Vol. 3 November 1991, pp.177 - 200

Hitch, Charles J./McKean Roland N. [Defense in the Nuclear Age 1960]: The Economics of Defense in the Nuclear Age, Project Rand – Rand corporation R-346, Santa Monica March 1960

Horowitz, Michael C/ Shalmon D. [The Future of War 2009]: The Future of War and American Military Strategy, In: Orbis 53:2, Spring 2009, pp. 300-318

Jones, Lawrence R./McCaffery, Jerry L. [Financial Management 2007]: Budgeting, Financial Management, and Acquisition Reform in the U.S. Department of Defense, 2007

Kaufmann, Daniel/Kraay, Aart/Mastruzzi, Massimo [Governance Matters VIII, 2009]: Governance Matters VIII – Aggregate and Individual Governance Indicators 1996-2008, The World Bank Development Research Group June 2009, Policy Research Working Paper 4978

Kancs, D'Artis/Siliverstovs, Boriss [Productivity of Heterogeneous Firms 2011]: R&D and Endogenous Productivity of Heterogeneous Firms, Paper – 3rd European Conference on Corporate R&D and Innovation – Concord September 14th 2011

Kaufmann, William W. [Assessing the Base Force 1992]: Assessing the Base Force – How much is too much, Washington 1992

Kaynes, John M. [How to Pay for the War 1940]: How to Pay for the War – a radical plan for chancellor of exchequer, New York 1940

Keegan, Paul [The Iraq War, 2004]: The Iraq War: The Military Offensive, from Victory in 21 Days to the Insurgent Aftermath, 1st Edition New York 2005

Knorr, Klaus [The War Potential 1956]: The War Potential of Nations, Princeton 1956

Kober, Avi [Change in Warfare 2005]: Does the Iraq War Reflect a Phase Change in Warfare? In: Defense & Security Analysis, Vol. 21 No. 2 June 2005, pp. 121 – 142

Lambeth, Benjamin S. [The Transformation of American Air Power 2000]: The Transformation of American Air Power, Ithaca 2000

Leach, John [Public Economics 2004]: A course in Public Economics 2004, Cambridge, UK

Leibenstein, Harvey [X-Efficiency 1966]: Allocaative vs. "X-Efficiency' In: The American Economic Review, Volume 56, Issue 3, June 1966, pp. 392-415

Lejeune, John A.: [Military Efficiency 1920]: https://www.mcu.usmc.mil/historydivision/Pages/Speeches/militaryefficiency.aspx, accessed: 25.03.2014

Lin, Patrick [The Ethics of Biologically Enhancing Soldiers 2012]: More Than Human? The Ethics of Biologically Enhancing Soldiers, In: The Atlantic 02/16/2012, quoted from: http://www.theatlantic.com/technology/archive/2012/02/more-than-human-the-ethics-of-biologically-enhancing-soldiers/253217/ accessed: 25.03.2014

Lippitz, Michael J./O'Keefe, Sean/White, John P. [Revolution in Business Affairs 2001]: Advancing the Revolution in Business Affairs, In: Keeping the Edge, Managing Defense for the Future, Cambridge 2001 pp.165 – 202

Lorenz, Andreas [Pyongyang's Provocations 2003]: Pyongyang's Provocations: What Motivates North Korean Threats? In: Der Spiegel March 8th 2013 http://www.spiegel.de/international/world/north-korea-responds-to-new-un-sanctions-with-nuclear-threats-a-887753.html, accessed 16.01.2014

Lovell, C.A. Knox [Production Frontier 1993]: Production Frontiers and Productive Efficiency, In: The Measurement of Productive Efficiency – Techniques and Applications, New York 1993 pp. 3 - 67

Mackubin, T. Owens [The QDR and Future U.S. Security 1997]: The QDR and Future U.S. Security – Strategic Review, Summer 1997

Mandl, Ulrike/ Dierx, Adriaan/Ilzkovitz, Fabienne [Efficiency of Public Spending 2008]: The Effectiveness and Efficiency of Public Spending 2008, European economy, Economic Papers 301, February 2008

Mahnken, Thomas G. [The American Way]: Technology and the American Way of War, Chichester 2008

Management of Defence [Mission of Armed Forces 2013]: The Mission of the Armed Forces, http://www.armedforces.co.uk/mod/listings/l0002.html 2013, accessed: 25.03.2014

Mann, Edward C. [Thunder and Lightning 1995]: Thunder and Lightning: Desert Storm and the Airpower Debates, 2nd Ed., Maxwell 1995

McCarty, Therese A./Yaisawarng, Suthathip [New Jersey School Districts 1993]: Technical Efficiency in New Jersey School Districts, In: The Measurement of Productive Efficiency – Techniques and Applications, New York 1993 pp. 271 – 287

McKinsey& Company [The Future of European Defense 2013]: Aerospance & Defence, The future of European Defence: Tackling the Productivity Challenge, June 2013

Millet, Allan R./Murray, Williamson/Watman, Kenneth H. [Military Effectiveness 1986]: The Effectiveness of Military Organizations, In: International Security, Vol.11, No. 1 summer 1986, pp 37 – 71

Mount, Mike [More problems for F-22 2012]: More problems for F-22 beyond mysterious oxygen loss issue, CNN 16.07.2012, http://security.blogs.cnn.com/2012/07/16/more-problems-for-f-22-beyond-mysterious-oxygen-loss-issue/, accessed 25.03.2014

Murdoch, James J./Sandler, Todd [Free riding 1984]: Complementary, Free Riding, and the Military Expenditures of NATO Allies, In: Journal of Public Economics, Vol. 25 No 1-2, Amsterdam 1984, pp. 83 – 101

Murillo-Zamorano, Luis R. [Frontier Techniques 2004]: Economic Efficiency and Frontier Techniques, In: Journal of Economic Surveys Vol. 18, No. 1 2004, pp. 33-78

Naegle, Brad [Logistics and Sustainment 2008]: Logistics and Sustainment, In: Management of Defense Acquisition Projects, American Institute of Aeronautics and Astronautics, Virginia 2008

Naegle, Brad/Snider, Keith F. [Test and Evaluation 2008]: Test and Evaluation Management, In: Management of Defense Acquisition Projects, American Institute of Aeronautics and Astronautics, Virginia 2008

Nagle, James F. [A History of Government contracting 1999]: A History of Government Contracting, 2nd ed., Washington D.C. 1999

NATO [ISAF's Mission in Afghanistan 2013]:

NATO, ISAF's Mission in Afghanistan, October 2013, http://www.nato.int/cps/en/natolive/topics_69366.htm,

accessed: 25.03.2014

Niskanen, William A. [Bureaucracy 1971]: Bureaucracy and Public Economics, Atherton 1971

O'Hanlon, Michael E. [The Science of War 2009]: The Science of War - Defense Budgeting, Military Technology, Logistics, and Combat Outcomes, Princeton 2009

Olson Jr., Mancur/Zeckhauser, Richard [Theory of Alliances 1966]: An Economic Theory of Alliances; In: The Review of Economics and Statistics Vol. 48, No. 3, Cambridge 1966, pp. 266-279

Organski, Abramo F.K. [World Politics 1958]: World Politics, Knopf 1958

OSD Cost Analysis Group [Cost Estimating Guide 1992]: Operating and Support Cost-Estimating Guide, prepared by the Office of the Secretary of Defense (OSD) Cost Analysis Improvement Group (CAIG) for use by Department of Defense (DoD), 1992 cited from http://www.dtic.mil/pae/paeosg02.html, accessed: 25.03.2014

Osmundson, John S.: [Software Project Management 2008]: Software Project Management, In: Management of Defense Acquisition Projects 2008, pp. 63 – 83,

Diagram cited from http://software.ssu.ac.kr/SE_page/06_class1.ppt#13, accessed: 25.03.2014

Owens, Bill. [Fog of War 2000]: Lifting the Fog of War, Baltimore 2000

Parkin, Michael/King, David [Economics 1992]: Economics, Wokingham 1992

Paul, K. Davis [Planning Under Uncertainty 1994]: Planning Under Uncertainty Then and Now: Paradigms Lost and Paradigms Reemerging, In: New Challenges for Defense Planning: Rethinking How Much is Enough, Santa Monica, Rand 1994

Pentagon Papers [Kennedy Commitments 1971]: The Pentagon Papers Gravel Edition Volume 2 Chapter I, "The Kennedy Commitments and Programs,1961,", Boston 1971, pp.1-39 https://www.mtholyoke.edu/acad/intrel/pentagon2/pent1.htm, accessed: 25.03.2014

Pivetti, Massimo [Underconsumptionist 1992]: Military Spending as a Burden on Growth: an 'Underconsumptionist' Critique, in Cambridge Journal of Economics Vol. 16, No.4, Oxford 1992, pp. 373-384

Poast, Paul [Economics of War 2005]: The Economics of War, 2005

Poutvaara, Panu/Wagener, Andreas [Ending Military Conscription 2011]: Ending Military Conscription, In: DICE - Ifo Institute for Economic Research at the University of Munich, Vol. 9 Issue 2, 2011, pp.36 - 43

Press, Daryl G. [Lessons from Ground Combat 1997]: Lessons from Ground Combat in the Gulf: The Impact of Training and Technology, In: International Studies Vol. 22, No.2, Cambridge 1997, pp. 137-146

Pugh, George E./Mayberry John P. [Effectiveness General-Purpose Military 1973]: Theory of Measures of Effectiveness of General-Purpose Military: Part I A Zero-Sum Payoff Appropriate for evaluating combat strategies, In: Operations Research: The Journal of the Operations Research Society of America, Vol.21 No. 4, 1997 Linthicum, pp. 867 - 885

Rendon, Rene [Contract Management 2008]: Contract Management, In: Management of Defense Acquisition Projects, American Institute of Aeronautics and Astronautics, Virginia 2008

Reuters [Pentagon says Israel improves arms-export controls 2007]: Pentagon says Israel improves arms-export controls, published 09.06.2007 by Reuters quoted from ynetnews.com: http://www.ynetnews.com/articles/0,7340,L-3446607,00.html,
accessed: 25.03.2014

Ricks, Thomas [Fiasco 2006]: Fiasco: The American Military Adventure in Iraq, New York 2006

Rizzo, Jennifer/Tapper, Jake [War games play out poorly 2013]: War games play out poorly http://security.blogs.cnn.com/2013/04/10/war-game-plays-out-poorly/?iref=allsearch posted on April 10th 2013, accessed: 25.03.2014

Royal Society [Brain Waves Module 3: Neuroscience 2012], Brain Waves Module 3: Neuroscience 2012

RS Policy document 06/11 Issued: London, February 2012 DES2419; http://royalsociety.org/uploadedFiles/Royal_Society_Content/policy/projects/brain-waves/2012-02-06-BW3.pdf, accessed: 25.03.2014

Russett, Bruce M. [Concentration in the International System 1968]: Is there a Long-Run trend towards Concentration in the International System? Comparative Political Studies, Vol. 1 1968, pp. 103-122

Russian Ministry of Defense [Mission and Objectives 2013]: Mission and Objectives of the Russian Armed Forces, cited: http://eng.mil.ru/en/mission/tasks.htm, accessed: 25.03.2014

Samuels, Richard J. [Rich Nations, Strong Army]: Rich Nation, Strong Army: National Security and the Technological Transformation of Japan, Ithaca, NY 1994

Samuelson, Paul A. [Public Expenditures 1954]: The Pure Theory of Public Expenditures, In: The Review of Economics and Statistics, Vol. 36, No. 4. Nov. 1954, pp. 387-389

Sandler, Todd [Sharing Burdens 1988]: Sharing Burdens in NATO, In: Challenge vol. 31, No.2, Armonk 1988, pp. 29-35

Scheel, Holger [EMS Analysis 2000]: EMS: Efficiency Measurement System User's Manual, Version 1.3, 2000-08-15, http://www.holger-scheel.de/ems/ems.pdf, accessed: 25.03.2014

Schneider, Peter [Die neuen Kameraden 1994]: Die neuen Kameraden – Eine Meisterleistung der Vereinigung: Wie die NVA aufgeloest wurde, In: Der

Spiegel 24/1994, http://www.spiegel.de/spiegel/print/d-13685964.html, accessed: 25.03.2014

Seiford, Lawrence M./Thrall Robert M. [Developments in DEA 1990]: Recent Developments in DEA, In: Journal of Econometrics 46, 7-48 North Holland 1990, pp 7-38

Sen, A. [Defense Spending as a Priority 1987]: Comment on A. Brody, Defense Spending as a Priority, In: Schmidt, C. and Blackaby, F., Peace, Defence and Economic Analysis, London 1983

Sherwood-Randall, Elizabeth [International Relations 2001]: Managing the Pentagon's International Relations, In: Keeping the Edge, Managing Defense for the Future, Cambridge 2001, pp.235 - 264

Shimko, Keith L. [The Iraq Wars and America's Military Revolution 2010]: The Iraq Wars and America's Military Revolution, Cambridge 2010

Singer, P.W. [Corporate Warriors 2007]: Corporate Warriors: The Rise of the Privatized Military Industry, Updated Edition, Ithaka 2007

SIPRI [China 2013]: SIPRI database of military spending and armament, http://www.sipri.org/research/armaments/milex/copy_of_faqs, accessed: 25.03.2014

SIPRI [Definition of Military Expenditures 2013]: SIPRI Definition of military expenditure http://www.sipri.org/research/armaments/milex/milex_database/definitions, accessed: 25.03.2014

SIRPI [Import/Export 2012]: SIPRI database of global arms transfers, http://www.sipri.org/databases/armstransfers/background/explanations2_default, accessed: 25.03.2014

Smith, Adam [The Wealth of Nations 1776]: The Wealth of Nations, Bantam Classic Edition based on 5th edition as edited and annotated by Edwin Cannan in 1904, New York 2003

Smith, Ron [Military Economics 2009]: Military Economics: The Interaction of Power and Money, Hampshire and New York 2009

Smith, R. Jeffrey/ Nakashima, Ellen [Changes in Programs, Defense Budget 2009]: Gates Planning Major Changes in Program, Defense Budget, In: The Washington Post April 4th 2009

Smith, Ronald P. [Military Expenditures 1977]: Military Expenditures and Capitalism, In: Cambridge Journal of Economics, Vol. 1 1977, pp. 61-76

Snider, Keith F. [Defense Acquisition 2008]: Defense Acquistion's Public Policy Imprint, In: Management of Defense Acquisition Projects, American Institute of Aeronautics and Astronautics, Virginia 2008

Snider, Keith F. [Initiating Defense Acquisition 2008]: Initiating Defense Acquisition Projects, In: Management of Defense Acquisition Projects, American Institute of Aeronautics and Astronautics, Virginia 2008

Spicer, Tim [An Unorthodox Soldier 2000]: An Unorthodox Soldier: Peace and War and the Sandline Affair, Edinburgh 2000

Strategypage [Database 2008]: Armed Forces of the World Database http://www.strategypage.com/fyeo/howtomakewar/databases/armies/default.asp, accessed: 25.03.2014

Sullivan, Gordon [A Vision for the Future 1995]: A Vision for the Future, In: Military Review Vol. 75 No.3 May/June, Fort Leavenworth, KS 1995

Tellis, Ashley J./Bially, Janice/ Layne, Christopher/McPherson, Melissa [Measuring National Power 2000], In: Rand Paper MR-1110-A, 2000

Tirpak, John: [Air Campaign 1999]: Short's View of the Air Campaign, Air Force Magazin Vol. 82 No.9, September 1999, published by the Air Force Association, 1501 Lee Highway, Arlington, VA 22209-1198

Troxell, John F. [Force Planning 2001]: Force Planning and U.S. Defense Policy, in US Army War College Guide to Strategy, Chapter 12 http://www.au.af.mil/au/awc/awcgate/army-usawc/strategy/ 2001, accessed: 25.03.2014

Tucker, David [Confront the Unconventional 2006]: Confronting the Unconventional: Innovation and Transformation in Military Affairs, Carlisle Barracks, PA: Strategic Studies Institute, U.S. Army War College, 2006

US Government [Federal Budget 2014]: Report on Federal Budget estimate http://www.usgovernmentspending.com/federal_budget_estimated, accessed: 25.03.2014

Van Creveld, Martin [The Changing Face of War 2006]: The Changing Face of War: Lessons of Combat from Marne to Iraq, New York 2006

Von Clausewitz, Carl Phillip Gottlieb [On War 1831]: On War translated by Peter Paret, Princeton 1976

Warner, John T./Asch, Beth J. [All-volunteer Military 2001]: The Record and Prospects of the All-volunteer Military in the United States, In: The Journal of Economic Perspectives Vol. 15. No. 2, Nashville 2001, pp.169-192

Weitz, Richard [Jointness and Desert Storm 2004]: Jointness and Desert Storm: A Retrospective, In: Defense & Security Analysis Vol. 20, June 2004, pp. 133-152

Wilson, Georg C. [This War Really Matters 2000]: This War Really Matters: Inside the Fight for Defense Dollars, Washington DC 2000

World Values Survey [Introduction 2012]: Introduction to the World Values Survey-2012

http://www.worldvaluessurvey.org/wvs/articles/folder_published/article_base_46, accessed 25.03.2014

Woodall, Pam [Military-Industrial Complexities 2003]: Military-Industrial Complexities The defence industry will not be the biggest beneficiary from the war, The Economist: March 29th 2003, p.55

Zemin, Jang [On National Defense and Army Building 2002]: lun guofang yu jundui jianshe – On National Defense and Army Building, Beijing: Jiefangjun Chubanshe 2002

www.ingramcontent.com/pod-product-compliance
Lightning Source LLC
Chambersburg PA
CBHW051407200326
41520CB00023B/7139
* 9 7 8 0 6 9 2 4 1 6 3 9 6 *